# KAREN KAIN

*Movement  Never  Lies:  An  Autobiography*

M&S

# KAREN KAIN

with Stephen Godfrey and Penelope Reed Doob

Cloth edition published 1994
First published in trade paperback 1995

**Canadian Cataloguing in Publication Data**

Kain, Karen, 1951-
Karen Kain: movement never lies

Includes index.
ISBN 0-7710-2320-0 bound ISBN 0-7710-4575-1 pbk.

1 – Kain. Karen, 1951 –    . 2. Ballerinas – Canada –
Biography.    I. Godfrey, Stephen, 1953-1993.    II. Doob,
Penelope Reed.    III. Title.

GV1785.K28A3 1994    792.8'092    C94–931889–2


Designed by Kong

Every effort has been made to identify and contact the copyright holders for
the illustrative material in this volume. Upon notification, any credits
will be corrected in subsequent editions.

The support of the Government of Ontario through the Ministry of Culture,
Tourism and Recreation is acknowledged.

Printed and bound in Canada on acid-free paper.

McClelland & Stewart Inc.
*The Canadian Publishers*
481 University Avenue
Toronto, Ontario
M5G 2E9

1 2 3 4 5  99 98 97 96 95

*To my mother and father, for helping me make my dreams come true.*

# Contents

CHAPTER ONE ✢ *First Positions* 1

CHAPTER TWO ✢ *Getting into the Company* 25

CHAPTER THREE ✢ *The Gold-Dust Twins* 57

CHAPTER FOUR ✢ *Rudolf* 91

CHAPTER FIVE ✢ *Branching Out* 123

CHAPTER SIX ✢ *The Private Cost of a Public Life* 155

CHAPTER SEVEN ✢ *The Bruhn Years: A New Maturity* 181

CHAPTER EIGHT ✢ *Putting It All Together: A Dancer's Life* 211

CHAPTER NINE ✢ *Now and Then* 245

*Acknowledgements* 275

*Photo Credits* 276

*Index* 277

First Positions

*"When I grow up I am going to be a ballerina. I could go out every night and dance. I will be in* Giselle. *It will be so much fun being a ballerina."*
– Karen Kain, age eight

In ballet, if you don't start training before you're a teenager, you probably can't have a serious career. I was lucky: on the night of my eighth birthday, I knew I wanted to be a ballerina. As a birthday present, my parents took me to the old Palace Theatre in Hamilton to see the National Ballet of Canada perform *Giselle*, with Celia Franca in the title role. It was March 1959, and the company and I were the same age.

*Giselle* was a perfect choice for my first live performance; a classic from the Romantic Era, it contains some of the most affecting moments in all of ballet. It's the story of a young village girl, Giselle, who falls in love with a handsome stranger (actually, a nobleman in disguise). When she discovers he's engaged to someone else, the shock of his betrayal unhinges her fragile mind, and she goes mad and dies. She spends the rest of the ballet in the land of the Wilis, the malevolent ghosts of women betrayed on their wedding day, and here she triumphs over these evil spirits to save the life of her repentant lover. This intense melodrama, with its glorious music and exotic costumes, went straight to my heart.

Celia Franca, founder of the National Ballet of Canada, was an astonishing Giselle. One of the best dramatic dancers England has ever produced, she could communicate Giselle's emotions even to an eight-year-old. I can still see her reaction when she understood that her lover had betrayed her. She tore the

*(Previous page) Even at a very early age, I was exhibiting interesting* port de bras *(and expressive acting).*

wildflowers out of her long black hair, which came cascading down around her shoulders. She spun wildly across the stage, and even though I could hear only the music, I knew she was sobbing in anguish.

The second act, ghostly and gloomy, didn't affect me as much; it would take years for me to appreciate its complex, mysterious message of the power of the love that survives beyond the grave. But the whole evening was so mesmerizing that I determined to enter that world on the stage. At this point, I had been taking ballet lessons for a year, but now I was serious, although it took a while for my parents to accept my new dedication; most little girls want to be dancers at some point, and there was no particular artistic tradition in my family. In retrospect, however, I see that my family offered a fertile environment for a career in dance.

Like most Canadians, I come from adventurous stock – in my case, Scots-Irish – people who were willing to risk a future in a new country. My paternal grandfather came to Winnipeg from Ayrshire, Scotland, at the turn of the century; his great-grandfather had been a ship's captain who had changed his name from Robertson to Kain (his mother's maiden name), probably to avoid prosecution for smuggling. My mother's great-grandfather, Thomas Alexander Stewart, was a settler in Peterborough and a member of Parliament, and his wife, Frances, had a literary bent: her journals and letters to friends back in Ireland were published as *Our Forest Home* in 1902. She was related by marriage to two other famous pioneer women, Susanna Moodie and Catharine Parr Traill. All three are featured in *At My Heart's Core*, a 1950 play by Robertson Davies.

Henry Louis Stewart, a son of Thomas and Frances, was also a surveyor who settled in Marquette, near Winnipeg. My mother, Winifred, his granddaughter, grew up there, a real tomboy, who rounded up cattle on horseback and milked fourteen cows by hand every day before school. She put herself through business college, moved to Winnipeg, and there met my father, Charles.

He had grown up in Winnipeg's north end, a pretty tough area. Like me, he was a rebellious teenager; at seventeen, he was sent off to Sacramento, California, to learn discipline as a farmhand. Soon after he returned to Winnipeg, war broke out, and he served as a wireless operator on the West Coast for five years before studying engineering at the University of Manitoba.

When Charles and Winifred met in 1945, on a double date, my father was wearing a flashy zoot suit that he'd ordered from a catalogue by mistake, and, while my mother wasn't too impressed with his fashion sense, she thought he

*My mother at the farm on her favourite palomino.*

3

*My mother and father with me on the day of my christening.*

was a great dancer – perhaps the first clue of what lay ahead for me. They married and moved to Hamilton, Ontario, when my father got into a postgraduate training program at Westinghouse Canada. When he retired in 1984, it was as senior vice-president of the company.

It's always fascinating to reflect on what you have inherited from your parents. Mine have always been physically active. They were superb square-dancers, and you still can't keep them off the dance floor. That's reflected in the general encouragement they gave me and my siblings in sports and perhaps in my own love of athleticism in dance. My twin sisters, Sandra and Susan, excelled in sports. Susan, who became an exercise therapist after a career as a horse trainer, was one of the few women who completed the Paris–Brest–Paris cycling endurance race in 1991. Sandra, a registered nurse, has taken quadriplegic patients through Europe and Russia for specialized treatment. My brother, Kevin, a tropical disease specialist and a consultant for the World Health Organization at the University of Toronto, runs, hikes, and helicopter-skis, and has backpacked around the world twice.

I shared my siblings' passion for sports, particularly track and field, and that probably contributed to my athleticism and willingness to take risks as a dancer. My most vivid memory, however, is not of success in the hop, step, and jump, but rather of the humiliation I suffered in a self-taught gymnastics feat with which I'd hoped to impress a family audience – hanging from the basement water pipes and putting my legs through my arms before pulling them back again safely. After considerable practice I was ready for an audience, but, while my performance was spectacular, it was hardly perfect: my arms gave way and I landed on the cement floor, stunned, winded, and completely crestfallen. Ever since, I've lacked confidence in the strength of my arms and have been slightly nervous doing big lifts in ballet. Fortunately, I've also learned to work through the fear and, when I fall, to get up and carry on without dwelling on the embarrassment.

Although a career in ballet for me would have been the farthest thing from their minds, my parents both cared deeply about music, and this passion, which I inherited, is at the core of my love of dancing. When my father came to see me in ballets in my early years, he remembered them by their music, not their stories. Sometimes he would close his eyes to listen, until my mother spotted me hidden in the back row of the corps and gave him a good nudge to draw his attention back to the stage.

Temperamentally, my father is calm and logical, qualities I wish I had in greater abundance. In fact, I seem to have inherited 99 per cent of my personality – and my physique – from my mother, who is intuitive, restless, and energetic. My father claims she has two speeds: "high" and "off." I'm much the same – driven, determined, and able to work to the point of exhaustion – which has served me well in my chosen profession, when not taken to extremes.

Something else she has taught me by example is empathy with other people's feelings and predicaments. I treasure this gift, though at some points I've carried it too far: I've often felt paralysed in making decisions or negotiating contracts because I see the other party's point of view only too well. But, by the same token, my ability to identify with others has helped me enormously as an actress. Like many gifts, this has been a double-edged sword.

My mother certainly needed her energy. We children were all so high-strung and rambunctious that babysitters refused to come back after one night. Later, as the eldest, I had to babysit for my sisters and brother, and I came to understand our babysitters' defections completely. And as if we weren't rowdy enough, there were always the animal visitors I insisted on bringing home – another instance of empathy. We nursed baby birds, squirrels, rabbits, raccoons, and various reptiles, to the annoyance of my mother, who, having been raised on a farm, felt that animals belonged in a barn. At one point, I wanted to be a veterinarian, but a vet we knew cured me of that notion by pointing out that the job consisted mainly of sticking needles into sick, frightened animals.

I knew about frightened, injured animals. When I was about six, my own dog – a beagle named Puffer, who was full of bounding energy and loved to chase cars – was run over. His pelvis and hind legs were badly broken, and as I ran to him in horror he tried to wag his mangled tail. We rushed him to the vet, but so much damage had been done that he couldn't be saved. Even a miracle would have left him badly crippled. Most parents would have made the decision themselves to spare their child the pain, but mine

*We were a very close family: (front to back) Kevin, Susan, Sandra, and me.*

showed a rare sensitivity to my feelings. Puffer was *my* dog, and I had a right to be consulted. With the greatest tenderness, my parents explained the options and told me that the decision was mine. I knew that Puffer loved running better than anything; I saw his agony; I knew what had to be done. Although I cried for days afterwards, I was sure I'd done the right thing for Puffer, and to this day I'm grateful to my parents for having had the insight to allow me the responsibility for his well-being until the end.

My love for animals has lasted; I bring pictures of my cats out of my wallet at the slightest excuse, plaster them all over my dressing room, and still regret that the travel demands of my career mean that I can't have a dog as well. Incidentally, many dancers share this passion; animals somehow bring a sense of stability, of family, into lives that can otherwise be quite lonely. At one point early in my career, I had twelve cats. One stray led to another, and soon there were plenty of kittens as well. My flatmate quite rightly objected – it was a two-bedroom apartment – and I sorrowfully found homes for eleven, settling the twelfth, a tom named Jeffrey, with my parents, where he became a treasured resident for almost two decades.

*With my mother in our first formal group portrait.*

My mother and I may have disagreed about the merits of stray animals, but in most respects I was a typical eldest daughter, trying very hard to please both parents. Not surprisingly, given the stock from which I come, praise was hard-won in our family. No matter how well any of us did at anything, we always felt we were expected to do better. This attitude certainly prepared me well for the rigours of being a professional dancer, since praise is surprisingly rare in the inner sanctum of a ballet school or company, but it also contributed more than a little to the insecurities that have plagued me throughout my career. I have seldom felt that I have really done well enough.

I was very shy, retreating to my room when neighbours came over so I could avoid having to talk to them. This trait continues to this day; in 1976, McKenzie Porter of the *Toronto Sun* wrote, "Socially, Karen Kain is a flop . . . she lacks the grace of entertaining small talk." I couldn't agree more, and in fact I don't feel that this is a deficiency. I hate the superficiality of small talk. I've dedicated my career to getting to the heart of communication in body language, stripping off whatever is superfluous. Embellishment isn't my style; I try to distil the essence, and remain uncomfortable with frills and excesses in language and movement alike.

My parents were determined that we should have all the opportunities they didn't have, so, since money was limited, they set an example of hard work and discipline – another aspect of my upbringing that would serve me well as a dancer. While my father strove to climb the corporate ladder, my mother made three hot meals a day, sewed many of her own clothes, as well as ours, made jams, jellies, chili, and did all of the other things expected of a homemaker in the fifties. Even at the time, it wasn't totally enjoyable to be the beneficiary of so much activity; I felt some vague responsibility for the perpetual exhaustion that my mother's valiant efforts cost her. As I grew older, I became aware that I myself could never embrace a life of traditional domesticity; it's a nice place to visit, but I wouldn't want to live there. Knowing the price a woman pays in a traditional family, and freely deciding whether or not it's worth it, is part of what feminism is all about.

I didn't make the choices my mother made, but her choices led obliquely to my eventual career. With four active children around the house, my mother needed somewhere to park me to give herself a break, so, when I was six, she enrolled me in ballet class. She also felt – quite rightly – that dancing would be good discipline and good for my posture. After a bit of homework, she found a ballet teacher who was only a twenty-minute walk from the house. I was acquiescent rather than eager; at that point, I'd never seen any ballet and had no great desire to dance, but I was quite willing to try.

In those days – and even today – anyone who could point a foot could claim to be a ballet teacher. This particular teacher conducted classes in a dark, damp basement that had two focal points: a smelly box of kitty litter, around which we tiptoed or ran, and a big sofa, onto which we flopped after a tough exercise. I particularly enjoyed practising wild spins around the floor, my pony-tail smacking me in the cheek as I turned. What I did *not* like was the fact that this woman apparently had only one record, Patti Page singing "The Tennessee Waltz." For eight months, I heard that music so incessantly that the song was totally ruined for me. People tend to forget that even children can have an artistic sense.

Even worse for my artistic sense of myself was my practice costume. My mother thought I looked adorable in green tights and sweater with a green ribbon in my hair, but I felt like an elf. I was so humiliated that, on my way to and from class, I crept from tree to tree, camouflaging myself when anyone came by, in terror of being recognized. What I feared most was being conspicuous in any way.

Fortunately, my mother had read in an article in *Chatelaine* that girls shouldn't be put on pointe until they are at least twelve. So, when my teacher suggested that I be given pointe shoes for Christmas at the age of seven, my mother whisked me out of her class for good. It was then that she entrusted me to the woman who really pointed me in the right direction.

Betty Carey, now Betty Carey Love, a licensed ballet teacher with a certifcate from England's Royal Academy of Dancing, gave a far more structured and correct training at the nearby Ancaster Town Hall. For the next eighteen months, until we moved to Mississauga, I learned the real basics of ballet, starting with the five positions. It was at one of the class demonstrations that my parents realized I might actually have some talent. Betty had a terrific figure and sexy fishnet stockings, and attracted more fathers to these events than might have come otherwise, so both my parents were there. They distinctly remember hearing the other parents discussing the budding talent in front of them. These other parents weren't focusing on their own children; they were talking about me. "They all wanted to know who the little girl was who seemed so serious," my mother recalls. "You seemed to be really inhabited by the music, in some kind of trance. We were almost embarrassed that you were getting so much attention." Of course, I was completely oblivious to all of this at the time.

Betty suggested that I audition at the National Ballet School. If it hadn't been for her, I would probably never have gone to the school and had a career as a dancer, even though, by this point, not long after seeing Celia Franca in *Giselle*, I'd put my commitment to dance in writing. In a Grade 3 assignment entitled "When I Grow Up," I had drawn a stick-figure ballerina with these words, "When I grow up I am going to be a ballerina. I could go out every night and dace [*sic*]. I will be in *Giselle*. It will be so much fun to be a ballerina."

This determination wasn't entirely shared by my family. My sisters had taken ballet and hated it. My brother, on the other hand, wanted to continue his ballet classes, but, as too often happens with boys, he was steered into more "practical" pursuits. My mother was wary of the ballet world; she thought theatre people led disreputable lives, used bad language, worked too many nights, and were poorly paid. Like most women of her generation, she felt the smart thing to do was to choose a sensible job that would put you in the path of "Mr. Right." My father simply wanted me to be able to earn a living. But Betty Carey's insistence that I had talent moved my reluctant mother to take me to the National Ballet School auditions in Toronto in 1961. I was ten and would be entering Grade 5 the next fall.

The school was run by Betty Oliphant, a tall, imperious woman with swept-back grey hair, who had been born in London in 1918 and studied classical ballet with the great ballerina-teacher Tamara Karsavina. When she was only eighteen, Betty opened a dance studio on Wigmore Street in London. She had choreographed and peformed in London musicals, but in those days she was considered too tall for ballet.

In 1948, Betty came to Canada with her husband and two children, and she taught ballet and tap-dancing to support her family after her marriage broke up. In 1951, on behalf of the Canadian Dance Teachers' Association, she

*Betty Oliphant teaching in the main studio at the National Ballet School.*

approached Celia Franca to urge that promising local students, not just the professional dancers from Boris Volkoff's Toronto company, be considered for the new National Ballet of Canada. Betty and Celia hit it off instantly (a rapport that unfortunately deteriorated in the seventies), and Betty was invited to teach at the new National Ballet's first summer school. She became the company's first ballet mistress while still running her studio at 444 Sherbourne Street, where future company members Lorna Geddes, Victoria Bertram, Vanessa Harwood, Nadia Potts, and Veronica Tennant were still students. In 1959, she was the founding principal of the National Ballet School, an adjunct to the company that became fully autonomous in 1963.

When I auditioned in 1961, the National Ballet School consisted of two residences and one main building, an elegantly proportioned former Quaker Meeting House on Maitland Street, with impressive columns, high ceilings, huge arched windows, and a soft wooden floor, excellent for dancing. Over the next seven years I'd get to know this hall well, and its serene beauty would sometimes be the only tranquillity in my life. It was here that I joined the Grade 11 students for a regular class – at that time there were no big public auditions with newspaper photographers. Intimidated by the presence of students five years older than I, and rattled by another girl who sobbed throughout, I shyly showed as well as I could the simple steps I had learned from Betty

9

Carey. Stern during the class, Betty Oliphant was warmer in the solo audition afterwards. Even then, I sensed one of her greatest qualities as a teacher: she insisted on treating children as people, as responsible creatures.

During the solo audition, Betty asked me to leave the room. When I returned I was to pretend I was a royal princess, greeting the members of my parents' court as I approached their thrones at the end of a grand ballroom. Apparently I slunk out the door as a frightened little girl and came back confident and composed, graciously acknowledging my grateful subjects. My mother was so stunned by the transformation of her daughter into a regal being that she burst into tears. Betty didn't cry, but she did accept me into the school. Since I was too young to start that year, I studied with Iris Giggs, an RAD-trained Mississauga teacher, at Betty's recommendation. Then, in 1962, I moved to Maitland Street.

It seems strange to people outside the dance world that talent can be spotted in children so young, but, even at ten, bodies manifest the physique and flexibility, the natural grace and ability to create beautiful movement through space, without which it is simply too difficult to succeed as a ballet dancer. But, as I would learn later, the physical instrument can change radically with age, and your natural grace with it. I certainly wasn't an ideal shape for dance. Already taller than most girls, I also had more curves than was considered appropriate for ballet, but I wouldn't find out until later the pressures put on many dancers – including me – to fight against their natural weights.

My parents were understandably concerned about how they were going to pay the school fees, which were then $1,700 a year, even after I earned a scholarship worth $800 for room and board. This was no small amount for a couple with three other children to support. They were also shaken to learn that the school uniform – white blouse, green blazer, tartan skirt, knee-high green socks, camel-hair coat, and brown Oxfords – had to be purchased at Holt Renfrew, a very expensive store. But when Betty assured them that I really had the talent to make it as a dancer, they swallowed hard and reluctantly agreed.

On my first day at school, my initial delight at being accepted was tempered by reality. I had fallen asleep the night before in a room with four other girls and an orange crate as a night table. When I awoke in the morning, I realized that my mother had always done my hair. I didn't know how to do it myself, which suddenly made me feel homesick and frightened.

Life at the National Ballet School was concentrated, even cloistered. Jolted from our beds by a loud bell at seven, we staggered around looking for our uniforms, competed for space in the bathroom, and ran down to breakfast by eight. At nine, we took ballet class for an hour and a half, wearing identical regulation black leotards and pink tights, each duly name-tagged. After a full day of academic classes, we took another dance class – perhaps in folk-dancing or contemporary technique – for an hour and a half, then had dinner, did homework, and put our lights out by nine.

Betty wisely insisted that even the most talented dancers keep up their schoolwork in case a career in dance turned out to be impossible, for whatever reason. I enjoyed the academic classes, doing well in courses I liked, such as history and English. Some of the teachers were wonderful. In particular, Lucy Potts, whose daughter Nadia would become a principal dancer with the company, made French and Russian come alive, and later in my travels I would be especially grateful for her inspiration. In contrast, I had no talent for math or science, which my father insisted I take in case I failed at dance and needed to go to university. It was typical of my dogged determination to please that I repeatedly sought out special tutoring in math and struggled hard, but to no avail; over the years I've come to accept that I don't have a mathematical bent.

Surprisingly, even in ballet class, my life was miserable for part of the first year because all of the other students saw that I was the teacher's pet – and the teacher was Betty. Although she was only one of our teachers, she inspired the most respect because she was the principal. Clearly excited when she had a raw new talent to work with, she singled me out, giving me a dozen corrections every class, while everybody else got two or three. Nobody thought for a minute that these frequent corrections meant I was making more mistakes than anyone else; in the élite world of dance, only those who have promise are given these attentions. Betty's comments on my first full report card said that I had "the talent, the physique, and the opportunities to become a first-class dancer, the rest is up to her." I was well aware that not everyone was getting that assessment.

Betty has always been open and frank – perhaps sometimes too frank – in expressing her opinions, and her singling me out made me very unpopular. Icy stares greeted me in the corridors, and I was ostracized for the first few months. By temperament I wanted to please everyone, so I was miserably unhappy and lonely, painfully aware of the other girls' hostility and envy. It was a severe but important lesson in living with people who didn't seem to like me. Although my desire to be a dancer overpowered my desire to be liked, I was at a loss in dealing with the situation and cried myself to sleep, longing for my home and family.

My obvious distress intensified my mother's misgivings about the school. When I innocently mentioned that the matron in our residence had disappeared again (later we discovered the cause: periodic benders), my mother immediately phoned Betty to tell her what I had said. Betty flatly told her to

*At age twelve.*

mind her own business. The next day, Betty phoned her to say that the matron had been fired, but after that incident my mother was understandably miffed; she felt Betty assumed that parents should simply fork over their money and not interfere.

It didn't help when my mother returned me to school after a weekend in Mississauga to find that a new matron had piled all the clutter in the room I shared with the four others onto my bed, insisting that I was the untidiest of all. Shoes, skirts, dustballs, everything was on my bed – and none of it actually belonged to me. Furious, my mother began to understand why I felt a little persecuted. Every week I would phone her, burst into tears, and tell her how miserable I was. She would respond, "You've really tried hard, and it's just not working. Why don't you just pack your bags and we'll pick you up tomorrow?" At that point, after a good cry, I would say, "Well . . . it's really not all that bad. Maybe I'll just give it another week." Gradually things improved. Once I'd made a few friends, like Doris Ruther, Susan Harris, Christy Cumberland, and Kate Shaughnessy, the rest of the school warmed up to me. The fact that Betty stopped favouring me so obviously after the first year also helped.

I even scored a few points when I finally learned how to do my hair properly. I found I could flatten my statutory bun, which had a tendency to get lopsided or stick out like a rat's nest, by banging it against the wall. Soon dozens of girls were banging their buns on the walls before class.

Even after I began to feel I belonged there, however, I still felt awkward in other ways. For one thing, by the age of twelve I'd reached my full height of five foot seven and towered over all of my classmates. That's why I was never allowed to dance in the annual Christmas production of *The Nutcracker* at the O'Keefe Centre in Toronto and on tour. Most students got their first stage experience in the Party Scene in Act I or in the dance for Mother Gigogne and her children in Act II, and every year one lucky girl got to be Clara, who travels to exotic places with her nutcracker doll-prince. Not only was I too big to play Clara, I was too big to be a plausible child at all. Of the eight children at my level, I was the only one who never danced in *The Nutcracker*.

My public performances at the time were somewhat more modest in scope. At home in Mississauga I could sometimes be coaxed to show what I'd learned. One neighbour – Alex Read, known on "The Tommy Hunter Show" on television as Alexander "Ragtime" Read – would play ragtime, and I would dance around his house while he laughed at my antics. Years later, he cried when he saw me dance *Swan Lake*, thinking of the girl who had twirled around his living room. Much later, I built on this early experience in Sir Kenneth MacMillan's ragtime ballet, *Elite Syncopations*.

Many ballerinas impressed me deeply in those early years when my mother took us to the National Ballet at the Royal Alexandra Theatre. I saw magical performances by dancers like Lillian Jarvis in *Coppélia*, Angela Leigh in Grant Strate's *Pas de Chance*, and the sublimely elegant Lois Smith, who danced Myrtha to Celia's Giselle. Later, I was thrilled by an amazing performance of *Romeo and Juliet*, with the eighteen-year-old Veronica Tennant as Juliet, Earl Kraul as the most passionate Romeo ever, Yves Cousineau, cool and disdainful as Tybalt, and Lawrence Adams, electrifying as Mercutio. Performances like this would keep me dancing through what were to be turbulent teenage years.

My parents kept asking Betty, "Is she really good? Will she have a career?" I think they half-hoped she would say, "No, you can take her home right now." But Betty was always encouraging, despite a few reservations. When I was thirteen, she told them, "If she's going to be on stage, she has to have her teeth fixed." So, to counteract prominent buck teeth, I wore braces for the next two years. This made me even more excruciatingly self-conscious than usual, and I wailed uncontrollably when I learned that I would have to wear an awful harness wrapped around my head for a year. The only thing that consoled me was that my best friend, Susan Harris, had to wear the same miserable appliance. The next year, we graduated to bite-plates with rubber bands, which we flicked endlessly with our tongues during academic classes to irritate our teachers.

Betty also had reservations about my physique. Ballet is custom-made for highlighting every little flaw, and it was obvious that I needed some reshaping. My turnout wasn't naturally good, my hip joints weren't particularly flexible, and my back was stiff. In her typically frank way, Betty said I had "the tightest tail in town." If I did everything by the book when I tried to perform an arabesque, my raised leg would go only about one inch off the ground behind. Sometimes I argued with Betty about this frustrating arabesque business. "I can't do it your way," I'd whine when she told me to get my leg higher. She was sure I could; I was sure I didn't have the strength or the flexibility. Once, forcing me into the correct position, she shouted (for the class's benefit), "You have to work like this every day!" Then, very quietly, she murmured to me, "But when you get on stage, you can cheat." I can and I do cheat every time I do an arabesque, perhaps by bending forward or by opening my hip more than is textbook-correct. I've spent most of my career trying to stretch my ligaments to get more flexibility, but I've also learned that a good line is the most important thing, and every dancer has to make the most of the facility that comes naturally. The biggest physical problem, though, was my weight, of which more later.

Gradually, the combination of steps that we learned and then linked together in class became increasingly complex. We had to translate strange incantations in French – *glissade, assemblé, pas de bourrée, sissonne, jeté, gargouillade, pas de bourrée en tournant, soubresaut* – into precise and effortless movements. We had to know both the spoken language of ballet and the semaphore. One teacher demonstrated the combinations she wanted by fidgeting her hands together like knitting needles; we'd stare intently at her tiny hands to read the movement she wanted. Later, I'd discover that many choreographers worked the same way, and that "marking" a movement with your hands is a valuable tool to prevent utter exhaustion in the long days of rehearsal.

But the most important thing I learned – and I'd really always sensed it – was the absolute centrality of something that was even more critical than the perfect step: musicality. True sensitivity to music involves much more than dancing obviously on the beat, though many dancers seem incapable even of that, and some misguided critics assume that *only* dancing exactly to the beat is true musicality. At school we learned that the music comes first, no matter how difficult the accompanying steps. As we became proficient with the steps, we experimented with the musical inventiveness that characterizes the greatest dancing, when, depending on what the steps are saying, on the style, and on your mood, you can dance on, before, or after the music.

Dancing just ahead of the beat – or "on top of the music" – can give the impression that your heart is racing with emotion, or that you're madly impetuous, or that you're totally alert and in command, depending on the context. I find myself doing this as Juliet, when I want to convey her sense of wonder, the pounding of her excited heart. Dancing just after the beat can make an audience feel that you're being pulled by the music or clinging to something that you've lost, and this can create feelings of longing, nostalgia, or pathos, an effect I strive for as Alice Liddell Hargreaves in Glen Tetley's *Alice*. Such tensions between the heard musical rhythm and the visible rhythm of the dancer's actual steps can convey emotion, conflict, teasing, playfulness; you have to have a dialogue between music and dance, not a slavish relationship. What's best of all, however, is feeling the music's pulse so deeply that you and the music are one. Very few dancers are instinctively musical, and most dance students need help to develop their rhythmic and emotional response to music. This imposes an additional layer of difficulty at a time when you're still trying to perfect the steps, but the development of musicality must start early, and it's part of what separates good dancers from great ones.

Whenever I grew discouraged with the difficulty of what I was learning or the refusal of my body to do it correctly to the music, there was one teacher who kept egging me on and never let me give up. This was Daniel Seillier, who had been a dancer with the Paris Opéra Ballet and Roland Petit's Ballets de Paris, and a soloist and ballet master at the Grand Ballet du Marquis de Cuevas before emigrating to Canada. "Don't give up! *Courage! Courage!*" he'd say, and then he'd give me an intense series of combinations that ensured I was always on the move, unable to think long enough to lose my nerve. A tiny man, he called me *"ma grande fille"* because I towered over him.

*Daniel Seillier.*

He gave me confidence at a time when I most desperately needed it, and my strength, attack, and precision as a dancer came from him. He also taught me to take risks, to dance with my full power and strength. I'm not a natural turner, but he'd say, "What's the worst thing that can happen to you? You fall!" I *did* fall, twenty-four out of twenty-five times, but the twenty-fifth time I'd turn perfectly and gain confidence from my success. In the perfectionist world of dance, teaching traditionally emphasizes "corrections," which tends to destroy rather than create confidence. Unfortunately, many dancers – and I'm one of them – are naturally such perfectionists, so hard on themselves, that they need encouragement at least as much as they need criticism.

By my second year at the school, not only was I making friends easily, but I had also become a ringleader for certain activities frowned upon by the staff. One of these in particular got me into trouble in more ways than one. There was a piece of paradise called The Dutch Shop nearby, which sold almond cookies guaranteed to fatten you up beyond your wildest nightmares. I couldn't get enough of them and frequently organized bingeing expeditions. Finally, Betty grounded me in no uncertain terms, though this didn't prevent my developing what would become a persistent weight problem by the time I was fifteen. And I still kept adopting stray pets. Once it was a squirrel, fallen out of a tree. Another time it was an injured pigeon. My most daring move was to keep a puppy that a boy on the street had given me. For two days, with my roommates sworn to secrecy, we spread newspaper on the floor and gave the puppy secret feedings. Unfortunately, he kept yelping, and one night the matron stormed in to demand an explanation.

National Ballet School matrons were often intimidating creatures, and this one was no exception. She might have been Myrtha, Queen of the Wilis, ordering Giselle to relinquish Albrecht. In a booming voice, she commanded, "Give me that dog immediately!" As my friends huddled in their nightgowns, sobbing, I made a desperate stand. With tears streaming down my face and all the outrage and melodrama that a twelve-year-old would-be Giselle could muster, I clutched the dog to my heart and retorted, "Over my dead body!" It was a good try, but the puppy went.

The ballet school may have been a cloister, but it was in a tough part of town, and we often had glimpses of how close the real world was to us. Church Street and Jarvis Street were a lot rougher then than they are now, and late at night, if we couldn't sleep, we'd look out our windows to catch the entertainment. Propped up on our elbows, we watched wide-eyed as drunken men bellowed and swatted their girlfriends in front of The Red Lion tavern across the street. While no parent would wish his or her child to be exposed to this world, it gave me early insights into some of the seamier roles I'd later tackle: Louise, the Mother in Ann Ditchburn's *Mad Shadows*, or the Mother in James Kudelka's *The Miraculous Mandarin*.

Sometimes the street-life came a lot closer. Occasionally, we'd sneak out on a Saturday night and stroll down Yonge Street; in retrospect, I'm amazed that we weren't harassed as we walked by strip joints and bars looking our ballet-school freshest. But it was exciting, partly because we were sure we'd be expelled if we were caught. One night, someone broke into the residence, took all the kitchen knives, and, for some unimaginable reason, stuck them into the kitchen and dining-room doorframes. We never saw the intruder, but his handiwork created quite an impression when we came down for breakfast. Finally, after one man managed to get into the dormitories, bars were put on our windows. The school has an excellent security system now – and more-alert matrons.

By grades 8 and 9, I wasn't having fun any more. I sank into a blue funk, chafed against what seemed the overly regimented system at the school, became cranky and stubborn, and wrote dark, soulful poetry. A Grade 11 report card was a somewhat belated model of understatement when it noted that I was "listless and melancholy." "To become truly mature," it said, "Karen must learn to conform in ways which are demanded by those in authority in her chosen profession." At the time, my distress must have seemed to be a case of typical melodramatic teenage misery, but I now realize that it was a foretaste of the serious depression that would plague me later on. Despite my apparent successes early in my career, until I was about thirty, life would continue to seem bleak and happiness unattainable.

My parents, quite conservative people, were alarmed to learn that I was a girl with dark moods – and, even worse, raging hormones. The only real distraction from my brooding thoughts during this period was my discovery of boys. I kept getting caught kissing them in corners and corridors, and while I came in for my share of lectures, Betty was amused. "They're just like bees to honey with you, aren't they?" she said. But my mother was distressed at my adventurous spirit and activities. It didn't help when she would call me in the residence late at night and someone would exclaim, "Oh, but she said she was going home to see you!"

My first serious boyfriend was Tim Spain, a student two years older, with whom I fell madly in love when I was fifteen. My parents, even though they quite liked Tim, thought I was far too young for such a relationship and did their best to separate me from temptation on the weekends by securing me in my suburban bedroom. As it happened, however, this was an intensely important relationship that was to last for six years, despite parental disapproval. Later, dancing Juliet, I found myself drawing on that first intense love and my despair at our separation. Juliet's passion was easy for me to communicate; I'd felt it all in Mississauga.

Not surprisingly, relations with my parents at this time became so strained that for almost a year we barely spoke. So deep was my melancholy that Betty sent me to a private psychiatrist to see if anything was seriously wrong with me. My first and only visit was a failure. Furious at being coerced into the appointment, I sat in outraged silence, arms crossed, fiercely refusing to answer a single question. As I discovered later, therapy is only effective when you're open to it.

It may seem odd that, although I was rebellious, depressed, and frustrated about my dancing as well, I never seriously considered leaving the school or indeed taking up any other career options. I wasn't happy, but there was something I wanted more than happiness. Unlike most teenagers, National Ballet School students know exactly what they want to do in life: dance. It's been said that the only possible justification for a career in dance is that you can't imagine any other life, and that's how most of us felt. That conviction – or perhaps that tunnel vision – made us different from others our age, both more dedicated and more insular. For one thing, we weren't as plugged into pop culture. In residence we never watched television during the week, and the only program I ever saw regularly was "The Ed Sullivan Show."

Still, my rebellious feelings were fanned by the general mood of protest and defiance of the late sixties. Perhaps because I was looking for new outlets, I found myself part of an exciting and creative group at the school, not as a creator but as a willing interpreter. I have never had the slightest desire to choreograph, but I have admired my friends who could. To her credit, Betty encouraged creativity in her students and did everything she could to give aspiring choreographers like Ann Ditchburn and Tim Spain a chance to show their work in public. In May 1968, a year before I graduated, a group of young choreographers received Canada Council grants to create new pieces for a workshop performance at the MacMillan Theatre, and I was lucky enough to be in several pieces.

The Toronto critics came, and I received my first published reviews. The evening as a whole was seen as quite novel. Ralph Hicklin of the Toronto *Telegram* wrote, "Last night, I spent the most rewarding, exciting evening in a theatre that I have experienced in at least the last twelve months." The nature of that excitement was evidently not entirely aesthetic. Both Wendy Michener in the *Globe and Mail* and Nathan Cohen in the *Toronto Star* alluded to the works' sexual content, not least "the sexual consolation of Karen Kain" (Michener) and performances (including my own, at age sixteen) that "aspired to an erotica altogether alien to the Canadian ballet tradition, and all the more welcome" (Cohen). After the intensely structured atmosphere of the school, it felt good to be treated as if we were bringing something unexpected to the Canadian dance scene.

🙚

In all, I spent seven years of my life at the National Ballet School. In many ways it shaped me as a dancer, for better or worse, and I've finally reached the stage where I can assess its impact on me.

Almost everything at the school emanated from Betty's strong personality, beliefs, and background, which had both advantages and drawbacks. What I now value most about the school's training was its double emphasis on a clean, pure style and on the overwhelming importance of musicality. Betty had seen enough dance styles, techniques, and training methods around the world to be able to incorporate at the school what she felt were the best qualities of each. She realized that dancers with mannered and rigidly coordinated training can neither adapt to contemporary dance styles nor work with choreographers who create novel, unfamiliar movements. Wanting her students to experience a broad range of movement styles, she exposed us to character dancing, yoga, flamenco, and Martha Graham technique, among others. We may not all have become very proficient in these styles, but our exposure to them helped us cope with contemporary choreography and opened the door to careers in other kinds of dance, so that some NBS graduates, like Robert Desrosiers and Claudia Moore, went on to excel in modern dance. One of Betty's students, James Kudelka, negotiates the worlds of classical and contemporary dance with equal skill and in my opinion has become the foremost choreographer in this country. Another, John Alleyne, now the artistic director of Ballet British Columbia, is increasingly recognized as one of the country's most exciting and inventive young contemporary choreographers.

In her insistence on combining a mastery of ballet with exposure to other techniques, Betty was surely forward-thinking. I completely agree, too, with her emphasis on musicality and the search for purity of line, which also make the school and its training so fine. (I should say that I am on its board, so obviously I'm biased to some extent.) If you were a genius, you might emerge from Betty's training as a dancer like Erik Bruhn, whom Betty always held up to us as a shining embodiment of the ideal *danseur noble*. As a student in the rebellious sixties, I wasn't so enthusiastic about Bruhn's talents. I saw him as a dancer like Fred Astaire, cool, elegant, and refined. I preferred Rudolf Nureyev, dangerous, sensual, and mesmerizing. In my early years as a dancer, I strove to be like Nureyev, passionate and athletic; it took me years to appreciate the more subtle artistry of Erik Bruhn, who would later play an important part in my life.

*Aged fourteen, posing in a borrowed costume for a newspaper article on the National Ballet School.*

Betty was also keenly attuned to the pitfalls of the ballet regime. At first we had weekly weigh-ins, but when she realized that this kind of monitoring encouraged anorexia, she had it stopped immediately. She put in place a comprehensive support system for students, with psychologists assigned to every grade level to help not only with the inevitable crises of adolescence but also with the special, competitive pressures of being a performing artist.

As well, Betty carefully observed other schools of dance to try to avoid their mistakes. For example, she was convinced that overtraining in England had given her overdeveloped calf muscles that were inappropriate for classical ballet, and she believed that the Russian habit of forcing turnout also tended to create overdeveloped legs. She was against an excessive pelvic tilt for the same reason, and we lived in dread of her constant correction, "You're tucking under." Unfortunately, as a result, some of us in my era did not develop our turnout as fully as we might have done, and we are instantly recognizable as NBS products, because we tend to dance with sway-backs, which cause improper alignment and faulty technique, especially for turns. I've spent much of my professional career trying to rework some of these early problems, though in fairness I should say that there probably is no perfect universal training.

Later, when I first started to dance in Europe, I realized with a shock that the school had not equipped me with all the technique I would need in the international world of ballet. After seeing extremely turned-out dancers who lifted their legs very high, I knew I had to catch up or get out of the running on the international scene. We had never been encouraged to go for high extensions; in the traditional British style, exemplified by Dame Margot Fonteyn, anything above an ear-high extension was considered vulgar showgirl material. Because Betty's background had been in music hall and musical comedy as much as ballet, she was particularly vigilant about good taste. But whatever her views on high legs, and however beautiful a line Fonteyn could achieve without lifting her leg much more than ninety degrees, I realized that a high extension was expected in most choreography, especially George Balanchine's.

In some ways, I agree with Betty that an insistence on perfect turnout in certain physiques, like my own, can contribute to problems of the hips, knees, and ankles. Later on, I created foot problems for myself by trying to turn out too much for my body. But that may be because I started trying for more rotation as a professional dancer in my early twenties, which is a bit late, considering that it's almost impossible to change joint mobility significantly beyond the age of eleven. This is another reason you have to start ballet training early.

In retrospect, I think Betty may have been a little too cautious with us. Although overtraining can contribute to bulky muscles, most muscle development comes from genetic predisposition and hormonal balance. I've seen young male dancers train with weights for years, trying desperately but in vain to develop precisely those large calves that Betty hated.

In my time, our training was so focused on purity of form that we advanced very slowly and far too carefully. We'd practise preparations for difficult turns for years, in the process losing the feel of the spin itself. For me, and probably for others, it's important to get the feeling of a difficult step first, and only then to start polishing the form.

It may be a more significant criticism to say that I don't remember a great deal of positive reinforcement from my days at the school. Of course, that, too, is the ballet tradition: you don't want people to think they're too good in case they stop working to get better, because the balletic ideal is impossible for any mere human to achieve. In all honesty, I may have received more positive commentary than I remember, but it's my perfectionist nature to hear only negative remarks. I vividly recall collapsing in tears of humiliation when someone compared me to a turtle, with my tense shoulders hunched up under my ears. This never-ending criticism and questioning, whether from others or myself, took its toll later on in my career, as it has done with many other dancers.

Surely it contributed to both my despair and my rebellion, and it's a factor in eating disorders like anorexia and bulimia. It was only with my beloved Daniel Seillier that I could blossom from a shy, awkward student into a real dancer, because he was loving and caring and created the atmosphere of trust and confidence I needed.

Over time, many of these deficiencies in physical training at the school have been rectified, and the school continues to evolve positively on many fronts. It's particularly significant that there's much more focus on the development of young dancers as well-rounded, well-balanced people, concerned not only with physical virtuosity but also with developing artistic expressiveness and self-confidence. Psychological and psychiatric support services continue to be important and readily available resources for young dancers facing the inevitable difficulties of being very contemporary teenagers learning a demanding and perfectionist art form. There are numerous consultants, from orthopaedic surgeons to podiatrists to nutritionists, who are sensitive to the special needs of dance students. To her lasting credit, it was Betty who first put many of these programs in place.

Most recently, under the directorship of Mavis Staines, there has been a steady flow of innovation. One of Canada's greatest modern dancers, Peggy Baker, now teaches regularly at the school, bringing not only an expansion of the students' artistic and technical horizons but also what Mavis describes as an awareness of the spiritual dimensions of the art of dance. The Vaganova method of ballet training, with its emphasis on fluidity in the torso, neck, and arms, now enriches the curriculum. Even more importantly, there is more concern for individual students' needs than there was in my day.

Traditionally, ballet has been taught in group classes, which limited the amount of individual attention any student might receive. In that context, the most obviously talented students attracted most of the teacher's care (and criticisms, constructive or otherwise). These students may have profited technically, but paid a price psychologically or socially, while other young dancers with one or two physical limitations may have slipped through the cracks because no one worked with them individually to solve their technical problems. I hate to think how many potentially great dancers were lost to the art through lack of sustained individual attention at the beginning.

Well aware that this is not an ideal situation, Mavis has made a concerted effort to change it. The atmosphere for students has become more supportive, more nurturing, as Mavis fosters a climate in which individual needs are respected and as much time as possible is found to respond to them. There are more private lessons now, for one thing. For another, an expert in biomechanics and neuromuscular training, Irene Dowd, makes week-long visits to the school to work intensively with teachers and students, identifying likely anatomical causes for difficulties students are experiencing and suggesting how teachers, the school physiotherapists, and the students themselves can work to overcome these limitations. In keeping with current methods in high-level athletics and with the new atmosphere at the school, Irene not only deals with biomechanical problems but also, rather like a sports psychologist, suggests appropriate ways to use mental imagery to enhance performance in class or on the stage. I attended one of Irene's seminars myself, and it's clear that professional dancers can benefit as greatly as ballet students from her insightful observation and practical commentary. I'm delighted that Mavis and Irene are collaborating on a review of the ballet curriculum that will include special exercises for students facing particular physical challenges that in the old days may have ruled out a career in dance.

But I'm getting ahead of myself; I knew none of this as I reached the end of my years at the National Ballet School. Instead, I was distraught with worry. Would I be accepted into the National Ballet of Canada? Could I pass the audition and get one of the two or three contracts available? Would I get to dance anything at the graduation performance that might impress Celia Franca? Depressed, rebellious, often feeling I was more trouble than I was worth, I thought for some time that Betty had totally forgotten me once I stopped being teacher's pet. She proved me wrong: for our graduation performance in May 1969, she cast me as the Swan Queen in the second act of *Swan Lake* (even though I was third cast behind two older, more-experienced post-graduates, Linda Maybarduk and Barbara Malinowski).

However, despite this vote of support, Betty's continued concern for me had a more demoralizing manifestation. In April, she took me aside to say, "Celia Franca has scheduled auditions for the company. You have two weeks to lose weight." There it was again. If there had been one deafening, discouraging reproach throughout my time at the school, this was it: my weight. Early on in my days at the school, I'd seen Betty talking to my parents during a break in a demonstration performance for families. Barely waiting until she'd finished, I rushed up and asked, "What did she say? What did she say?" My mother looked at me regretfully. "She says you're too fat." At this point, she had heard it all before. "Your daughter's talented, but she's too fat," Betty and the staff had said time and again.

*I am congratulated by Robert A. Laidlaw on my graduation from the National Ballet School.*

In fact, from any normal perspective, I was *not* fat. At five foot seven, even at my heaviest I had never weighed more than 130 pounds, which most physicians would think healthy and normal for that height. But in the ballet world, having a few too many curves is obesity, and I was continually convinced that my excessive weight, which I saw as a real deformity, would doom me.

To make matters worse, by conventional standards I was definitely too tall at five feet seven to be a ballerina. (Even though the rules have finally changed, thanks to choreographer George Balanchine's love of long legs, it's still a liability for a woman dancer to be over five feet six.) Having suffered from being too tall in her youth, Betty was keenly sensitive to the problem, so, perhaps to remind me that a spot in the company wasn't assured, she told me before the audition that, when she had pointed me out as a strong candidate, Celia had moaned, "Oh no, not another tall one!" The company had accepted Martine Van Hamel three years earlier, and she is even taller than I am, so Celia had had to audition all over Europe to find a partner tall and strong enough for her (which is how Hazaros "Laszlo" Surmeyan, a Yugoslav dancing in Germany, joined the company). Celia didn't think she could afford to traipse around Europe to find a partner for me, too.

For two weeks before the audition, all I ate was lettuce and tomatoes. I don't know how I kept my strength up, but on the day of the audition, I was a lot slimmer. We started off with class, just like every other day for the past seven years. But this time, a small, elegant woman with upswept hair – so different from the long, tumbling black locks that first inspired me as a small girl – scrutinized us from the far end of the studio. When it was over, I was sure I hadn't distinguished myself. A lot was going to ride on *Swan Lake*.

When the night, May 23, 1969, finally came, I was shaky and terrified despite a year's careful preparation (of which I remembered virtually nothing) and despite Lucy Potts's warm, motherly concern when she appeared in the dressing room to give me moral support and see that my make-up was right. I don't think my performance went well: I certainly didn't enjoy it much, and nobody seemed very excited about it. Suddenly, I was painfully aware of how little I'd performed in front of an audience – just the odd fund-raising lecture-demonstrations at a country club, a performance at Maple Leaf Gardens for a Shriners' Convention, and, of course, the new work at the MacMillan Theatre. That was it.

To my complete astonishment, and despite my own harsh self-assessments, I was accepted into the National Ballet. To celebrate, I went to The Dutch Shop and ate a dozen almond cookies.

# CHAPTER TWO

# Getting into the Company

*"You treat this art like a religion, and this is your life."*
– American ballerina Maria Tallchief,
in Anne Belle's film *Dancing for Mr. B.* (1989)

Ever since seeing Celia Franca's Giselle, I had admired the National Ballet of Canada from afar. Throughout my school years, my single goal had been getting into the company, and as far as we students were concerned, the National was the *only* company. Then, as now, company headquarters was the St. Lawrence Hall, a beautiful nineteenth-century building with an elegant ballroom where Jenny Lind once sang. As a result, when I reported for work as a member of the company in July 1969, the proudest day of my life, I was a little disconcerted to discover a real rabbit warren behind the harmonious façade. Squeezing past stacks of cartons and thick wicker costume boxes to find the locker room, I was sure my dreams would be fulfilled. Hadn't all the dancers I had idolized over the years made the professional dancer's life look easy and joyful?

I was in for a shock. Quite unprepared for the unglamorous reality of company life, I would become so exhausted by rehearsing, touring, and performing during my first year in the corps de ballet that for the first time in my life I would seriously consider finding another line of work. Maybe I should have taken the contrast between the hall's external harmony and the crammed untidiness within it as an omen.

A few things were deceptively familiar that first day. Like all other days, it began with class, and I soon spotted some good friends: Linda Maybarduk, who

*(Previous page)*
*Baby swan queen, aged nineteen. This was my first major full-length role.*

had come to the school in her teens from Florida, and Tomas Schramek, who had left a professional career in his native Czechoslovakia during the Russian invasion in 1968 and had taken postgraduate training at the school. But much was new to me, including the teacher, Joanne Nisbet, the ballet mistress and the wife of ballet master David Scott. Joanne would play a major part in my future with the company, and I was anxious to please her. To dispel any illusions about how easy that would be, my intimidating classmates included prima ballerinas Martine Van Hamel, Veronica Tennant, and Karen Bowes.

As I slunk into the back row, my old insecurities surfaced instantly, for it was always during class that I was most tormented by seeing in the floor-to-ceiling mirror – a dancer's constant corrector and reference point – how much my body and its ways of moving differed from the classical ideal. I knew I was too tall, too heavy (or so everyone kept telling me), and poorly turned out, and my back and hips were too tight for high extensions. I wasn't a complete disaster, but if I had an acceptable head, a long neck, and tolerable proportions, so did many other girls. Now I realize that most of the dancers I admire, like Marcia Haydée, Suzanne Farrell, Dame Margot Fonteyn, Veronica Tennant, Carla Fracci, and Evelyn Hart, don't have perfect bodies either; it's by their extraordinary talent and passion that they transcend those thousands of perfectly shaped dancers who somehow can never seize your attention on stage. Physical perfection is never enough by itself – in fact, if you are too physically perfect, you may be a little lazy – and physique certainly isn't what makes a great dancer. But that knowledge came later and didn't console me on my first day.

As a perfectionist, I've never had trouble spotting and admitting my deviations from the physical ideal; it's harder for me to remember that I do have qualities that fit that classical ideal, and for the record I should mention them. I do have a long neck and well-arched feet, although these have been banes as well as blessings. Since flexible areas tend to be weak, I've had repeated neck and foot injuries, even after training hard to develop strength. My third classical virtue is *ballon*, a large natural jump, which depends on timing and strength as much as on the flexibility of the Achilles tendons.

I had discovered early on that I loved jumping – the energy of it, the exuberance, the feeling of hovering in the air. If I had to choose just one thing to illustrate the joy of dance, this would be it. I had always tried to jump as often and as high as the boys at school. I didn't have to think, analyse, or dissect the movement, as I did with turns; I could just jump and enjoy it. I still envy the flamboyant leaps in male solos. That's one reason I often take men's company class to this day, along with other women who share my passion for big jumps.

Most women like a quick tempo in jumping solos to get them out of the way faster and because you don't have to jump so high to fill out the music. But I always want the music slower so I can luxuriate in the height and reach of the jumps. Giselle and Aurora in *The Sleeping Beauty* have always been among my favourite roles precisely because there's so much jumping in them.

Early in my career, in 1973, writer Tobi Tobias gave a very accurate assessment of my deficiencies and talents in New York's *Dancemagazine* – perhaps the more complete because I'd reeled off to her a huge catalogue of my flaws in an interview.

> Kain is the first to itemize her God-given physical faults. She's too short-limbed – the arms especially – and her legs are *stocky*. Well, if she doesn't have the requisite slender ankles, her feet are serviceable and strong, with a good high arch, and her surefootedness is particularly satisfying, part of her aplomb. She's got a long – "too long" – handsome torso which she doesn't use yet with much expansiveness. "I've got a tight back. I have to work on it," she says matter-of-factly. "That, and my acting," she sighs, aptly connecting both deficiencies under the category of "expression."
>
> She looks womanly and athletic, and the contradiction in the schoolgirlish way she uses her hands – stiffly, with the index finger pointed and the other fingers glued together – is absurd and charming. Her greatest gift is invisible when she's standing still. But when she's in full flight . . . she looks as if she's impelled by a spontaneous vitality.

Of course, Tobias couldn't know how much of that vitality came from sheer nervousness and fear of failure rather than pure love of dance. I was still a young dancer learning how to fit the pieces of the technique I'd learned into a coherent whole.

That first day with the company, and virtually every day since, I've struggled to put the pieces together in the dancer's most sacred ritual: daily class, with its time-honoured progression from the barre and simple pliés – the springboard for jumps, the cushion for soft landings, and the impetus for turns – to the challenging combinations of big jumps in the centre. Morning class at ten is the cornerstone of a dancer's life. People sometimes wonder why I have to take class as if I'm still a student, but how else can you maintain the strength, precision, coordination, and flexibility you need? The older you get, the more important class is. Of course, class would be intolerable if it were *only* a workout, a mechanical tune-up, as boring as compulsory figures in skating. Instead, there's something almost mystical about this always-familiar,

*A grand jête from* Don Quixote.

always-new process that really defines a dancer. The quiet, companionable, almost-meditative exertion of class reminds us why and how we dance. The great modern dancer and choreographer Merce Cunningham, who is still dancing well into his seventies, put it best in an interview I found recently in my clipping file:

> The dancer spends his life learning because he finds the process of dance to be, like life, continually in progress. That is, the effort of controlling the body is not learned and then ignored, as something safely learned, but must go on as breathing does, renewing daily the old experiences and daily finding new ones.

If class is the dancer's trusty, constant, beloved companion through the years, the rest of the dancer's day, which runs until half past six at the earliest, and much later on performance days, provides the element of unpredictability. Until recently, rehearsal schedules weren't posted until the day before, so outside appointments were virtually impossible to plan. It was a given assumption that the company came first, with the rest of your life – if any – squeezed into the corners. This seemed perfectly natural to us; dance was a privilege and an honour, and if we weren't prepared to make it the centre of our lives,

*Even on tour, daily class is a must. This one is taking place in New York's
Metropolitan Opera House.*

other dancers were. We could be replaced. In those days, we were so thrilled
to be deemed worthy of dancing that we demanded neither free time nor a
good salary.

Despite my insecurities, the sheer excitement of being a professional dancer
carried me through those first days, and, three weeks later, at the end of July, I
made my debut with the National Ballet of Canada. It was far from the magical experience I had dreamt of as a girl in Mississauga.

The ballet was Roland Petit's *Kraanerg*, with a score by Iannis Xenakis and
designed by Victor Vasarely and Victor Yvaral. This avant-garde work, commissioned for the opening of the National Arts Centre in Ottawa, had been
premièred just before I joined the company, but while I had enjoyed doing
contemporary choreography ever since those workshops at the MacMillan
Theatre, *Kraanerg* wasn't exactly *Giselle*.

Rehearsals were less than promising. I had been paired with a young male
dancer we called "the King of Garlic" because of his hearty appetite for spicy
foods and his apparent inability to wash his dancewear more than once a

30

week. At one point in the ballet we had to lie curled up together for almost five minutes, and although I'd sneak up for air every now and then, I finally had to have a word with the ballet master to get my partner to clean up his act. So much for the glamour of dance.

Petit's choreography involved moving large clumps of people around the stage to rhythms that had nothing to do with the music. To keep us all together in this difficult counterpoint, the ballet master stood in the wings with a microphone, screaming out the counts. Theoretically, the music should have masked the sideline commentary, but theory and practice in this case were as unrelated as the music and the movement; the strictly-metred counts penetrated loud and clear to the back of the auditorium whenever the music softened. Reducing chaos to comedy, one dancer always refused to hear the counts and followed his own tempo, making our massed movements about the stage not only unpredictable but even perilous.

My own inadvertent contribution to the festivities might have been more appropriate on the Yonge Street strip. We wore white unitards, and I was to wear a costume that had been made for someone else. At my first fitting, noticing that the crotch was a good five inches too short, I mumbled shyly that the legs weren't quite long enough for me. "It's fine," the wardrobe person snapped. I shut up. Wasn't I too tall? Did I really want to bring those extra inches to everyone's attention? So it was that, on my very first entrance in my very first performance with the company, I did my very first large split to the side – and "split" was the operative word. As my increasingly revealing unitard tore from front to back, the pop of rupturing stitches competing with the shouting of counts all the way to the back of the auditorium, I was struck by an unexpectedly cold and sudden draft. Since then, I've tried to rehearse in my costume before performing in it, and I've been a little bolder in requesting alterations.

After my moment in the spotlight, the relentless drudgery of the professional dancer's life set in with preparations for our fall tour. Casting for the ballets – the Kingdom of the Shades Scene from Marius Petipa's *La Bayadère*, Erik Bruhn's controversial production of *Swan Lake*, Sir Frederick Ashton's *Les Rendezvous*, and Sir Kenneth MacMillan's *Solitaire* – was announced and daily rehearsal schedules were posted. You would find your name, jot down your rehearsals and fittings, and show up on the dot if you knew what was good for you. Complaints, carelessness, and haphazard behaviour were unthinkable; our strict regimen was enforced by the very existence of our seemingly omnipotent artistic director, Celia Franca. That fragile, tender Giselle who had lured me into all of this ten years before would sometimes seem more like Myrtha, Queen of the Wilis, as she dominated the next five years of my life.

*With Celia in the rehearsal room, early 1970s.*

Born in London in 1921, Celia had held her own with the best in England. Having studied at the Royal Academy of Dancing with choreographer Antony Tudor and the indomitable Dame Marie Rambert, she joined Ballet Rambert in 1937 at fifteen, moving to the Sadler's Wells Royal Ballet in 1941. That other *grande dame* of British dance, Dame Ninette de Valois, recommended Celia as an ideal founding artistic director for the National Ballet of Canada in 1951, not least because Celia was, in her words, "probably the finest dramatic dancer the Wells has ever had" – something I'd sensed even at eight. New ballet companies in the fifties couldn't count on magnificent technique, so dramatic power was all the more critical to fill the house. Celia's flare for the dramatic contributed heavily to her unquestionable authority in the company.

Celia had earned the right to be demanding. She had known tremendous hardships founding the company, working as a filing clerk at Eaton's while she scouted for dancers and making do in fourth-rate rehearsal and performance conditions throughout those early years. As our artistic director until 1974, she made the National a far larger and more respected company than anyone could have imagined in 1951.

I now realize that Celia had a gentle, caring side, but at the time she didn't appear to take any personal interest in us; perhaps her own sacrifices had made her a little impatient with our unhappiness over the sacrifices that were sometimes expected of us. The nurturing role was dele-gated to David Scott, Joanne Nisbet, and the principal pianist, Mary McDonald, who genuinely worried about us when we were sick or unhappy. Celia had her hands full keeping the company going, and she knew exactly what she wanted. She could be demanding and manipulative in getting it, and everyone was terrified of her.

Like most artistic directors of her generation, Celia had strict standards for the most minute details, from jew-ellery and nail polish (not allowed in rehearsal or per-formance) to appropriate practicewear (no sweatpants or colourful leg warmers). She checked before performances to make sure the parts in our hair were straight, and had been known to hold the curtain until some anguished girl's hair was redone. She made us wear Wet White body make-up for every performance, classical or contemporary, and she'd rub our arms to make sure that we hadn't cheated by using baby pow-der. Now, as ballet inches closer to the real world, we wear Wet White only when we're swans, ghosts, or other exotic creatures.

*One of the early ballets in which I appeared,* Solitaire, *by Sir Kenneth MacMillan.*

Within the hierarchy set up by Celia, the National fell into the three dis-tinct ranks common to most classical companies. First came the principal dancers, who usually danced the leading roles and therefore got most of the public attention. Beneath them came the soloists, favoured with supporting roles and individual variations. At the base of this artistic pyramid lay the corps de ballet, quite literally the core of the company. Probably the least-appreciated dancers, they create beautiful group formations and lively crowd scenes, bringing atmosphere and colour to the big ensemble numbers. These ranks still exist, though soloists now come in two categories, first and second.

As a new member of the company, I was in the corps de ballet, but, as I found out after my first year, that didn't limit my opportunities. At least in recent decades it has been possible for talented corps members to dance leading roles, and, while every artistic director claims to be unique in giving young dancers chances above their official station, it's really never been any different. Choreographers, in particular, may almost always use any dancer they choose, and I'm one of many young dancers who first came to public notice that way. Corps dancers need to believe they can move up; if I hadn't felt that, I wouldn't have lasted more than a year.

I was thrilled to be in the company, but I hated being in the corps. For one thing, corps members in those days had to be in every ballet, often dancing eight performances a week. During my first two months, I reeled from the effort of learning hundreds of steps for every ballet. Bewildered during the day, I'd dream the steps at night and still get confused. Even worse, I sensed the frustration of the older dancers, who had to repeat steps they could do in their sleep until we knew what we were doing. Feeling guilty about this made the learning harder and the stress worse.

Learning the steps was only part of the task; we also had to learn the right style, for you can do the same step in many different ways, and there's a different style – and sometimes, as with Balanchine ballets, a different technique – for different companies, different traditions, and different choreographers. Like other NBS graduates, I had an advantage over outsiders, because we had already learned the basic National Ballet style, which is really much like the British style: neat, precise, and tasteful. But as the company repertoire expanded, and as other choreographers mounted productions, we had to learn more about the other schools, or traditions, of ballet.

One of these was the Danish school, the legacy of the nineteenth-century choreographer August Bournonville and the birthright of Erik Bruhn. Characterized by musically flowing allegro dancing, Bournonville style (*La Sylphide*, *Napoli*) features buoyant jumps linked together in tight, organic sequences and performed with effortless *joie de vivre*. In contrast, the Russian school of choreographers Marius Petipa and Lev Ivanov – which is what most people have in mind when they think about classical ballet (*Swan Lake*, *The Sleeping Beauty*) – stresses slow adagio movements, spectacular partnering, and large, powerful jumps. While this style is very grand and impressive, Russian training doesn't produce as light-footed, speedy dancers as are produced by the Danes or the Americans.

George Balanchine's style of dance was a drastic reaction to the Russian style in which he'd been trained in St. Petersburg early in this century. Russian by birth and education, he was inspired by the fast-paced, jazzy world of the United States in the thirties, where he forged a style of neo-classical dance for the New York City Ballet that covers more space faster than any of the styles before him. The speediness and occasional quirkiness of Balanchine's style requires a modification of normal ballet technique; for instance, the preparation for turns is often quite different, and you can't always put your heel to the floor between jumps.

Over the years, I learned the fine distinctions between these styles, but as a young dancer, I clung desperately to the basic steps and techniques I knew.

What I remember most from those days is being exhausted mentally, physically, and spiritually, and the panic of always having to learn more, more, more. Because I'm a crier – and I've come to see weeping not as a weakness but as a highly effective form of stress release – there were plenty of tears, too. And then, as if the worries at work weren't enough, there were the financial problems all dancers face. For the first time in my life I had a salary – about $80 a week. But after paying for food and a shared apartment (young dancers still have to share accommodation to reduce expenses), even if I had had the energy to go out, I wouldn't have had the money. I usually collapsed into my small bed at night.

It wasn't exactly the bohemian life my mother had feared. It was more like the arduous and blinkered life of an élite athlete, constantly in training. We had to spend most of our time watching our diets, the state of our every muscle and tendon, our sleep, and our equipment. And many of these things were frustratingly outside our control, either because personal and company finances were limited or because we lacked knowledge of the best training and performance conditions.

*The endless task of preparing pointe shoes.*

As a young dancer, I had much to learn about the tools of my trade, and at the top of the list were my shoes. One of the major things that distinguishes ballet from other forms of dance is the ballerina's pointe shoe. While it's possible for someone with strong feet to balance on the tips of her toes without special aid, to be able to run, turn, and even jump on pointe requires special support. To achieve the long, clean line and ethereal quality of romantic ballet, a highly specialized instrument of potential torture was developed: the pointe shoe.

Pointe shoes are handmade from cotton-backed corset satin, with support provided by a block on the point that sometimes sounds like wood but is actually made of layers of canvas, brown paper, and glue that is hardened overnight in a hot oven. Shoes must be as precisely built as machines, and even more individually tailored than an elaborate costume, because dancers' feet, like their bodies, are very different. Some, like me, are lucky to have toes of roughly even length, which distributes the weight throughout the foot more equally; others have a particularly prominent big toe, which takes all the pressure, or a longer second toe, which creates a hammer toe and makes balancing tricky. Dancers have to learn how to take all this into account in ordering the right shoes, or they wind up with poor balance, ugly feet, and considerable pain caused by bunions, blisters, and corns. Over the years, I've experienced such agony from some of these ailments that I could hardly concentrate on the choreography. It took years, and much experimentation with lamb's wool, Kleenex, and other innovations, to learn how to avoid these problems.

Proper shoes are more important to ballet dancers than to any other artist or athlete, because they have to provide the perfect blend of balance, grip, and flexibility. Moreover, aesthetics are as important as is proper function; shoes have distinct visual personalities, which are dependent on the colour, the shape, and even the fabric. Since dancers want their feet to be as expressive as their hands, shoes that help us dance well and look good are extremely precious to us.

The quest for the perfect shoe can take a dancer's lifetime. When I joined the National, I thought Mary Jago had the most beautiful, expressive feet in the company, so I ordered shoes exactly like hers from Freed of London. (Mary, in turn, had chosen that shoemaker because Lynn Seymour used him; the great tradition of ballet extends even to shoemakers.) Like fine silversmiths, shoe-makers, too, have their mark. Mary's used an eyebrow with a dot underneath, so we knew him only as Eyebrow and Dot. For a time, all went well. Wonderful shoes arrived in large batches, and I'd examine each batch and categorize differ-ent shoes for different ballets, saving the softest ones for *Giselle* and pulling out the hardest, firmest shoes for *The Sleeping Beauty*, which is so demanding that it turns shoes to mush in short order (as Aurora, I often go through three new pairs in each performance).

But shoemakers retire. I had to find a new cobbler, and unfortunately the replacement wasn't as reliable as Eyebrow and Dot. There was one impossible batch of shoes: the block wasn't tapered enough at the bottom, and the inside was so crooked it threw me off balance. I decided it was time to meet my maker, so, when the company went to London, I jumped in a taxi and headed for Freed's. At a large conference, which included the head of the company, I explained my problems. The staff nodded their agreement, murmuring "Oh yes, you're absolutely right!" and "We see what you mean!" But all this must have made my maker try too hard, because the next shipment was even worse: clunky, badly balanced, and ugly. I had to switch makers and start over again.

Shoes have to be well made and perfectly fitted, but that's just the begin-ning of the story. Even perfect shoes have to be rather violently adjusted by the dancer, and learning just how to do this is another aspect of the dancer's art. Dancers often bang the shoes furiously against the floor or crush them in a door to soften the block. You don't want the shoes to be noisy on stage, and, while you need support, you don't want the shoes so hard that you can't move smoothly from full pointe to the flat foot – a soft, subtle movement called "going through the foot" and an extremely fine point of female technique. You may also cut away bits of the fabric, inside or out. And then you have to sew elastics and ribbons on each pair in just the right place, an activity that fills many of my "free" moments to this day.

In those early months, I also had to learn about handling a second major factor affecting both the quality of my performance and my ability to stay injury-free: the floor. In Russia and Europe, floors are usually wooden and "sprung" – cushioned with an air space or steel coils – and that flexibility more than makes up for the bumps, splinters, and lack of traction that can cause falls. In North America, however, most floors are made of concrete set on steel – perfect for industrial trade shows but terrible for dance. There's no "give" when you land from a jump; it's like doing high-impact aerobics on a sidewalk, without the shock absorption that even a simple running shoe provides.

The floor's surface is almost as important, and dance companies have (and travel with) different kinds of linoleum to provide the right traction. Sometimes, a surface that's just right for the women in pointe shoes is too sticky for the men in their soft canvas or leather shoes, so young dancers need to be adaptable.

Only in the past few years have we had a consistent surface no matter where we danced. Realizing how many dancers were sustaining back, knee, and ankle injuries from hard floors, and concerned that careers were being cut short, our current artistic director, Reid Anderson, found a special sprung floor that we can use both in Toronto and on tour. It has saved us a lot of wear and tear.

*Performing on a concrete floor for a television special.*

🙟

That first year, even on the rare occasions when shoes, stage, and surface were right, the experience of dancing fell short. Much of what we did wasn't dancing at all by my definition; it was just staying in line, trying to look like everybody else. Success – or should I say survival? – in the corps requires a certain temperament, starting with patience, and that I didn't – and still don't – have. Because you usually have to move or pose exactly like everyone else in the line, corps members have to develop a sixth sense. You learn to look to the side while making the audience think you're gazing modestly at the floor. As you turn your head to the left, you have to peek to see what's going on to your right. You must know if your shoulder is in line with the others, if your leg is too high

*(Following pages) These shots from* La Bayadère *show the discipline and precision necessary for the corps de ballet.*

37

or at the wrong angle. You smell who's had garlic for dinner, and you sense the nervousness of the newcomer beside you.

Despite my lack of enthusiasm about all of this, however, there was one ballet I enjoyed doing even when I was in the corps: *Swan Lake*. I loved the challenge and variety of the dancing; I'd be a courtier in the first scene, a swan in the second, a Spanish dancer in the Ballroom Scene, and then a swan once more. The steps were hard, and when the final curtain fell, you knew you'd done some real dancing.

The hardest ballet for the corps is the Kingdom of the Shades Scene from *La Bayadère*, which starts with a famous (or, depending on your point of view, notorious) sequence of arabesques, in which one girl after another, twenty-four in all, starts down a long ramp, tilts forward perilously into an *arabesque penchée*, balances, arches back again, and then begins the combination all over again. You do this down the ramp and back and forth across the stage, and if you're the unlucky first girl, you do it twenty-four times. It's hard enough to balance on one leg under normal circumstances, but as you leave the gloom backstage to descend the ramp, you're suddenly dazzled by a blazing spotlight directly in your eyes and total darkness everywhere else. This is the most terrifying and exposed kind of dancing, since everyone in the audience can immediately notice the slightest wobble, and I always shook with fear when I had to do it. Anybody who's ever been in the corps in *La Bayadère* must have applauded when, in the mid-seventies, London's *Evening Standard* gave its award for excellence in dance – usually reserved for the likes of Fonteyn or Nureyev – to the Royal Ballet's corps in recognition of their performance in this ballet.

But if *La Bayadère* is terrifying, it's even more ghastly to have to stand on one foot for agonizing minutes while the principal dancers have a great time in centre stage. The worst ballet in this category is the second act of *Giselle*, in which Giselle and Albrecht dance their magnificent, sad adagio centre stage for what seems like hours, while the corps looks implacably in the other direction. It was excruciating to stand immobile, my weight on one leg, for at least thirty-two bars, my wrists crossed in front as if in chains, my head averted to show my disdain for the heartbroken lovers. Imagine the disappointment of sharing a stage with Lynn Seymour and Peter Martins, two of the greatest dancers of our time, and not being able to see them dance. Gazing soulfully into the wings, inwardly furious at missing the performance, I became obsessed with a recurrent outrageous fantasy: I'd break out of formation, rush to centre stage, perform some crazed but oddly appropriate improvisation, and charge out of the theatre, never to return, lest Celia impale me with her piercing eyes. But, of course, I never did any such thing. I was far too well-behaved.

*La Bayadère with Frank Augustyn after I moved on from the corps.*

41

Corps work can be as painful as it is boring. Dancing eight *Swan Lakes* a week makes for some pretty sore feet. In the last act, the swans mourn the betrayal of their Queen; all in line, they bourrée on pointe back and forth across the stage. It looks ethereal, but on stage the effect is somewhat dissipated by a symphony of muffled groans and sobs as the pain of continuous pointe work aggravates bruised toenails and painful corns. We passed the bottle of Bufferin around with some frequency after that.

Years later, sitting out front, I came to appreciate the importance of good corps work. As a corps member, I would persuade myself that I could get away with a so-so turn and disguise a certain wobble in the leg, but I discovered, to my surprise, that it all shows. Whether you're in the back line or not – and because of my height, I usually was – you can't ever really hide.

If a small flaw or a moment of inattention in the corps shows clearly, however, corps members also contribute memorable individual grace notes to a performance. In *La Fille Mal Gardée*, Lorna Geddes, a career corps dancer who is now one of our ballet mistresses, regularly stole the show. In the second scene, a group of villagers enjoys a day in the country. Way off in a corner, far from the central pas de deux of Lise and Colas, Lorna would eat her imaginary picnic with such gusto and good humour, licking her fingers and dabbing her mouth clean, that you couldn't take your eyes off her. My mother once came backstage after I'd danced Lise, and when I asked her how I'd done, she said, "I'm sorry, dear. I'm sure you were very good, but I couldn't take my eyes off Lorna eating her picnic. She was marvellous!" It's not just rhetoric to say that everybody counts on stage, and imagination and creativity make a performer rise above the rest.

Of course, it's fine to be noticed when you're a villager meant to have personality, but it's not so good when you're part of a group that's meant to look the same. In my corps days, I kept getting corrected for raising my leg too much or jumping too high. There's an interesting tension between striving for personal excellence and seeking the perfection of the whole, and, while I'm well aware that things can't change much in the classics, it has always concerned me that so many ballets enforce uniformity for the corps. Many contemporary ballets – William Forsythe's *the second detail*, for instance, or John Alleyne's and James Kudelka's works – are far more democratic, allowing all dancers to do their individual best with what they're given.

Despite these reservations, and despite my discomfort at the time, I learned something profound in the corps: the satisfaction of being a good team player. I discovered the pleasure, the real sense of accomplishment, of working with other dancers to create one powerful image. That's why I continue to enjoy dancing in ensemble ballets like Balanchine's *Serenade* or Hans van Manen's *Four Schumann Pieces*, where I'm one of a group, not "a star." So often in ballet, the whole is far greater than the sum of its parts.

ॐ

In my first year in the company, two different sides of my personality emerged. On-stage, I was frisky and eager to show what I could do (I'm not very competitive in real life, but on-stage I've always been determined to do my best). In contrast, in rehearsals I suffered an almost-crippling shyness. Celia consistently corrected me, "Look up! You're looking at the floor again." Maybe I also didn't look up much because there didn't seem to be a great deal to see. I was nearsighted, and it took me ten years to get a pair of contact lenses.

I didn't get or expect any real encouragement at first; usually no one noticed me, and on balance I was pretty thankful for that. But one day after class during my first month, Veronica Tennant came over. She was already the star of the company, having been plucked from the school four years earlier to dance Juliet in John Cranko's *Romeo and Juliet*, a role with which she would always be closely identified. Having admired her in so many ballets, I was both thrilled and terrified when she approached me, and, smiling warmly, told me that I had done a really good adage, the slow, controlled section in daily class. I was astonished that she had noticed me, let alone liked what I had done, and then that she had had the generosity to tell me so. This was the first of many joyful encounters with a woman who would inspire me in many ways over the years.

It was a good thing that there were some moments of delight that year, because otherwise life was dismal. In the fall of 1969, we went on a U.S. tour, and if my company debut in *Kraanerg* had been a nightmare, my first performance on tour was a disaster. I was one of the Melancholic dancers in Balanchine's wonderfully inventive *The Four Temperaments*, and as soon as I got out on stage, I froze. Perhaps it was because the choreography is so eccentric and unusual that I couldn't remember a single step. Miserable, humiliated, and panic-stricken, I limped along just a shade behind everyone else, copying their movements as best I could.

The pitfalls of touring are a constant theme in a dancer's life. It's an adventure trying to get along with sixty other artists for anything from six weeks to four months. You rehearse together in stressful conditions, perform together through utter exhaustion, eat together in whatever restaurant is open late and is affordable, and sleep together, as roommates or as lovers. Separated from close friends, sweethearts, families, and pets, with one bland hotel room blending into the next, you struggle to keep up your morale. To make matters worse, both dancers' and stagehands' unions severely limit the amount of time you have to rehearse on an unfamiliar stage or to perfect what you're there to do in the first place: dance.

The National Ballet wasn't exactly a major box-office attraction, so we endured a string of one-night stands, often in smaller towns. This U.S. tour began well enough with a week in Milwaukee, but then the whirlwind began as we gave single performances in places I'd barely heard of: Oshkosh, Wisconsin; Waverly, Iowa; Rockford, Illinois; Terre Haute, Indiana. On and on it went, until I couldn't tell if I was in Kokomo or Kalamazoo. Crossing the Smoky Mountains three times in as many days, several male principal dancers got so nauseated that they lay on the floor of the bus as it lurched and twisted on the mountain roads.

After riding the bus from ten in the morning until five in the afternoon, we were delivered in crumpled heaps at less-than-luxurious theatres. In Red Bank, New Jersey, the single dressing room had two light bulbs, a curtain to separate the men from the women, and wardrobe crates to change on – something that struck us as odd until we noticed an inch of water on the floor. The tour lasted only a little over a month, but it seemed to go on forever. Back in Toronto, I thought, "That's it. If this is what life in the company is like, I'm just not up to it."

But unbeknownst to those of us in the corps, the principal dancers felt just the same. One day in class, Karen Bowes, a principal dancer whom I admired enormously (her Juliet regularly moved me to tears), spoke up to management. "On behalf of the principal dancers," she said, "I would like to state that we will never undertake a tour of that intensity again." And she explained why, in no uncertain terms: the gruelling pace, the inadequate stages, and the exhaustion. I was delighted. It was the first time I'd seen dancers protest about company policies (thank goodness, it would happen more frequently in years to come, and I myself would become involved). And speaking out seemed to work: we never had quite that bad a tour again, which is fortunate, since touring would become a staple in my life. We performed in Eastern or Western Canada every year (a tradition that has been made impossible by financial problems in the nineties, and that's a shame; taxes from all Canadians subsidize the company, and we should appear where they can see us). And every January, we toured Ontario.

There's nothing quite like touring northern Ontario in the dead of winter. Ask any dancer who's done it. Once the furnace for the high-school auditorium in North Bay broke down and the audience wore winter coats for the whole

*One of my first Juliets, with Celia Franca as Lady Capulet.*

performance. We wore ours in the wings until the last possible moment before we went on stage, where our breath was clear for all to see. That couldn't happen now; union rules specify temperature limits within which we're allowed to dance.

But problems with the physical conditions weren't always the worst of it. Those January tours were a particular nightmare because, every New Year's Eve, Celia would try to quit smoking, and she'd be at her most stingingly sarcastic until she succumbed and started smoking again. Eventually, she quit for good, but during those early attempts, we avoided her as much as possible – not an easy thing to do on tour.

ℰℛ

Throughout that first year, instead of dancing the performances of my dreams, I was learning the ropes, adjusting to the discipline and the odd blend of frenzy and tedium that characterize the sheltered life of most ballet companies. I had rebelled against constraints at school and hoped for freedom, only to find myself in another highly structured environment that was both protective and oppressive, a shield against the reality of the outside world, but also an invisible barrier to personal maturity and independence. Traditionally, ballet dancers – even grown men and women with children of their own – are called "boys" and "girls." For many of us in those days, these words both reflected and created the reality. We were positively encouraged to be boys and girls because our lack of independence made us easier to handle and less likely to have disruptive opinions of our own. We didn't think of objecting to our diminished status because we had worked so hard to become dancers that our innate confidence and independence of spirit had withered from inattention. Seldom hearing praise, all but the strongest of us internalized criticism so eagerly that we thought we were lucky just to be allowed to stay in the company. More than once after a mistake in performance, I cowered in a cubicle in the communal washroom, standing on the toilet seat so Celia couldn't identify me by my feet and bawl me out. When we were in really big trouble, we'd bolt from the theatre before she could catch us. These were hardly the actions of mature adults.

We were the more easily intimidated because we saw what happened when you went your own way. Soloist Howard Marcus grew sideburns, and Celia ordered him to shave them off. He refused, and Celia fired him. Nowadays, many of us have enough self-assurance to laugh at ourselves by "baaa-ing" like sheep as we're herded through train stations and airports, but in 1969 our lives revolved around the company. Every part of our professional lives was carefully governed, and in retrospect Karen Bowes's courage in speaking up to Celia was amazing. Most other principal dancers wouldn't have dared, and for a soloist or a corps member it would have been unthinkable – and probably terminal.

An unfortunate side-effect of our habitual subservience was that our dancing, too, was regimented and unimaginative. No matter how awkward or ugly an arm movement might look or feel, it couldn't be changed in the slightest. You did it the way it had always been done, because tradition couldn't be improved upon. Just as there was an ideal physical type for ballet, so there was an ideal way of posing and moving, and the logical outcome of those ideals was a stage full of flat cookie-cutter versions of the same dancer. Our well-drilled consistency gave us a unified, professional look (or so we were told), but it also smothered the personal creative expression that makes a company exciting to watch on-stage. We were sound and respectable, but seldom much more. The rigorous company style gave me polish, but it was the extent to which I unconsciously broke the mould that would take my career beyond Canada's borders.

☙

While I was conscientiously trying to cope with new rules, new ballets, new styles, a new environment, shoes, tours, and all the rest, a far more mysterious and unconscious kind of learning was taking place. As a willingly adopted child of the theatre, I was exploring the strange ways of my new home and finding my own place and rituals within it. Because I'd had far less performing experience than many young dancers, this was a baptism by fire.

By day, the stage is a cavernous, chilly warehouse. Transformed by lighting, audience, and the clear focus of performers, it's a hallowed place, set apart from the normal world. It's here that the dancer comes to life.

Between the familiar studio, with its daily classes and rehearsals, and the intensity of the stage lies a transitional space that is both magical and mundane: backstage. Whether you are in the corps or are a principal dancer, in your dressing room you apply your make-up, arrange your hair, prepare and put in place all the tiny details that will transform you into someone else and transport you to another time and place. As your face becomes the character's, your mind begins to inhabit that other world. Outside in the hallway sit the dressers, calmly knitting or reading, attendants awaiting their moment to help you with your costume.

*Sharing a dressing room with Nadia Potts.*

You warm up in the studio, check once more that your shoes and ribbons are tightly secured, and proceed to the threshold: the wings of the stage. This is a strange, sometimes-unsettling place, a cluttered cave, a forest of cables and wires and pulleys, with props – from goblets and swords to strings of sausages – laid out amid pieces of scenery, anticipating their own moment on stage. In the dim light, you see other dancers watching from the wings as stagehands pull cables, shift props, and clear a path for the dancers' entrances. Off to one side, a few stagehands sit playing cards. One stagehand at the O'Keefe Centre always tells me a joke just before I go on. Sometimes I laugh, but more often my concentration is elsewhere.

I'm always nervous backstage. I'm waiting for my cue, and trying to focus my concentration. In the last few moments before I make my entrance, I've learned to erase my doubts and fears, mustering all my courage to convince myself that I'm really capable of achieving what I'm about to attempt. In my first years with the company, that nervousness was often sheer dread. But when my cue came, I had no choice but to get out there and get on with it.

What is it like to be out on a stage? The feeling has changed remarkably little over the years. When a strong spotlight hits you, sometimes you feel like a tiny animal on a deserted road, suddenly paralysed by the headlights of an oncoming car. For a moment you can't see the wings, the floor, your partner. Nothing in the studio prepares you for the way the light affects your balance. When the stage lights are very low and you're in the spotlight, for a few seconds you feel vaguely disoriented.

The spotlight is a lie detector. Every thought is transmitted to the audience: every quiver betrays your doubts, every smile lends confidence – unless, of course, it's not an honest smile but that taut facsimile you sometimes paste on to hide the fear. You know that the audience can sense the falseness of *that* smile, and the knowledge makes you all the more nervous. This is one reason I've always had to believe I really am the character I'm dancing when I go on stage; if I don't believe it, I'm sure that no one else will. That's why it's so difficult when the character I'm playing is herself uncertain and unsure, like Juliet entering the ballroom for the first time in *Romeo and Juliet*. Showing the audience the character's nervousness, rather than your own, is an art that takes years to master, and on that art your credibility depends.

My need to become the character on stage means that, unlike some dancers, I don't and can't plan my performances completely ahead of time. I have to be open to react to whatever actually happens. Usually, I'm not conscious of everything I do on-stage, and I don't necessarily remember what I've done, because I'm concentrating so completely on the music, my partner, and the immediate situation.

And then suddenly it's all over; off-stage, trying to breathe normally but often doubled over, panting, I realize how exhausted I am. My stage smile has disappeared; the character's stylized, elegant gestures have simply melted away.

A constant problem for any dancer, novice or seasoned principal, is nerves. I'm always tense before performing, but I often find myself yawning just before a big solo. For years I couldn't understand it; boredom was the least of my problems, and I certainly wasn't sleepy, even though I might have lain awake for nights thinking about a part. What was even stranger was that I noticed other dancers yawning, too. Finally, Marcia Haydée told me that yawning increases your oxygen intake. You're going to need as much breath as possible, and this is your unconscious physical response to that demand.

Jittery nerves are probably inevitable; there's so much that can go wrong, and you're terrified of disappointing the audience and yourself. But you have to be professional in the face of any disaster. At school, this was drilled into us. The halls echoed with Betty's words, "Remember, you're *professional* children," whenever our shoes came untied or our buns disintegrated. One teacher, Juliet Fisher, reminded us never to let personal problems show on stage, never to deliver the infinitely tempting "Dear Audience" letter. That metaphor is often enough to get us through a bad patch; at times I've fantasized about popping out in front of the curtain and announcing, "Dear audience, please understand why I'm not going to dance well today. I have a terrible cold, a sprained ankle, a corn, and a blister that's killing me. I've had only one rehearsal with my partner, and I'm not crazy about him anyway. This isn't my favourite music, and I'd rather be home washing my hair. But since you insist . . ."

But excuses are unprofessional, and you dance unless you're so ill you can hardly stand. In my first year, Suzanne Farrell, the great Balanchine dancer, was a guest artist in *Swan Lake*. She was breathtaking, but as I watched, I noticed that her feet turned out much more than her knees. I knew that that was the perfect recipe for an injury, and unfortunately I was right. Seated to one side as a Spanish dancer in the Ballroom Scene, I was admiring her panache in getting through that dreadful circus trick, the thirty-two fouettées, when her knee twisted badly. I winced with her pain as she struggled to finish the variation, her legs buckling, and then limped off-stage with as much dignity as she could. It was clear she wasn't coming back.

Her partner, Laszlo Surmeyan, madly improvised the finale of the pas de deux, wondering whether someone would materialize in the wings to take Suzanne's place. Filling out the music as best he could, he surreptitiously cast desperate looks at Celia, the Black Queen. As always, she was in complete command. Descending from her throne with a great flourish, she whispered loudly, "Follow me, darlings, we're going to do a *grande promenade!*" and led us all around the stage with haughty gestures, as if this was how the scene always ended. Reaching the wings, she hissed to the stage-manager, "Bring the curtain down! Bring it down! Now!" As conductor George Crum continued to play, the curtain came down and the audience enjoyed an unexpected ten-minute intermission. After some hasty coaching, an astonished Nadia Potts made her debut in *Swan Lake*, replacing Suzanne for the last act.

The sheer unpredictability of performance makes it nerve-racking. No matter how well-prepared you may be, almost anything can happen on stage. There are almost as many ways of coping with pre-performance anxiety as there are dancers. When Natalia Makarova was a guest artist in Toronto a few years ago, she had candles in her dressing room and chanted a strange invocation to Russian spirits before she went on. I was so unsettled by this that I avoided disturbing her as much as possible – which was a problem, since it was my dressing room, too. Andrew Oxenham, now a successful dance photographer, threw up like clockwork before going on stage. Like children who have just been zipped up in their snowsuits, many of us also feel the urge to make a quick trip to the bathroom seconds before our cue. Margot Fonteyn used to take a few Aspirins for her nerves, and British ballerina Antoinette Sibley once admitted to me that she sometimes downed a little emergency scotch in *The Sleeping Beauty* – "Just a thimbleful before the Rose Adagio." Suffering from Rose Adagio anxiety myself, I once tried a nip of cognac (I hate scotch) before my entrance. It felt rather good going down, but I doubt that it helped my nerves or my performance. I didn't repeat the experiment, partly because I didn't want my partners to smell liquor on my breath and come to the wrong conclusion.

Of course, I didn't have to face the Rose Adagio in my first few years with the company; there were far more mundane occasions for trepidation, such as mastering the prescribed traditional hairdos. My school trick of banging my head against the wall wasn't universally applicable to the various styles: the "classical," the high bun, the low bun, and the French roll. Stage make-up was another delicate art that escaped me for some time, if early photographs of me with Yvonne de Carlo eyebrows halfway up my forehead and bright red "Bride of Frankenstein" lipstick are any evidence. Bodies had to be made up as carefully as faces. For instance, if swans don't put pale pancake make-up on their pink ballet shoes, their feet turn orange under the blue stage lights and look more like a duck's than a swan's. And swans with too much red lipstick or rouge find that those same blue lights, turning the red to purplish-black, make them look like vampires. To complete the ghastly picture, when a good tan is concealed with the requisite Wet White body make-up, the skin looks grey. All this is great for comedy, but it doesn't convey quite the right mood for *Swan Lake*.

In my early years, I also learned how dramatically an audience affects your mood and your dancing, how wrong you can be in sensing their response accurately, and how differently audiences behave in different countries. Less-knowledgeable audiences, especially in North America, can be so quiet that you hardly know they are there. For instance, Toronto opening nights are often filled with corporate guests who are seeing their first ballet and reacting cautiously. And it can be disappointing to see people scurrying up the aisles to get to the parking lot before the rush.

Sometimes a performance seems to be going badly because the applause is faint and dutiful, but then, at the final curtain, when that same audience shouts bravos, you know they were just waiting to show their enthusiasm. Too

*Taking a curtain call with Rudolf Nureyev in* The Sleeping Beauty.

much reticence is a shame; when audiences express their enjoyment all along, dancers ride the crest of their pleasure and perform far better. Of course, audiences that are vocal in delight can be equally straightforward in disapproval. In France, I've heard people boo and hiss if they didn't like a new piece of choreography or music, and I've seen a Moscow audience laugh an amateurish dancer right off the stage.

Although I like feeling appreciated, however, I'm not comfortable bathing in endless adoration. If I can take the bow in character, I have no trouble relishing every second of applause. But when the story is over, so is the trance; I'm myself again, and the inherent shyness that used to make me stare at the floor in rehearsal returns. I always imagine that I hear the applause dying out, so I try to get off the stage as soon as possible. Perhaps Celia, who believed in tasteful, sparse curtain calls, had something to do with this attitude. When a prominent guest ballerina ended her calls by blowing kisses to the audience, Celia shot me a steely glance and said, "I pray that I never see you do something like that." Rudolf Nureyev taught me to take bows more graciously and without embarrassment, but that was partly because he'd grip me firmly by the wrist to be sure I didn't rush off. Frankly, he also liked to prolong the applause to catch his breath for the next variation.

Sir Frederick Ashton managed to have the best of both worlds. When he mounted *La Fille Mal Gardée* for us in 1976, he demonstrated what must have been simultaneously the most modest and the most outrageous of curtain calls. Backstage, the curtain closed, he'd wink at us, as if he were about to divulge a great secret. After letting the applause die down a bit, he'd start poking the curtain with his hand. Poke, poke. "That should keep them going," he'd say. "You've got to let them know something's going on back here. Gives them a sense of anticipation." As the applause began to swell again, he'd walk out ever so slowly, as if he had just enough energy to make one more little bow. Clinging to the curtain with one hand as if for support, he would toss off an elegant *port de bras*, a little wave like the Queen Mother's. It was very restrained, very funny, and it worked brilliantly. Years later, in the film *The Dresser*, the Shakespearean ham actor played by Albert Finney did exactly the same thing. It must be a British tradition.

However, I had few occasions for curtain calls in my first season. My most exciting solo was a ten-second Mazurka in *Swan Lake*, in which I was partnered by Earl Kraul, whom I had idolized for years. But I had no hope of rising above the corps until Peter Wright mounted his production of *Giselle* in the spring of 1970. I found out later that Peter had considered me for the Queen of the Wilis – a role I've never done – but Celia didn't think I was ready: I was only eighteen.

That summer, by no means certain if I wanted to continue dancing, I studied in London and Paris on a short-term Canada Council grant. Reluctantly, I made a decision: if my second season at the National wasn't more challenging than my first, I'd find another line of work. But that fall, Peter Wright returned to Toronto to create a new contemporary ballet, *The Mirror Walkers*, to music by Tchaikovsky. The four principal roles had been cast, but when Nadia Potts decided to take a year off, Peter auditioned three dancers – a principal, a soloist, and me, a lowly member of the corps de ballet – to replace her as the White Girl. I got the part. As one might imagine, this made me fairly unpopular with some of the more-senior dancers, but I was so elated that I barely noticed their resentment.

Here was a real chance to achieve something on-stage. One of the work's highlights was a pas de deux for Jeremy Blanton and me, and dancing with him was pure pleasure; he was an excellent partner, with such sure instincts, such sensitive musicality, that for the first time I could really relax and give my best. Rehearsals went well, and the first performance was October 31, 1970, at the National Arts Centre. Well-received by audiences (if a little less so by critics), *The Mirror Walkers* survived for the next two years.

The Mirror Walkers *with Sergiu Stefanschi, who partnered me in this ballet after Jeremy Blanton.*

Having tasted a role I could really dance, I was depressed when I found myself back in the corps after *The Mirror Walkers*, so, to keep myself motivated, I got up the nerve to ask Celia for a small solo. Our meeting was short and shocking. At the appointed hour, I tapped timidly on her door.

My heart was pounding, and I was not at my most articulate, but I managed to ask if I could learn one of the smaller soloist roles in *Swan Lake*, or perhaps the Neapolitan Dance. I wasn't prepared for the response.

Looking at me with a strange smile, she asked, "How would you like to learn the Swan Queen?"

I swallowed hard. "The what?"

"The Swan Queen. We'll start soon."

Speechless, I fled. Surely I was imagining things. She couldn't be serious; after my unmemorable graduation performance at school, even I knew I wasn't ready for one of the most demanding roles in the repertoire.

In ballet, sometimes you're in the right place at the right time. As it turned out, another U.S. tour was scheduled for early 1971, and Veronica Tennant, scheduled to alternate as the Swan Queen with guest artist Angelica Born-hausen, had injured her back. Celia needed a second cast. Although several principal dancers would have loved the opportunity, and Celia had been irri-tated by my complaints about the miseries of life in the corps, she thought I had the talent and presence to bring it off. It was one of many times I would be grateful to Celia for having faith in me.

I had only a month to prepare, which might have been sufficient for a dancer with plenty of technique and experience. Having neither, I was lucky to have an able Prince in Laszlo Surmeyan. Both technically and dramatically demanding, especially in Erik Bruhn's controversial production, the role of the Swan Queen requires great stamina and a Jekyll and Hyde personality change between the gentle, trusting White Swan and the cunning, malicious Black Swan. Learning the role at the last minute, I had to focus on the difficult steps; there was no time to spend on the role's complex emotions, and the only thing that saved me from disaster was my instinctive response to the music.

In early rehearsals, exhausted and forced to confront my inadequacies daily, what I seemed to do best was explode into tears of frustration. While others consoled or berated me, Celia responded with sensitivity, "Leave her alone," she would say. "She needs a good cry." In fact, Celia was watching me closely: if I didn't have the fortitude to deal with this pressure, I wouldn't make it as a dancer. And I almost didn't.

I was pitifully grateful that my big debut, on January 16, 1971, was far from Canada and the major U.S. dance centres – in the Grady Gammage Memorial

Auditorium in Tempe, Arizona, the last large building designed by Frank Lloyd Wright. I know that fact only because it was on the postcard I sent my sister Sandy; at the time, I wasn't sure where I was. We arrived for the matinée performance after a two-hour bus ride. Trembling, barely fending off a flood of tears, I was trying to wrestle my rebellious hair into submission when there was a knock at the door, and there was Veronica Tennant.

Without a hint of her own disappointment, she dextrously worked on my hair, suggesting how to cope with the incredibly quick costume changes and warning me not to stumble over a fake rock during my entrance. But what she taught me most that day was the value of generosity and professionalism.

I've given better performances – even my graduation performance may have been more accomplished. Predictably, I was so excited about my first leading role, and so inexperienced at proper pacing, that I used up all my energy in the second and third scenes, leaving nothing for the last scene. By then I was terribly weak and wobbly, but Laszlo was wonderful. Whenever my legs buckled, he'd sweep me off my feet into a lift and pretend it was the choreography. He literally carried me through much of the last act, shielding me from major humiliation. In my changing room afterwards, I could barely stand up.

Apparently, the whole performance wasn't much better than my own, because everyone was so concerned about me that they didn't dance well themselves. The nondescript local review hardly mattered; the review that counted was Celia's. She told Canadian Press that I had done "marvellously. . . . It was a thrill for us behind the scenes, because Karen has come right up through the school, and we have watched her grow through all the stages, including puppy fat."

Privately, Celia took me by the hand for "a little walk and a little talk." Obviously pleased, she warned me that now I'd have to start taking my work more seriously: fewer late nights and parties. (I'd never considered myself much of a party girl, but apparently I'd acquired that reputation from my rebellious ballet-school days.) Celia also hinted that I had better wear a little make-up for the receptions I would be attending (at nineteen, I didn't think much of make-up, except for the stage). Then, in a truly perceptive comment, she said that I didn't understand the difference between *rubato* and *legato*, that I tried to do every step with equal and maximum intensity, ignoring the shadings that make a performance interesting for the audience. I had to learn to shape a phrase with sensitivity.

That talk has haunted me over the years. She was right. I was so determined not to slight any step that, while I built up terrific stamina and vitality, there was too little dynamic contrast in my dancing. It's taken me years to get the right balance.

At my second performance, two weeks later in Berkeley, California, I was so nervous I felt nauseated before the Black Swan pas de deux, but I danced fairly well. Martin Bernheimer, music and dance critic for the Los Angeles *Times*, wrote: "Miss Kain is undoubtedly a find. . . . She commands a natural stage personality, sharp theatricality, impeccable musicality, a fine line, astonishing elevation, and an elegant sense of phrase. Not bad for a start."

Reading that now, I'm delighted that he noticed what was perhaps my greatest virtue then – my musicality. But it's typical of my ability to hear only the negative that for years all I remembered was his comment that I gave "the primary impression of a bird whose vulnerability lies in too scrawny wings." From puppy fat to scrawny wings; I'd never realized I had skinny arms, and that was one more flaw I had to worry about.

Reviewing that same performance for New York's *Dancemagazine*, Olga Maynard praised what she saw as: "great technical brilliance and the beginnings of a deep sensitivity. Her Odette was lyric yet elegant, emotionally not fully developed but absolutely true in what was there. Her Odile is already complete – exultantly sly and as sharply beautiful as a finely cut diamond."

I couldn't believe Maynard was writing about me, even though she had hinted that she had enjoyed the performance when she sent me a note with a small gift, a figurine. Her kind gesture touched me even more than the review, for I was hardly a star; for seven performances out of eight, I was still in the back line of the corps de ballet.

Typically, when I danced the role in Toronto three months later, the Canadian critics were less generous. In the *Globe and Mail* (April 22), Barbara Gail Rowes castigated my "stilted emotions," adding, "Miss Kain is so cold she is almost frigid. She makes no use of her eyes or facial expressions to convey a character." Bernheimer and Maynard praised a very young dancer for what they thought she had; Rowes emphasized what was missing. I would later discover that I had begun to experience the difference between Canadian and American critics.

All this attention was new to me, but over the next few years I would have to come to terms with what critics, the public, and the dance world thought of me. I was about to be singled out in ways that I had never imagined.

# CHAPTER THREE

# The Gold-Dust Twins

*"The difficulty with relationships is that they involve other people."*
– Choreographer Eliot Feld

Love at first sight – or something very much like it – certainly exists, but more often than not the people who will play the most extraordinary roles in your life don't make much of a first impression. The first time I saw Frank Augustyn, he looked so unprepossessing that I almost laughed out loud, yet he would become both my partner and the man in my life for most of the seventies, and forever one of my dearest friends.

Part of my initial disappointment at our first encounter, when I was about fifteen and Frank over a year younger, was Betty Oliphant's fault. She had rushed up to me in the hall, bursting with excitement, and asked, "Do you want to see the next Erik Bruhn?" This was obviously a rhetorical question, because what budding ballerina would *not* want to see another cool, elegant Scandinavian god of dance? Despite my personal preference for the exotic Nureyev, I followed her eagerly to the studio, and she cracked the door open just a bit so I could peek in.

I couldn't believe my eyes. Here was no golden boy – just a skinny kid with thick glasses, stringy hair, and chipmunk cheeks. This creature was hardly a candidate for the stage, I thought, let alone for a celebrated career, and I would never have imagined him as a partner for me. In fairness, he didn't think much of me at the time either: he remembers me with braces and exceptionally small ears, something he has teased me about ever since.

A few years later, in 1969, Frank and I were both cast in Celia Franca's ballet *Eh!*, to music by Francis Poulenc. I had a minor role, Frank had an even smaller one: a corpse. He was very funny in rehearsal, wearing white make-up with dark circles under his eyes and lying around with his feet flexed in rigor mortis. But because he was younger and intensely shy, and because *Eh!* was being performed on the same bill as my graduation *Swan Lake*, I didn't really pay Frank any attention. It wasn't until he joined the company and we danced together a few times that I became aware of him as anything more than a funny kid. It's a good thing I noticed him then, because on one occasion he saved me from complete embarrassment.

It was during a performance of *The Nutcracker* during my second and his first season with the company. Vanessa Harwood, Frank, and I had just finished the Spanish pas de trois in Act II. Waiting in the wings for our appearance in the finale, Vanessa and I were gossiping up a storm, completely oblivious to Frank's timid-but-persistent attempts to interrupt. "Excuse me, oh, excuse me," he whispered with increasing urgency. We simply ignored him. Suddenly, we realized what he'd been trying to tell us: we had missed our entrance, and the stage was completely empty except for the poor child playing Clara, twitching and smiling nervously on her throne in front of three thousand people and hoping desperately for something to happen. We raced out in a panic and did our three remaining steps brilliantly. Quaking in anticipation of Celia's wrath, we were reduced to the hiding-in-the-bathroom routine to evade detection until she had cooled off.

The first serious dancing Frank and I did together came a little later. Eliot Feld, then an extremely talented rising New York choreographer, arrived in the summer of 1971 to set his ballet *Intermezzo* on the National. This work is a masterpiece, a moving, imaginative series of duets to Brahms intermezzi and waltzes. Eliot auditioned the whole company for a gruelling three days to select three leading couples, and when the marathon was over, the names on the cast list were Veronica Tennant and Sergiu Stefanschi, Jacques Gorrissen and Mary Jago, and Frank Augustyn and Karen Kain.

I was overjoyed, but not for long. Although he was only in his late twenties, Eliot was the harshest taskmaster I'd ever worked for. Nothing we did was ever good enough, and he let us know that disheartening fact in terms that were both perceptive and sometimes devastatingly personal. Sensing exactly where we needed improvement, and speaking truths in the most direct fashion, he told Veronica – a marvellous dance-actress even then – that she wasn't letting the movement speak for itself, and that if she wanted to act, she should become an actress. He attacked the exquisitely reticent Mary Jago for hesitance and self-consciousness. I tried to ignore the trauma by luxuriating in the music, and he accused me of self-indulgence, of letting my feelings overwhelm the steps.

59

Intermezzo *with Frank, 1972.*

We were wounded by these comments and frustrated that, no matter how hard we tried, it seemed we couldn't please him. Worst of all was our confusion: why had he chosen us, if he hated those very qualities that made us special as dancers?

I've since learned that a number of choreographers get their best results by challenging dancers to give something they didn't even know they had. Perhaps Eliot had learned his method from his choreographic mentors, Jerome Robbins and Antony Tudor. For the first time I recognized that, if I turned myself over to a gifted choreographer completely, I would discover qualities in myself as a dancer that I could never have found alone. Eliot was worthy of my trust; his taste and guidance, his tremendous personal and professional integrity, have influenced me greatly over the years.

This was the first time Frank and I had done any complicated partnering together, and some of the tensions we would continue to experience through the years were apparent the first day. *Intermezzo* involves many variations on the waltz step, and for some reason Frank had trouble with even the simplest waltz (a dance they'd neglected to teach us in ballet school). It remained a constant source of irritation to us both that I picked up the steps more quickly than he did. Not that I was smarter or more intuitive; rather, I was so nauseatingly conscientious that I'd rehearse alone at night, going over and over what we'd learned that day. The next day I'd be ready to move on, but my partner would not. "Don't you *remember* this?" I would whisper furiously as he hesitated in a sequence. Affably, casually, he'd say that, sorry, he didn't; could I show him again?

As it happened, Frank missed the opening night of *Intermezzo* (February 18, 1972). He had injured himself, and indeed throughout his career he would be a frequent casualty of hard stages and overwork. Tomas Schramek filled in, and by the time Frank and I performed several weeks later, our stormy beginnings were eclipsed by a developing friendship.

ço

Frank was born in Hamilton, Ontario, into a first-generation German and Polish family. He had started training as a gymnast, but, when his interest in ballet began to grow, his parents discouraged him – they didn't think it was an appropriate career for a man. Finally, they let him enrol at the National Ballet School to get this foolishness out of his system. But Frank has a deeply artistic soul. He draws beautifully; at a school reunion several years ago, our art teacher, Pat Goss, recalled how very talented Frank was, and, just as sweetly, how terrible I was. Frank's gentle, poetic nature shows in his dancing; dancers really do reveal who they are by how they move on-stage, and Frank had a special lyricism that was somehow intensely virile, a rare combination in a male dancer.

In April 1972, two months after *Intermezzo* opened, our potential partnership was put to a stringent test. I was to dance my first Juliet with Laszlo Surmeyan, who had got me through *Swan Lake*. Laszlo's experience and consideration made the rehearsals easy, and I was fairly optimistic I'd get through the performance. But a week before my debut, Laszlo was injured. I was terrified that I wouldn't get to dance at all, but Celia had another inspiration born of crisis: Frank would learn Romeo – and in record time. We rehearsed for endless hours every day, and while Frank was seldom a quick study, this time he showed how well he could manage under pressure.

Our first performance went surprisingly well, except for two calamities. In the bedroom scene, as we ran towards each other for a difficult step, Frank, in his eagerness to partner me well, veered too close. Our legs got so hopelessly

entangled that we fell flat on our faces, and sheer momentum sent us skidding across the stage. That rattled our confidence a little, but things picked up until the final scene, where Juliet stabs herself in grief upon discovering Romeo's body. Forgetting just how much spring there can be in a retractable knife, I let go too early; the knife recoiled, sailed over the bed, and bounced across the floor. These rather spectacular problems excepted, we were rather pleased with ourselves, until we read Barbara Gail Rowes's devastating review in the next day's *Globe and Mail*:

> If you think Romeo and Juliet had trouble, you should have seen these two young dancers. . . . Twenty-year-old Karen Kain and eighteen-year-old Frank Augustyn just weren't made for each other, at least not on ballet's stage. She is simply too much woman for him. . . . the performance was close to amateurish.

By this time, Frank had shed the glasses and chipmunk cheeks, but he still struck me as more of an Afghan puppy than a noble prince. Since he was younger than I, I often played the officious elder sister, Lucy to his Linus, constantly nattering about what he should do next. Nevertheless, he steadfastly and gradually made the transition from a cautious and slow learner to a great partner. Even that first year, his musicality was amazing and his reflexes swift. I particularly marvelled at his strength; he lifted me so effortlessly, and he wasn't much bigger than I was.

It was *The Sleeping Beauty* that established us as a partnership in the dance world's eyes. Rudolf Nureyev came to the National in 1972, bringing his lavish, demanding production of the ballet, which was a milestone in the history of the company, launching it into a new era of achievement (and debt: the costs were as extravagant as the production values). Although I would soon be dancing Aurora with Nureyev himself, it was in the Bluebird pas de deux that Frank and I first made our mark on the world stage.

This pas de deux, a highlight of Aurora's wedding festivities, reveals how a bluebird teaches a princess to fly. One of Petipa's greatest achievements, choreographed in 1890, the piece calls on every bit of delicacy, precision, and grace the woman can muster, and the Bluebird's high-flying leaps, skimming *brisés volés*, and fluttering hands and arms are as spectacular as anything in the repertoire. Frank had such wonderful elevation and such fluid hands and arms that this pas de deux was a show-stopper from the moment it premièred in Ottawa in September 1972. To show us off (or perhaps to keep success from going to our heads), Celia looked around for an even greater challenge.

*Romeo meets Juliet.*

Frank and I were overjoyed but apprehensive when Celia told us in January 1973 that we would compete at Moscow that coming June. The Moscow International Ballet Competition had been held only once before, in 1969, when a young dancer named Mikhail Baryshnikov won the gold medal, but it was modelled on a competition in Varna, Bulgaria (where Martine Van Hamel took a gold medal in the junior division in 1966 and Evelyn Hart took a senior gold medal in 1980). The mere thought of dancing on the Bolshoi stage was thrilling, and we were eager to meet and learn from other young dancers from around the world. But the prospect was also daunting: four different pas de

deux were required, and Celia had selected particularly challenging ones. Three of them called for impeccable classical technique and bravura: the grand pas de deux and the Bluebird pas de deux from *The Sleeping Beauty* and the Black Swan pas de deux from *Swan Lake*. The fourth pas de deux was from a contemporary ballet, Roland Petit's *Le Loup*. By that time, at home at the NBC, I had danced the leads in *Swan Lake* and *The Sleeping Beauty* with Rudolf Nureyev, who had galvanized the company as a guest artist the previous year, but Frank and I had never danced *Swan Lake* together, and I had never danced *Le Loup* at all. It diminished my anxiety only slightly to realize that Frank and I were at the ideal stage for a competition like this: we'd had some experience, but we weren't so well-known that early elimination would damage our careers.

*(Above and following pages)* The Sleeping Beauty.

The company was taking *The Sleeping Beauty* on extensive Canadian and U.S. tours that spring, so we had only two weeks to prepare for the competition. Much of that time was dedicated to a necessary-but-very-disorienting task: learning to dance on the raked stage that's typical of European opera houses. To help us out, the production department built a steeply sloped, four-by-six postage-stamp surface, but our fears were intensified because the small area made the slant feel even more exaggerated. My confidence wasn't increased when, two days before leaving for the competition, Frank and I did a special performance of the Black Swan pas de deux as guests in the school's graduation program, and I pulled my groin badly.

On May 23, Frank and I flew to Moscow with Celia, principal pianist Mary McDonald, and three dancers who were combining a holiday at the competition with moral support for us: Nadia Potts, Linda Maybarduk, and Wendy Reiser. In my jet-lagged excitement, I was pleasantly surprised to find Moscow

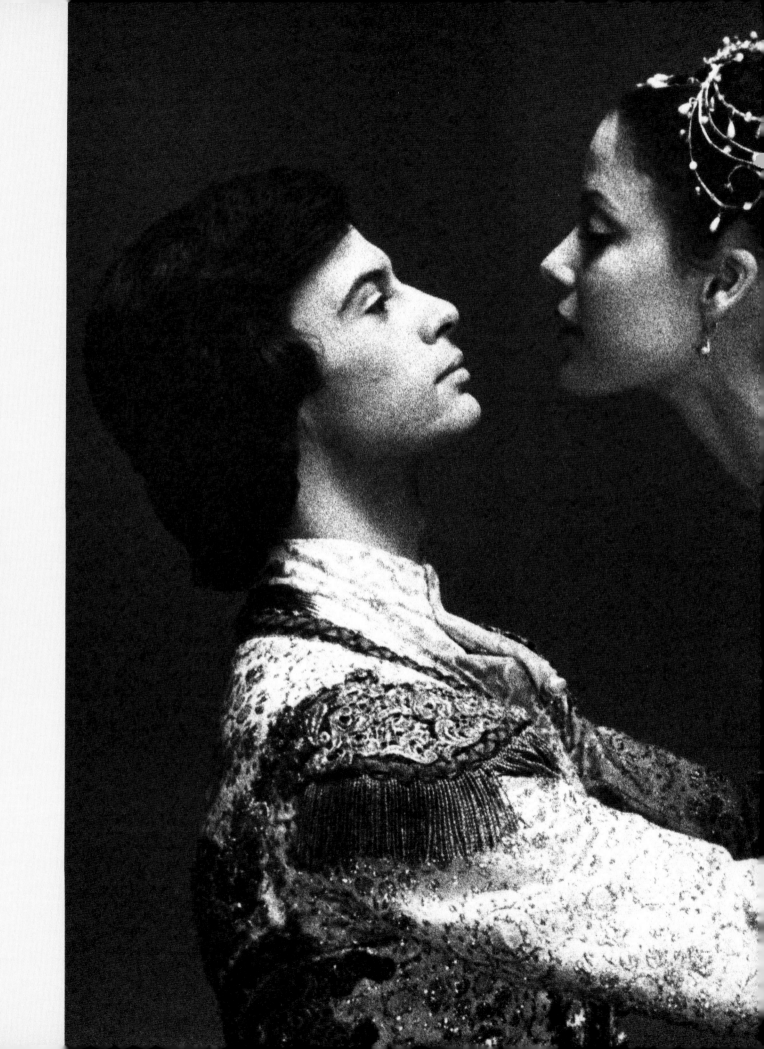

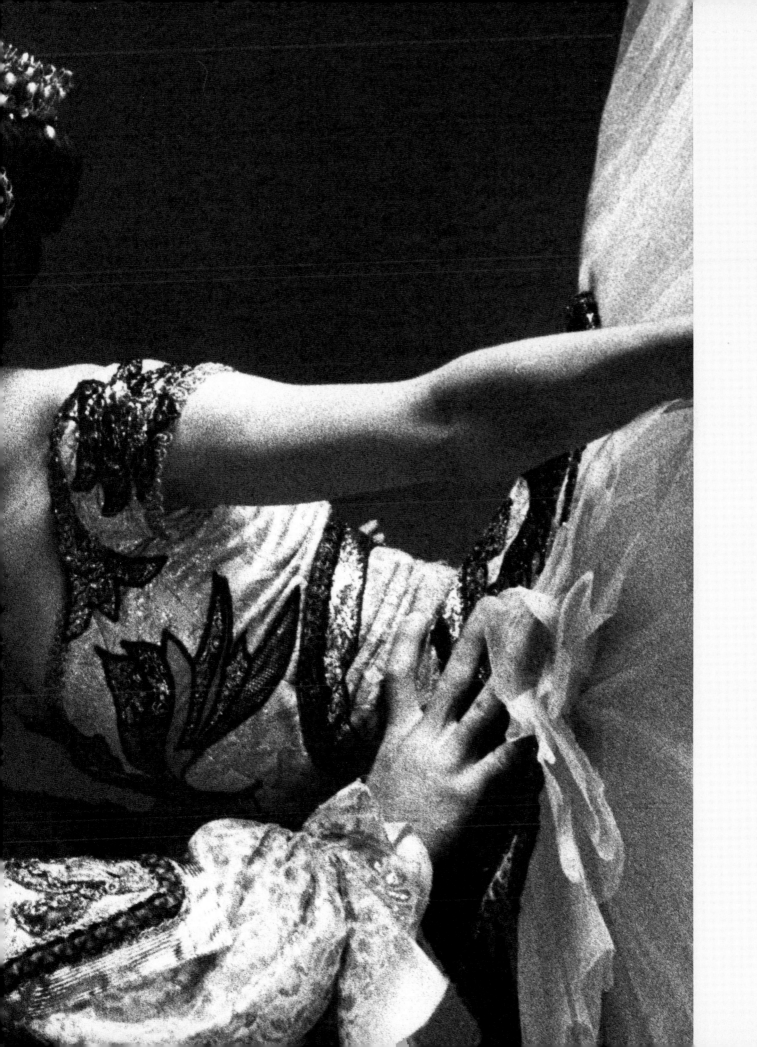

*In front of the
Bolshoi, 1973.*

warm and sunny, but dismayed to find the accommodations far from luxurious and the food worse.

At that time, the Rossiya Hotel was the largest hotel in the world, with over three thousand rooms and a labyrinth of corridors in which I regularly got lost. The rooms were small, and the plumbing was appalling, its odoriferous contents gurgling up into the toilet and bathtub with some regularity. It was hardly worth struggling through the halls every morning to find the cafeteria on our floor: breakfast consisted of either black bread or ancient fried eggs swimming in a pool of stone-cold grease. I must have looked pale and hungry, because the cafeteria women took pity on me one morning. From underneath the cash register, they extracted a dry, flat fish, as hard as a rock. Their concern was touching, but the smell of cured fish at eight in the morning almost sent me back to the fried eggs.

Unappetizing as it was, however, breakfast was a necessity. Then, as now, getting enough food in Moscow was a major preoccupation. Never mind the competition, the important thing was finding enough carbohydrates to keep up our strength. Within days, Mary, Frank, and I were lining up for the privilege of buying a single cucumber to split between us. Wonderfully practical and maternal, Mary elbowed Soviet shoppers out of the way whenever a long line-up at a store appeared to signify the existence of green vegetables. But apart from that cucumber, we never saw another vegetable on the streets of Moscow.

Finally, we phoned the Canadian Embassy in despair, begging for food. TANG flavour crystals, crackers, and other supplies arrived almost immediately, and Ambassador Robert Ford invited us to dinner, where Frank and I amused ourselves by speaking directly to the KGB through the hidden microphones that we pretended were everywhere (Frank used a completely unintelligible Russian accent). A few days later, we tried a plush restaurant just off Red Square, which had been recommended by the ambassador. The menu was extensive, but our optimism was dampened by the knowledge that the fact that an item was on the menu seldom guaranteed its existence in the kitchen. This time, the very first thing I ordered – chicken soup – was "on," and I bounced in my chair with excitement as the waiter marched off to the kitchen.

I was delighted too soon. After a fairly short wait (sometimes we had to wait two hours for a cup of coffee), the soup arrived: a thin, grey broth garnished with a complete-but-emaciated chicken wing, its feathers waving weakly in the liquid. My uproarious laughter suddenly turned to uncontrollable hysteria and racking sobs. Mary and Frank bundled me out of the restaurant and back to the hotel, where I calmed down only after a few oatmeal cookies. During the competition, our somewhat peculiar subsistence diet would be cookies, yoghurt, ice cream, and champagne.

But our Russian starvation wasn't entirely negative; in fact, it had one highly significant result early in our stay in Moscow. Our only rehearsal on the Bolshoi stage had been scheduled for one in the morning the night before the first of the competition's three rounds. Celia was worried that the combination of jet lag, lack of food, and a miserable hotel would make it hard for us to take full advantage of that one chance. As a member of the jury, Celia was in a better hotel, so when she saw our dreadful state she took us to her hotel, fed us a proper meal, and ordered us to rest before the rehearsal. She led us to her room, which had two single beds, and said, "Now you two darlings just have a nap for an hour." And then she left, locking the door behind her so we wouldn't be disturbed. The scene was straight from *La Fille Mal Gardée* – and with much the same consequences.

Frank and I had developed a wonderful camaraderie over the past year. We had come to love and respect each other as artists and as friends. We had laughed together helplessly and constantly (his talent for mimicry is truly uncanny), and we had comforted each other in times of need. But nobody had ever locked us in a bedroom together before, and neither of us was inclined to pass up a good opportunity. Lack of food hadn't diminished our hormones noticeably, so we were soon taking advantage of the situation. When Celia returned an hour later, she found us napping quietly, each on our own bed. We thought we were pretty good actors, and Celia didn't appear to notice anything, even though the windows were steamed up and my hair was an unruly mess. This was the start of a more intimate relationship that would continue, off and on, for the next eight years.

Meanwhile, we had serious business quite apart from our hunger for food and each other. For one thing, we had to grow accustomed to the Bolshoi. We attended performances for the first four days, and I was dazzled by Yuri Grigorovich's *Spartacus*. Vladimir Vasiliev, who had the role of Spartacus, struck me as equal to Nijinsky, Nureyev, and Baryshnikov, and Maris Liepa, as Crassus, was masculine in a way I had rarely seen in ballet. In fact, I had never seen so many powerful men on-stage together; the vast Bolshoi stage seemed to be filled with gladiators, not ballet dancers.

The theatre itself is wonderful. The troika of three great horses in front, the warm, musty feeling that no modern theatre can duplicate, the red velvet and gold leaf, the nineteenth-century lighting, all this conveyed a profound sense of history, making me intensely aware that, as a dancer, I was part of a great tradition.

Because the Bolshoi is a state theatre, conditions were far different from those I'd experienced in company tours. Proper food was still hard to find, but hundreds of employees offered us services that were inconceivable in any other theatre. Women delivered tea, helped me with my hair, gave massages, and kept the stage spotless. It was just as well, too, that this artistic factory was supported by an extensive organization, because there were seventy-five contestants from twenty-three countries at the competition, with back-to-back rehearsals. The Bolshoi never closed; the competition went on all day, there were operas and ballets in the evening, and rehearsals filled the night.

Despite our practice on the tiny facsimile stage in Toronto, the Bolshoi's raked stage – duplicated in the rehearsal studios – was unnerving, to say the least. When Frank turned me in a supported attitude, he would be shorter when he was in front of me and much taller when he was behind me. This not only looked peculiar, occasioning more nervous laughter, but it also strained my supporting arm and foot. In every *manège* of pirouettes around the stage, I'd accelerate dangerously as I neared the orchestra pit, only to struggle as I moved upstage. This kind of thing has strange effects on the musicality of the dancing. In the vast expanse of wood that was the Bolshoi stage, with its obstacle course of trapdoors, there was only one safe place: the main trapdoor upstage. Flatter than the others, it was made of newer wood that was easier to turn on, so I quickly learned to head in that direction before fouettés and other tricky turns.

As if we didn't have enough to worry about, our Bluebird costumes still hadn't arrived two days before the first round. Designed by Nicholas Georgiadis, they were truly opulent, with their rich blue brocade and feathered head-dresses, and an inspiration for a good performance. Eugen Valukin, a teacher from the Bolshoi School and a frequent visitor at the National Ballet School, was helping us prepare, and he tried to alleviate my panic by offering the Bolshoi's costumes. We'd seen these costumes in a performance of *The Sleeping Beauty* a few days before, and they couldn't compare to ours. Fortunately, our costumes arrived just in time for the first round on June 7, but the confidence they instilled was dissipated when the young Japanese dancer who appeared just before us was literally laughed off the stage by the discerning and vocal Moscow audience.

The gasp of appreciation that greeted our entrance demonstrated that I wasn't the only one who loved the Bluebird costumes, but our dancing pleased them even more. That day it seemed we could do no wrong, and the audience – the most supportive I'd ever heard – carried us to greater heights. Even my

*Princess Florine from the Bluebird pas de deux.*

tenuous pirouettes on that treacherous floor made them happy, and when Frank did a more challenging variation than they were used to – two diagonals of high, soaring jumps, instead of just one – the theatre erupted. Most of the Russian dancers were short, stocky, and powerful, so this slender, long-limbed, elegant young Canadian with his extraordinary leaps and difficult variation brought down the house.

Even pratfalls couldn't break the spell. When I ran out for a solo bow after my variation, I slipped and ended up flat on the floor on centre stage. But it didn't matter. The audience paid us the highest compliment by breaking into rhythmic applause after every section of our performance. Never having heard this before, we had to ask people in the wings if it was good or bad. Unfortunately, Celia hadn't known ahead of time that the first-round performances weren't marked – dancers were simply eliminated or allowed to proceed at that stage – so our best performance came when it could help us the least in our quest for medals. Forty-nine dancers survived the first round, and although we were among them, we were too nervous about the upcoming rounds to feel particularly pleased.

I was especially worried about *Le Loup*. At a stage rehearsal one day, a man wandered into the wings and watched intently. Afterwards, he strode over to Celia and, indicating me, announced loudly, "I must have her for Marseilles!" Thunderstruck, I realized that this must be Roland Petit, the choreographer, and indeed it turned out that, hearing the Henri Dutilleux music from *Le Loup* as he was leaving a rehearsal with Bolshoi legend Maya Plisetskaya, he'd come in to see what was going on. Annoyed that Frank and I had overheard his comments, Celia murmured firmly, "Roland, we'll discuss it later," but he was quite persistent, and his determination would pay off several years later when he would provide me with some of the most exciting opportunities I had as a dancer.

Although Roland was concentrating on me, *Le Loup* was primarily a showcase for Frank, as the wolf who craves human love, and it required a strong dramatic touch. Frank didn't think he'd done at all well in our second-round performance, and for a change it was he, not I, who suffered an agonizing crisis of self-confidence. Although he said he would continue to partner me, he wanted to give up his own place in the male division on the spot. But, perhaps with a little help from me, he found the courage to continue, and this incident marked the beginnings of a pattern of mutual encouragement and support that would continue to this day and that I was never to find so strongly with any other partner.

To our surprise and delight, we made it into the third round. There were now only twenty-three dancers: eight pairs, of which we were one, and seven people competing as soloists. As luck would have it, all eight couples had chosen the Black Swan pas de deux for this round. While this coincidence probably made the competition easier to judge, it was less than ideal for the audience, and it was too late to change the repertoire; none of us had anything else prepared. Frank and I were quite edgy, because we'd danced the traditional

*The Bluebird pas de deux.*

Petipa choreography only once. Our National Ballet production uses Erik Bruhn's quite-different version, with different music, and the Bolshoi orchestra didn't have the scores to play it. To make matters worse, we were scheduled to dance last. We had come too far to give up, but the stress was enormous as we fretted backstage, trying to stay warmed up, listening to the same music over and over again, hearing the audience applaud all the tricks and turns of the other dancers, and working ourselves into a frenzy.

*Afternoon of a Faun,* with choreography by Jerome Robbins.

It felt like hours before our names and country were finally read in Russian and we heard a great cheer, but when it was announced that we, too, were doing the Black Swan pas de deux, the cheer became a collective groan. Already distracted by our long wait, we were completely unnerved when the conductor took the tempo twice as fast as we'd rehearsed it; probably the orchestra was eager to put an end to its boredom on this eighth repetition. As is often the case with high-pressure performances, I don't remember much about what happened on-stage or how the audience reacted, except that they gasped audibly when I began my variation with double turns *en attitude* instead of the traditional single turn – something Nureyev, with his characteristic love of difficulty, had suggested. Afterwards, we felt utterly deflated. We returned to our dismal hotel sure that we were out of the running; we'd known all along that the competition was highly political, and virtually from the moment we'd arrived, everyone had known which Russians would win gold medals. The most we'd hoped for was an exciting performance, and we thought we'd failed.

Celia couldn't console us, because she was on the jury, along with Bolshoi Ballet artistic director-choreographer Yuri Grigorovich, the legendary Russian dancers Irina Kolpakova, Natalia Dudinskaya, and Maya Plisetskaya, Cuban ballerina Alicia Alonso, American choreographer Jerome Robbins, Romanian ballerina Magdalena Popa, and many others. Later we learned that the jury had been up all night haggling over the division of the spoils, with the Russians supporting the Cubans outrageously, and the flamboyant Alonso – widely rumoured to be blind as a bat – suspiciously adamant about her own dancers' brilliance. Robbins must have liked us: later he allowed us to dance his *Afternoon of a Faun*, a favour he rarely granted.

Early the next morning Celia called to tell us that we'd done surprisingly well. Of the twenty-three prizes, the Soviets won sixteen, which was no great shock. The highest medals won by non-Soviets were silver medals in the male division for Kelvin Coe of Australia and Peter Schaufuss of Denmark, whom Frank and I would get to know very well when he joined the National Ballet of Canada some years later. Marilyn Rowe of Australia and I shared the silver medal in the women's division, and Frank placed seventh in the men's division. This may not seem impressive, but in fact it was amazing: at twenty, Frank was much younger and less experienced than most of the other men. Even more heartening, when his name was announced at the awards ceremony, there was a huge roar of approval, and he had to take several bows before the proceedings could continue. If the audience had been the jury, he would have won.

Best of all, while our Bluebird performance hadn't counted for the medals, it took first prize for best pas de deux. Careful coaching from Rudolf Nureyev and David Scott, who had given up most of his holidays to work with us, had left its mark, and the personal chemistry between Frank and me contributed something, too. In any case, the Soviet news agency, Tass, called us "a real discovery," and said that we had "won the sympathies of Moscow audiences." The next night, all the winners performed at a televised gala in the Kremlin Palace, which had a stage that was as big as a football field, but, to our immense relief, was flat, so we felt reasonably comfortable with our performance. The next day we travelled to Leningrad to perform at the Maly Theatre.

While we were touring the Kirov School in Leningrad, we met Mikhail Baryshnikov for the first time, when we stopped to watch him rehearse *Don Quixote*. His technique was absolutely stunning; his huge leaps and turns in the air looked so easy, and then he did five perfect pirouettes *à la seconde* from a single preparation, ending in a smooth plié, all before the music even started. He had seen us in the gala and came over to offer brief congratulations, but later we spotted him in the canteen looking so very melancholy that we weren't terribly surprised when he defected a year later in Canada.

As it happened, we'd already met another young Kirov-trained Russian who would eventually go West. Alexander Godunov won the men's gold medal in Moscow, and he made a point of practising his English with us whenever we saw him. With his outgoing nature, his obvious enthusiasm for all things western, and his distinctly non-Soviet appearance (a long pony tail, jeans, and cowboy boots), he seemed to be planning a break even then, and, after the notorious defections of Nureyev, Makarova, and then Baryshnikov, we were sure that the Kirov would never allow him to tour abroad. He didn't manage to get out until 1979, and, although he danced for a while thereafter, he became better known as an actor in films like *Witness*. It's odd that Nureyev, Baryshnikov, and Godunov were attracted to Hollywood, perhaps because they saw it as a quintessentially American industry.

In Leningrad, I learned first-hand about the emotional price of defection. I had a favour to perform for the Kirov's most famous graduate – Rudolf Nureyev, whose name was unmentionable in Russia. The night before we were to leave for Moscow, Rudolf had phoned. My heart skipped a beat; we had danced together, but I was still awestruck that he would actually call me.

"Would you mind buying a fur coat for my sister Rosa?" he asked. I was somewhat preoccupied with last-minute packing, but I would have done anything for Rudolf, so I rushed to Yorkville and bought what I thought was a lovely muskrat coat. Risking the wrath of Soviet Customs officials, I stuffed the coat – and, far worse, several dance books on Nureyev – into my luggage.

It was considered too dangerous to go to Rosa's home, so we met at our hotel. Laughing and crying, she spoke movingly about the brother she hadn't seen in years, and we knew that Rudolf's love for her and for his mother was just as profound. She was delighted with the coat and the books, and gave us a huge vat of caviar to take to Rudolf as a present. When we next saw him, in Paris, Nureyev wasn't particularly impressed with my taste in furs – "You gave her muskrat?" he asked, with a sniff of disapproval – but when he saw the size of the caviar container that we'd lugged all over Europe, he laughed. Obviously, the coat had met with Rosa's approval.

I don't think we fully realized how much our dancing had impressed the Russians until four years later, when we were invited back to dance seven performances of *Giselle* in Moscow, Tallinn (Estonia), Vilnius (Lithuania), and Kiev (Ukraine). It was wonderful to be back at the Bolshoi, where the masseuse, the tea lady, and even the stage-sweepers remembered us well. But the tour was almost as stressful as the competition. Despite assurances to the contrary, every staging of *Giselle* was different from the one before, and we never knew where the trapdoors or Giselle's grave were going to be, what cuts there were in the score, or how many repeats the music would be given.

*In front of the Bolshoi with Alexander Grant, 1977.*

I'd watch carefully for someone to mime an invitation to dance, and then I'd do what I hoped was the right variation. At the Bolshoi, a corps member who was playing a villager kindly served as prompter. He'd peek through the tiny window of Giselle's cottage, remind me what was coming next, and whisper encouragement, "Don't worry! Don't worry! It's going well!" In the Mad Scene, I slipped and slid across the stage to my Mother's feet as if I were stealing second base; I had only enough music to reach desperately to Frank/ Albrecht and die. Fortunately, the backstage ladies were as solicitous and numerous as before: it took a whole team of them to get the splinters out of my backside before Act II. Our artistic director, Alexander Grant, had accompanied us, and he consoled me in characteristically witty fashion by pointing out that I'd made history as the first Bolshoi Giselle to die flat on her back and so far from centre stage.

The remaining performances were less eventful, but in retrospect they gave us an inkling of the hidden instability of the Soviet Union. Even then, dancers in the Baltic countries and the Ukraine were vehement in their criticisms of the central Soviet government for suppressing local cultures and language. Little more than a decade later, in 1989, this festering resentment would erupt into full-fledged political revolution – and Frank and I would once again be in Moscow to participate in a benefit telethon for the children of Chernobyl. On a lighter note, we would arrive to find ourselves billeted at the Rossiya, which in the interval had grown even seedier.

But all that was far in the future. In 1973, we returned from Moscow relieved that we'd done well at the competition and were completely taken aback to discover that the competition had made us stars. Thanks to John Fraser's stories in the *Globe and Mail*, many Canadians had followed our progress with the rapt attention usually reserved for the Stanley Cup, and the public recognition we experienced was astonishing. Our timing was also right: the early seventies witnessed a dance boom in North America, and perhaps Canadians wanted to have some local heroes, as well as the great Russian defectors.

However, our sudden fame created tremendous problems both for us and for the company. Public expectations far exceeded our ability to deliver – we were only twenty and twenty-two – and while the next years brought new opportunities and satisfactions, they also plunged us into a secret nightmare: at that age, how could any dancer, let alone any partnership, possibly be as good as everyone seemed to think we were? When would we be found out, exposed, even ridiculed? These tensions and self-doubts were all the more destructive because we were unable to acknowledge them to ourselves, let alone talk about them, even to each other.

Troubled in ourselves, we were also the innocent cause of a major change in company policy that for a time made many people at the National unhappy. Before Moscow, we had been "promising"; now, with recognition from abroad, we had somehow "arrived," and suddenly audiences everywhere wanted to see Frank and me dance together. Celia had always believed that the company should be the attraction, and that every cast was equally worthy of the public's attention. Consequently, the National had never announced casting before the night of the performance. But our partnership's high profile changed this. People phoned the box office demanding to know when we were dancing, and, reluctantly, the company was forced to start publishing the principal casting in advance. The sold-out houses when we danced were welcome, but naturally there were resentments when our performances sold out and performances by equally talented dancers did not. Trying to walk the narrow line between giving the public what it demanded and treating all its dancers fairly, the company administration wisely made no efforts to capitalize on us as a star attraction. On the contrary, we danced the same number of performances as everyone else. If we were stars – and we were very uneasy with the title – the marketing was done by the critics, the public jumped on the bandwagon, and the company – and Frank and I – reluctantly went along for the ride. I sometimes wonder whether we'd have done better, both personally and as dancers, if we had done badly in Moscow. The hothouse of public acclaim is not the friendliest environment for young artists.

Meanwhile, finding ourselves treated as a "legendary" partnership after just a year, we actually had to continue to build that partnership, by no means an easy task in the best of circumstances and close to impossible when you know that many people in the audience assume you've already reached perfection. Some things came fairly easily to us. Physically, we were well suited; we were both blessed with dark good looks, and we had been trained in the same elegant, pure style. Our proportions were harmonious, even though I was a little too tall for Frank, and we had the same sense of line, so our movements together were symmetrical and pleasing. More importantly, we were both inherently musical, and we quickly learned to sense when the other was going to lengthen or accent a phrase, so that our ability to play with the music, to hear and dance it freshly in each performance, lent spontaneity to our dancing on-stage. Because of our sensitivity to the music, we may have mastered the tricks of timing so essential to good partnering a little more easily than many couples. Frank knew almost instinctively that the speed with which he'd lift my arm in a turn would dictate the rate of rotation, so we could control whether I finished just

*Trying to get it right in rehearsal.*

before, with, or just after the music, depending on the effect we wanted to create. The thousands of hours of rehearsal we had in those days helped a great deal; it's much harder to establish a close partnership in the company now, when the wider repertoire takes its toll on rehearsal time for any single ballet.

Frank and I quickly developed a certain ease with each other in difficult lifts. I'd jump and he'd catch and lift me with such precise timing that our lifts looked almost effortless. Of course, there were exceptions. When we danced Erik Bruhn's version of the Black Swan pas de deux for the first time, we unintentionally provided quite a touch of comedy. The choreography is different now, but then the pas de deux ended in a big lift, with the Black Swan held high over the Prince's head. Somehow Frank's hand slipped, and I started to slide downwards. A highly experienced partner would have known what to do: set me gracefully on the stage and strike a triumphant pose to the final chord. But, terrified that he'd drop me and break the cardinal rule of good partnership, Frank panicked and squeezed me tightly to his chest, leaving my feet dangling about a foot off the floor and my tutu in considerable disarray. Struggling like a maniac, I hissed, "Put me down! Put me *down!*" He only held me tighter as I vainly tried to assemble my feet into something resembling fifth position.

Despite the occasional inevitable mishap, Frank's strength and fast reflexes were a tremendous help. A male dancer must be exceptionally sensitive to tiny shifts in his partner's balance so he can correct problems before they're visible to anyone else; at school, the boys practised by trying to balance a chair on one leg. Frank had that attentiveness, that delicacy of touch, and that swift, unobtrusive responsiveness almost instinctively. On-stage we seemed to be dancing as one, and it's through such intangible perceptions that audiences come to believe that you are really partners. Much of our success came from the fact that we'd worked together so long. We grew with our roles together, and our similar instincts, combined with the sheer amount of work we put in, made for the special chemistry that truly equal partnerships have.

*Frank and I move as one in a comic shot by Barry Gray.*

At least as important was our shared sense of humour, our ability to relieve tensions by laughing together. Because of my size and some of my favourite roles, such as the Swan and the Bluebird pas de deux, Frank called me Big Bird. I called him Mr. Magoo because, without contact lenses, he was even more blind than I was. We played jokes on each other constantly. To give just two examples, in Leningrad after the Moscow competition, Frank swept into the room I was sharing with Mary McDonald dressed in my Black Swan tutu, clutching it shut with one hand while he struck grotesque bird postures with the other. Later, in a dress rehearsal of *The Sleeping Beauty*, Frank urgently made his way down the great stairs to seek the sleeping princess in the vine-covered castle, and when the spotlight fell on me, there I was in a straggly, unkempt wig and Groucho Marx glasses and mustache, with the absurdly flexed feet I remembered from Frank's school performance in *Eh!* The whole company found this hysterically funny, and it took Frank and me every bit of self-control to get through the scene the next night in performance.

However, this incident had its negative side. I'd always danced dress rehearsals full out to simulate performance conditions, and for years I'd been urged to save my energy for the opening. On this night, despite the company's having danced the ballet on tour steadily for the past few months, I once again

*Princess Aurora gone wrong. My attempt at levity did not meet with universal approval.*

set what I thought was a good example by dancing with total commitment. The wig and glasses, introduced in a mime scene at the end of an act, were my innocent attempt to introduce a little harmless levity into what was, in the circumstances, a rather boring exercise for everyone. Alexander Grant saw things very differently: he told me off vehemently, accusing me of setting a bad example for the rest of the company.

But humour served Frank and me well. Because we knew how to laugh at each other and ourselves, we were amused rather than dismayed by a less-than-glowing review of a *Sleeping Beauty* performance in 1974. *Vancouver Sun* columnist Alan Fotheringham wrote:

> Amidst perfection of third act, imperfection becomes news. Head fairy, the nummy Karen Kain, crowd favourite, takes flying half-gainer across stage aimed at partner Frank Augustyn. Frank unfortunately may have spotted aunty in gallery. Not ready. Karen shooting past like Concorde on test flight while Frank recovers. Ends up handling her like a bundle of kindling that's gone askew. Karen's pretty nose saved from slivers. Dangerous sport, this.

*The "glamorous" life backstage.*

It *is* a dangerous sport, but that particular tense moment was my fault. Energized by the audience's enthusiasm, I jumped so eagerly that I sailed right past Frank, who managed to seize my ankles as I flew by. Frank never ever let me fall.

If Frank and I had much in common by nature and found even more with time and practice, however, we also had major temperamental differences. Some of these helped the partnership by providing constructive tension and overall balance, but some were clearly harmful. For example, I tend to be stubborn and impatient: I want everything perfect, right away, and if it isn't, I want to keep working until the problem is solved. Frank is stubborn, but he's also patient, willing to bide his time until things fall or drift into place. I was often exasperated that he didn't seem to care about getting the steps right as deeply as I did; he often felt (with some justification) that I was a highly-strung work-aholic. Sometimes his good humour worked to calm my tendency to become overwrought when we weren't mastering the steps fast enough. At other times, nothing could have irritated me more than Frank's laid-back, smiling reassur-ances: "Karen, relax. It's okay. Everything will be fine." More often than not he was correct, but I always preferred to get it right in the studio; even after a string of perfect rehearsals, I've never been confident that the performance will go well.

In our early days, we sometimes fought so ferociously that ballet master David Scott literally had to hold us apart. I had rarely been this angry with any-one in my life, and I certainly had never shown my fury in public. I had been spoiled by Jeremy Blanton's experienced and solicitous partnership in *The Mirror Walkers*; it took thousands of hours of rehearsals to achieve the same ease and sense of security with Frank.

Another source of tension was Frank's susceptibility to the back, knee, and ankle injuries many male dancers suffer, because of all the lifting and jumping on hard floors. Losing him unexpectedly before a performance was always disap-pointing, but what made me particularly edgy was the loss of time and tech-nique that the injuries entailed. I'd be restless and irritable when he returned, upset that he hadn't somehow avoided the injury and that his recuperation took longer and longer each time. This wasn't his fault, of course; there was far less knowledge of proper conditioning methods then than now, and his training hadn't strengthened him adequately for the extraordinary workload he would face as a budding principal dancer. A hard and willing worker, he also let him-self unwittingly be pushed into too heavy a rehearsal and performance schedule.

To put these problems in perspective, they were far less serious than those of most partnerships in ballet, and, despite them, at least as early as the Moscow competition, Frank and I sensed we had something quite magical as a couple. Thinking back on those days now, I have a much better appreciation of what made us special to each other and to the audience when we danced together. First, there was an unmannered simplicity in our dancing and acting that is very rare in ballet, perhaps because most dancers are older when they start per-forming leading roles. I've seen so many young dancers "produced" by their coaches over the years that I'm all the more grateful now that our early coaches – Celia, David Scott, and Nureyev – had the courage and wisdom to let us appear to be as young and innocent as we were, without embellishment or feigned sophistication. Second, we forged an intense bond of emotional and

physical trust. We dared to be open with each other; if we hadn't, we wouldn't have fought so violently at times. There was a directness, an honesty, in our relationship that not only helped us create our roles together but also carried across the footlights. Nureyev once told me that when you're on-stage, the only thing you have to give your partner is yourself, and if you don't give that, your partnership is mere artifice. Frank and I were able to give ourselves to each other with total, unquestioning commitment. In fact, we probably were more generous and trusting on-stage than off, so that, in ballets like *Giselle* and *La Fille Mal Gardée*, we became the characters we danced, enjoying and some-how conveying the richness and depth of a love that transcended our off-stage relationship. What allowed – or perhaps forced – us to develop this trust was our isolation.

Our rapid rise to prominence, our awareness of the envy of some of the other dancers, and our shared and unspoken sense that we weren't as good as everyone thought conspired to make us feel that it was Karen and Frank against the world. We were determined to encourage and support each other, to make it possible for each of us to excel. We held hands in the wings before an entrance to give us the strength and courage we so desperately needed. We were a team; if one of us failed, we both failed.

Over the years, Frank and I learned which ballets suited us as a couple, both dramatically and choreographically. *Romeo and Juliet* was one of these, and it was here that I first realized what a fine and subtle actor Frank could be.

*Giselle's death, in rehearsal and performance at the Bolshoi.*

In the second act, Romeo suddenly realizes he must avenge the death of his friend Mercutio, who has just been slain by Tybalt. Romeo picks up Mercutio's sword and hesitates for a long moment before initiating a fight to the death, and I've never seen anyone show the point at which the gentle Romeo is

Giselle, *Act I.*

overcome by murderous rage as clearly as Frank did. When Rex Harrington danced his first Romeo with me in April 1993, he brought something of the same quality to that moment, and I asked him how he'd discovered it. "I remembered Frank," he answered.

When the time came to realize my childhood dream and dance *Giselle* in September 1973, it was the first full-length ballet Frank and I learned together in the studio from day one, and for once we both had ample time to learn, explore, and plan the roles before our debut. The ballet suited us because, while challenging, it wasn't beyond our reach technically or emotionally. It was the kind of dancing we loved: difficult but full of jumps and our other favourite

*A tender moment between Lise and Colas.*

steps. We had many arguments along the way (and so did Celia and David, who were coaching us), but the quarrels were constructive. We had confidence that we would do well, and we did – most of the time. Given our preparation and comfort with the roles, then, it was ironic that it was in a performance of *Giselle* in Winnipeg that Frank would have one of his most serious injuries. I noticed him wince a little in his variation in Act II and then start to squint a bit with one eye and look down at the stage. "Poor Frank. He's lost a contact lens," I thought, carrying on as usual and feeling as much amusement as sympathy. Only at the curtain call did I notice that his knee was the size of a melon: he had torn a cartilage and had completed the act in almost-unbearable pain.

One of the ballets I love most is Sir Frederick Ashton's *La Fille Mal Gardée*, in which I played Lise, a mischievous country girl with an undertone of sweetness, and Frank was her lover, Colas, full of country-bumpkin swagger and exuberance. Ashton coached us in this ballet in 1976, and although it had been created sixteen years earlier, I always felt it had really been made for us. We just hadn't been around at the time. With a plot full of minor spats that are overcome by good humour and love, that gem of a ballet conveys more joy to the audience than almost any other I could name, and what Frank and I did on-stage reflected exactly how we felt about each other. We didn't have to think about acting or try to be cute; we just regressed to our mid-teens and were ourselves.

There's a moment in the last act when Colas hides beneath some bundles of hay and surreptitiously watches Lise daydreaming; she mimes their marriage, her pregnancy, and how she'll bring up their children. When Colas bursts out of the hay, Lise is so humiliated that she starts to cry. Trying to console her, Colas plants kisses on her arm, shoulder, and neck with a teasing tenderness

*Frank and I dance* La Fille *for a CBC production.*

that perfectly defined not only Colas but also Frank at his most lovable. *Fille* will always be one of my dearest memories, both as a work of art and as a symbol of what Frank and I meant to each other as dancers and as people. Much of acting is reacting, and because Frank and I trusted and cared about each other so much, we could react on-stage with utter openness and spontaneity. We were completely believable in these roles, and the public loved to imagine our storybook romance both on- and off-stage.

We had a long run together, but I now see that even our off-stage relationship was defined by dancing. Had we not been partners, paired at an early age and isolated as Canadian celebrities, we would probably never have been lovers. We had one of those relationships that grows from and depends on being part of a team mutually committed to all-absorbing work. Perhaps because I've never been uncomfortable living alone, Frank and I never lived together, and on days off we often went our separate ways, seeing family, doing laundry, and sewing shoes. For long periods during the seventies, our off-stage relationship would pause while we were involved with other people, as I was, for a full year, with a dancer in France.

Finally, around 1980, the combination of frequent separations and ceaseless work when we were in the same city led to the unravelling of our partnership. Frank spent the 1980-81 season with the Berlin Opera Ballet. When he returned, we danced together several times with great pleasure, but the divisions between us were growing deeper. I wanted us to explore roles more fully – he would probably say "exhaustively" – and challenge each other more. He seemed content with the status quo and was increasingly irritated with my nagging. It was clear to me that we wanted different things at that stage of our careers, and the partnership wasn't progressing. After one performance that left me particularly dismayed by what was happening to us, Erik Bruhn, who had become our artistic director in 1983, took me aside and said firmly but with great sympathy, "Karen, you have to give your own performance."

Erik was right: at a certain point, even the best partnerships have to end if dancers are going to continue to improve, as individuals *and* as partners, and our time had come. Accepting this was one of the most wrenching experiences of my life, as devastating as the break-up of a marriage and in some ways even worse, because both our work and our emotional lives had been so completely enmeshed for so long. I had thought I would always dance with Frank, and I couldn't imagine a professional life without him. We were a team. I felt I was abandoning something infinitely precious, something on which my career depended, and for years, with new partners, it was indeed frustrating to have to spell out in words something that Frank would have understood immediately.

La Fille Mal Gardée.

Fortunately, I lost neither my friend nor my career; in fact, the end of the partnership was probably necessary to preserve them both. Frank and I found new challenges in dancing with other people – in my case, wonderful dancers like Rex Harrington and Serge Lavoie from within the company, and, from without, Laurent Hilaire, who combines Frank's amazing musicality with Nureyev's fine dramatic intelligence and technique. I've grown as a dancer through these new partnerships, but Frank remains my dear and trusted friend, with whom I share long phone conversations and the occasional gala performance, usually to benefit the Ottawa Ballet, of which he was artistic director until 1994.

I'll always miss Frank; the bonds we created are lifelong. We shared something truly extraordinary, something most dancers are never lucky enough to find, and I treasure those memories. Some ballets will never feel as good onstage as they did with Frank.

*Rudolf*

*"I am a dancer."* – Rudolf Nureyev

If it hadn't been for Rudolf Nureyev, I wouldn't have had an international career at all. Moscow alone wouldn't have done it for me; you need to perform regularly in major dance centres – New York, London, and Paris – to be remembered from one year to the next. The National Ballet has never received sufficient funding to allow frequent tours to these places, but Rudolf took me there. Even more importantly, he became my generous mentor, adored coach, partner, friend, and inspiration; his belief in me helped me believe in myself. He helped me find my own style as a dancer, combining athleticism with lyrical elegance.

Having defected from his native Russia in 1961 when he was only twenty-three, Rudolf later explained, "I came to the west wanting to know all that I could about dance. I was like a thirsty man wanting to drink knowledge. I wanted only to learn." His intent may have been to learn, but he taught dancers in the west more than anyone had since Diaghilev and Balanchine. Rudolf's dynamic influence on London's Royal Ballet and its prima ballerina, Dame Margot Fonteyn, sparked a worldwide renaissance of popularity for ballet, and the Nureyev–Fonteyn chemistry was all the more remarkable since Fonteyn, born in 1919, had danced Giselle before Rudolf was born.

I had been dazzled by the great Tartar in my earliest years at the National Ballet School, when he and his close friend Erik Bruhn had visited class, but I didn't see him perform until I was about fourteen, when he and Lynn Seymour danced *La Sylphide* with the Royal Ballet at Maple Leaf Gardens. Then, as now, Toronto had no ballet theatre worthy of the name, so an abysmal makeshift stage was built on scaffolding at one end of the rink, and the cheap seats for the ballet school were closer to the roof than to the stage. Even at that distance, I was stunned by Rudolf's charisma and the beauty of Lynn Seymour's feet.

Afterwards, I just had to see him up close, so I convinced a few friends to join me in the rash attempt. Evading our watchful chaperons, we stole back-stage, but my friends were apprehended by security guards. I barely escaped by hiding in the scenery, where a kindly stagehand found me quaking; offering me a pen and a program for Mr. Nureyev's autograph, he led me to the dressing room. I mustered enough courage to enter, but could scarcely breathe as I approached my idol. Fortunately, he was giving a radio interview, because if he'd spoken to me I would have fainted. Mute, almost paralysed, I stood gawking as he signed my program, and when Lynn Seymour waltzed in with a bouquet of roses, I thought I was dreaming. Reality hit me only when I was removed by one of the entourage and came face to face with a policeman on the lookout for a missing person in a green tartan skirt and a blazer. I was in trouble again, but it was worth it. Rudolf wasn't amused when I recounted this story years later, and now I understand perfectly whenever an attractive young man tells me he first saw me dance when he was five.

I didn't begin to appreciate the full extent of Rudolf's phenomenal impact on dance, however, until he came to the National to mount his production of *The Sleeping Beauty* in 1972. Along with Erik Bruhn (who never captured the popular imagination the way Rudolf did, and therefore never got his full share of the credit), he had made that previously second-class citizen, the *premier danseur*, the ballerina's equal. Rudolf and Erik danced so superbly that, almost singlehandedly, they created an insatiable public appetite for male dancing. They responded to this new demand in a way that pleased both audiences and themselves: by adding many more male solos to their new productions of the classics (for example, the Prince in Rudolf's *Sleeping Beauty* has five, while the Petipa original has only one). Moreover, the technical and musical difficulty of the new choreography was so great that younger dancers like Frank Augustyn were challenged to raise the level of their own dancing.

Rudolf and Erik were also deeply concerned with the dramatic plausibility of the classics. Virtuosity was a beginning, but it wasn't enough; they sought credible psychological motivation for the well-worn fantastic plots, and this resulted in some of the most daring and imaginative restagings of the classics imaginable, from Rudolf's *Nutcracker* to Erik's *Swan Lake*. The freshly conceived stories demanded a new kind of acting, and the heavily mannered clasping of hands and pained expressions, common to this day in most Russian male dancers, were replaced by honest, realistic gestures. Inevitably, purists chastised Rudolf and Erik for these innovations, but they were too creative and sensitive as artists to be willing to consign dance to a museum. As Rudolf said, "When I change, where I change is for reason, for good reason that we dance these ballets today, not yesterday."

Over the years, I've come to see that most Russian-trained dancers (Nureyev and Baryshnikov are remarkable exceptions) are trapped in an anachronistic style, both as dancers and actors; they're brilliant technicians but unconvincing characters, and they can't adapt to contemporary choreographic styles. Perhaps because Rudolf started dancing late and was always a rebel, he avoided those limitations of Russian training. In any case, he dedicated his incredibly agile mind, intricate musicality, and formidable physical talents to making an indelible mark on western ballet.

*Rehearsal with Rudolf in his customary woollen toque.*

When the legendary Nureyev arrived to begin rehearsals for *The Sleeping Beauty* in August 1972, we were well aware he'd chosen to work with us primarily to have a North American touring vehicle for himself and his choreography, but that didn't offend us; we knew we weren't considered a world-class company, and we wanted to learn from the best. Obviously, Nureyev wouldn't have us holding trees in the background: we'd dance, too, and we enjoyed the passionate discipline, the obsessive dedication to excellence, that he exemplified and inspired. Painstakingly, buoyed by anticipation and driven by the terror of falling short, we prepared for his arrival by learning the difficult steps from a ballet mistress who had worked with Nureyev at La Scala, Milan, where he first staged the production in 1966.

I'll never forget my first sight of him in the studio. In eighty-degree heat, he wore a woollen toque, layers of woollen clothing, support stockings, and large, clunky clogs. Later we'd learn that it was never too hot for him; he always insisted on having the air-conditioning turned off, something I understand perfectly now that I'm older and realize how much harder it is to keep the muscles warm enough to dance easily. Interestingly enough, Glenn Gould, also notorious for his bizarre attire, was one of Nureyev's idols.

Rudolf's handsome, exotic face was dominated by prominent cheekbones and the most penetrating green eyes I've ever seen, blazing with intelligence, humour, and restless energy. Even more attractive close up than he was on-stage, he had a captivating smile, enhanced by a fascinating scar on his top lip that came from childhood rough-housing. My schoolgirl crush on him immediately increased a thousandfold; I've never met a more vibrant human being.

In the first rehearsal, Rudolf began by watching all casts dance the fairy variations in the Prologue. As soon as I had finished the Principal Fairy's variation, Rudolf stopped, pointed to me, and demanded to know why I hadn't been cast as Aurora. In fact, Celia had good reason not to cast me in the lead: I'd been ill on our European tour that spring and hadn't quite regained my strength; I had little experience dancing under intense pressure (this was ten months before the Moscow competition); she thought it would be quite hard enough for me to dance with him in a ballet I already knew – *Swan Lake* – on the upcoming tour; and I was the youngest principal dancer in the company (to her credit, Celia was trying to distribute roles fairly). These considerations meant nothing to Rudolf, and he continually embarrassed us both by discussing his plans for me in front of everyone.

This wasn't the only disagreement Rudolf and Celia would have; on the contrary, despite their great mutual respect, they fought about virtually everything. Passionate arguments are common in the ballet world, probably because most people who work there care so profoundly about what they are doing. So, while both Rudolf and Celia demanded excellence and purity of style, Celia was deeply rooted in the tasteful, understated British tradition, with its reticence, its scorn for showy virtuosity, its soft, rounded line, and its exquisitely precise footwork. In contrast, Rudolf wanted to make dance more exciting by showing some of the effort involved, by highlighting its sheer vigour and athleticism. The catalyst for the development of a bold new technique for an entire generation of dancers, he also brought to his partnership with Fonteyn feverish intensity and magnetic sexual chemistry. To sum up the differences, Celia was British and Rudolf was Russian. Celia wanted good taste and Rudolf wanted intensity and daring.

Fortunately, the Fonteyn–Nureyev partnership had shown just how dynamic a mixed marriage of Russian and English styles and temperaments could be, and both Rudolf and Celia hoped this magic formula could transform a company of English-schooled dancers. Hadn't she invited him, and hadn't he agreed to come?

The British and Russian qualities that Fonteyn and Nureyev had brought individually to their partnership had, by 1972, also become the qualities that Rudolf wanted to see fused in a female dancer. While he always adored Fonteyn and her embodiment of British taste, the other Royal Ballet dancers he particularly liked, such as Monica Mason (born in South Africa) and Canadian Lynn Seymour, had a dramatic power, a total commitment, and an athleticism that weren't usually produced by purely British training. Rudolf saw Fonteyn as the definitive Aurora of her time, but for his own production of *The Sleeping Beauty*, he wanted dancers who could combine Fonteyn's refinement, warmth, and musicality with the energy and power of the Kirov's great prima ballerina Natalia Dudinskaya. No mean feat!

The Russian qualities Rudolf wanted in his Aurora extended to his vision of the production itself, and here, too, Celia took exception to some of his ideas. With her vivid memories of the gentler, more-traditional Petipa–Sergeyev Royal Ballet production (in which Fonteyn had captivated New York

*The Awakening Scene from* The Sleeping Beauty, *with Wendy Reiser (left) and Linda Maybarduk (right).*

in 1949), she didn't approve of the bold, assertive style Nureyev had adopted. Most productions of *The Sleeping Beauty* are filled with light and pastels; Rudolf's was dark and heavy, with the dancing itself the only ray of transforming brightness in the gloom. Later, Celia insisted that Nureyev had "ruined" me for some years by replacing my lyrical quality with what she called "one set, stiff position after another."

Celia's taste in costumes also differed from Rudolf's, and here aesthetic and financial factors started to merge. She rationed sequins like diamonds, but Rudolf insisted on an opulent production (designed by Nicholas Georgiadis) in which you weren't really dressed unless you had a lavish necklace and earrings. Veronica and I knew we weren't about to return to the days of the tsars, when ballerinas wore priceless jewellery bestowed on them by their admirers, but we

*Dancing the Principal Fairy in the Prologue of* The Sleeping Beauty, *with Sonia Pérusse (left) and Vanessa Harwood (right).*

were thrilled at the prospect of rhinestones sparkling under the spotlights, and we shopped happily for perfect earrings for every costume.

Still more alarming, it was clear that production costs – already extravagant by National Ballet standards – were soaring. When Rudolf and Celia weren't sparring about whether I should dance Aurora, they were having even livelier budget discussions. Celia finally convinced Rudolf and Nicholas to have fewer chandeliers, to make some costumes do double duty, and to replace seven carriages with one (pragmatic as ever, Celia pointed out that seven simply wouldn't fit on Canadian – or most American – stages).

But even with every possible economy, *The Sleeping Beauty* was the biggest gamble of the National's existence. The projected $250,000 budget mushroomed to over $350,000, and several members of the board mortgaged their houses to make up the difference. This unheard-off exorbitance captured the imagination of the Canadian press, and when the production finally opened at the National Arts Centre in September 1972, before Governor General Roland Michener, Prime Minister Pierre Trudeau, and a glittering audience, the reviews invoked accounting principles as much as they did aesthetics.

The gamble paid off dramatically in years to come. *The Sleeping Beauty* and its star, Nureyev, were the price of admission to a two-month, thirty-two-city U.S. and Canadian tour, arranged by impresario Sol Hurok and culminating in a long season at New York's Metropolitan Opera House. The production paid for itself many times over with hundreds of performances, and, far more importantly, it gave the company international recognition and critical acclaim. *The Sleeping Beauty* and our association with Nureyev launched a golden era, not least because the company grew in size by almost a third, to sixty dancers (the minimum for a classical ballet of this scale), and those dancers were given regular employment (until then, we were laid off for two months every year). Steady employment and almost-continuous dancing meant that our productions acquired a polish they've seldom enjoyed before or since; sitting out front, I saw quite a few performances that were both exciting and virtually flawless, proof that the company had really arrived.

As our tour started that year, however, I was preoccupied not with *The Sleeping Beauty* but with *Swan Lake*, for it was in that ballet, in Montreal (the next stop on the tour after Ottawa), that Rudolf and I would first be partners. There was almost no time for rehearsals, since *Beauty* got all the attention, so I was more terrified than I've ever been in my life. I had danced only a few performances as the Swan Queen, and I was completely in awe of both Rudolf and Erik Bruhn, who rehearsed us on the few occasions we had the chance. Neither was I particularly put at ease by the fact that Rudolf kept changing

*Act III of* The Sleeping Beauty.

the choreography to make it more difficult, and Erik happily agreed to all his suggestions, which meant that I had to relearn huge chunks of the ballet. Otherwise, Rudolf was kind and gentle, insisting only that I look him straight in the eye as we danced. He couldn't have known that that was the hardest thing he could ask: intensely shy as I was, having to look into those piercing green eyes was just too much.

That first performance was enthusiastically received by the Montreal critics and public, but for once reviews didn't matter at all: I had discovered what it was like to have real emotional and artistic rapport with my partner. My heart pounding, I dared to meet his eyes, and he responded by partnering me with ease, strength, and complete commitment. Our steps were words in an intimate conversation; the natural intensity and honesty of his acting drew me and the audience into his world. That evening in Montreal, each of us gave the other as much as we had to give – and then challenged the other to give more. This paradoxically

*The Black Swan.*

insatiable generosity characterized both Rudolf himself and our partnership over the years. His demands that I meet and exceed his expectations, coupled with his certainty that I could do so, enabled me to dance far better than I imagined possible. Our first *Swan Lake* was a revelation to both of us. Before, he had thought I had possibilities; afterwards, he looked at me with different eyes – he *really* looked at me. Before, he had tested me: can you do this? this? that? Afterwards, he knew I could, and he pushed me relentlessly to push myself.

I see now that I believed in *his* belief in me, not in myself. I'd say, "So Rudolf thinks I have something? Okay, then I guess I do!" I needed him to encourage me; when he was away, my confidence would slip, and so would my dancing. But when Rudolf was there, I existed in a gloriously expanding artistic universe. The more he asked, the more I gave; the more I gave, the more I discovered I had; the more I had, the harder I'd try to find still more – and, when I'd found and given that, he'd demand still more. I absolutely adored him. People used to say that Rudolf discovered me; the truth is that he helped me discover myself. He taught me the joy and the necessity of a bold, clear, fully committed kind of dancing. If I were going to err, it would be in the direction of too much strength and daring; nothing could be worse to either of us than careful timidity. Far better to give too much than too little.

After Montreal, Rudolf began to call me his "angel," praising me for my energy, musicality, and capacity for hard work. His affection and pride in me were almost embarrassingly clear, and it's a measure of the man, and of my fellow artists in the company, that his feelings about my dancing aroused no resentment whatsoever. That's probably because Rudolf treated everyone well – everyone, that is, who wanted to work, to grow, and to improve. He'd stay for hours after a performance giving advice and corrections to anyone who would listen, from principal dancer to the youngest member of the corps, even when he was almost fainting with exhaustion. If you shared his passion for dance and for excellence, that was enough: he'd help in any way he could, giving as much as you were able to take. The ferocious intensity of his dedication and commitment touched and inspired almost every member of the company, and I'm absolutely certain that we could never have danced half as well without his leadership. He drove himself even harder than he drove us. After all, he was the one doing seven performances a week. He had a superhuman capacity for work, and whenever we'd feel exhaustion setting in, we'd look at him and somehow find the strength to dance our hearts out – for him, with love.

Certainly I would never have reached my own potential as a dancer without Rudolf. An avid coach, he was so eager to help that he'd watch my White Swan solo from the wings, sacrificing the only time he had for a short rest. Then he'd give me corrections, and there was always something we both knew could be improved. As much as he favoured bold, athletic dancing, he helped me understand the equal – and sometimes even greater – strength and importance of still moments. (This is part of what Celia had meant when she'd talked about *rubato* and *legato*, but I really learned that lesson only with Rudolf.)

Back in the thirties, Rudolf told me, Sir Frederick Ashton had wondered why Fonteyn's presence and elegant line weren't reaching beyond the orchestra pit. Finally, he spotted the problem: she was such a beautiful *legato* dancer, melting each movement into the next so lyrically, that the result was almost monotonous. Together they worked on creating moments of stillness, of balance – the visual equivalent of holding your breath – to give the audience time to register and appreciate what they'd just seen. Rudolf passed this insight on to me. His success can be measured by the response of Martha Graham, the great pioneer of modern dance and a good friend of Rudolf's, who came to our *Swan Lake* at the Metropolitan Opera House and praised the power of my "still moments." Characteristically, Rudolf was as pleased at her compliment to me as he was by her praise of him.

We danced *Swan Lake* throughout the tour with the greatest pleasure – at least, most of the time. He'd threaten me with death if I didn't finish my thirty-two fouettés, and that was good incentive for me to complete them. In San Francisco, Vanessa Harwood, who alternated with me in the leading role, was ill, and Rudolf was too exhausted to rehearse with a new Swan Queen. I couldn't refuse when he asked me to do all five performances: after all, he was dancing them all as well. After three performances, I was utterly spent, but he was so gentle, caring, and downright grateful that, for the last two performances – both on the same day, so I was literally hallucinating from fatigue and kept seeing phantom dancers leap across the stage – he treated me like porcelain. After the final curtain, he grinned at me triumphantly, "I knew you could do it. You and Margot have guts. I was born with only two balls, but you two, you were born with three." I've never received a higher compliment.

Meanwhile, we were preparing for my debut in *The Sleeping Beauty*. I studied as well as I could during the tour, but I was dancing every performance myself, in a variety of roles, and rehearsals were limited. Between matinée and evening performances, when he should have been resting, Rudolf would pull on his layers of wool, sip steadily at his tea and honey, and observe me closely. When I showed him Aurora's entrance for the first time, jumping as high and fast as I possibly could, he nodded appreciatively, "That's how it should be done. She looks like little rabbit jumping over fence." Rudolf's similes weren't always flattering, but I learned to recognize a compliment when I heard one.

His attentiveness – and his blunt way with words – extended to my appearance. When I modelled Aurora's costume, he tackled my physical shortcomings so matter-of-factly and affectionately that, far from feeling humiliated, I seized his constructive suggestions with appreciation and have followed them throughout my career. "Your arms *not* too short," he pronounced, hitting one of my sore spots. "No. Is your body too long for arms. You must always stretch arms straight – no round arms, no bent wrist. Arms look longer." The catalogue continued, "Shoulders too narrow. Never wear sleeve on shoulder!" And he pulled the offending costume down my arm, creating the illusion of much broader shoulders. "And" – fluffing my hair out at the side – "face too long, too narrow. Do like Margot – puff up hair!" Only recently, in my last few Giselles, have I departed from this last piece of advice: wanting to look a little gaunt in the second act, I've reverted to smoothly slicked-back hair, which does indeed make my face look narrower.

I made my debut as Aurora in Houston, Texas, on a hot, muggy night, and the weather was the cause of another near-disaster that I feared would end our happy collaboration. I had carefully prepared two pairs of shoes, which I had thought would be enough, but when the humidity started melting the canvas-and-glue blocks partway through the Rose Adagio, I felt my shoes dissolving beneath me. During the intermission, I hastily sewed ribbons on a new pair of shoes, but the dressing rooms were so far from the stage that I didn't hear the

music for the start of Act II. Suddenly I realized I was late. By the time I had put on my shoes and reached the stage, my Naiad Attendants had had to make their entrance without me. Still worse, I hadn't had time to properly break in the new shoes; they were rock hard, and distinctly audible. Sixteen bars late, sounding more like a tap dancer than a princess, I made my entry, and Rudolf flashed me a look of outraged disapproval.

Rudolf's anger was brief, however, and Act III went very well indeed – with me in a fresh and well-prepared pair of shoes. Afterwards, Rudolf was delighted. "You have everything!" he exclaimed. "Nobody since Margot has been like this." It was clear that his broad smiles were not only for my performance but also for his triumph over Celia. Full of exuberance, he invited all my friends to an impromptu champagne dinner so I'd always remember this special night.

It was indeed special, despite the shoe débâcle, and Aurora was to remain one of my favourite roles. A little after my debut, Rudolf told *Time* magazine, "The way she does Aurora, there is no one like that anywhere. I don't think they have anyone in Russia like that." My confidence, ease, and joy in the role grew steadily, and, having been taught by Rudolf to borrow details here and there from Fonteyn, I was soon putting in new touches. Several years earlier, I'd seen Russian-trained Galina Samsova make a simple circle of *piqué* turns look tremendously exciting by jumping, rather than just stepping, onto pointe for each turn. Reasoning that, despite my physical deficiencies, I at least had the strong legs needed for that trick, I added it to my variation in the first act; that was an innovation, and a piece of obvious athleticism, that I would never have dared to attempt without Rudolf's example.

Rudolf's coaching and my efforts paid off. A few months after the Houston debut, Anna Kisselgoff wrote in the New York *Times* (April 27, 1973), "If all the National Ballet of Canada's Auroras are as successful as the young Karen Kain, the Toronto company has an outstanding reserve of talent for the future . . . . Her local debut in a principal part confirmed that she will be a true ballerina." A year later, the New York *Times* dance critic Clive Barnes declared that I was "one of the most talented ballerinas in the western world." Praise like this normally would have thrown me into fits of insecurity, but Rudolf's confidence in me was contagious, even to me.

We became very close over the five summers (from 1973 to 1976, and again in 1979) that the company toured extensively with Rudolf. Through those years, he coaxed, berated, inspired, and wooed us into our best, most-exciting, most-polished performances, not only in the classics (*The Sleeping Beauty*, *Swan Lake*, *Giselle*, *La Sylphide*, and *Coppélia*), but also in the more modern repertoire we acquired for these tours (*Don Juan*, in which I first worked with choreographer

*The Black Swan pas de deux at the Metropolitan Opera House.*

John Neumeier; Hans van Manen's *Four Schumann Pieces*, a sensitive ensemble piece, in which Nadia Potts and I happily described ourselves as "the Bobbsey twins"; Rudi van Dantzig's dramatic, controversial *Monument for a Dead Boy*; and Maurice Béjart's *Songs of a Wayfarer*). We all quite relished the other perks of these Hurok tours: the endless receptions with champagne flowing, musicians playing, and ice sculptures melting.

Sometimes we caught glimpses of Rudolf's volatile temper, which, in my experience, was far more evident in the Nureyev legend than in fact. We had heard rumours that he had once slapped an Italian ballerina, but we saw him do nothing worse than call one of our dancers "a cow." True, he may have picked a fight with a lazy dancer or an incompetent technician, but that was to raise his adrenalin before a performance.

(Above) Giselle
and Albrecht
with Vanessa
Harwood as
the Queen of
the Wilis.
(Opposite)
Giselle and
Albrecht.

Far more characteristic of him was his generosity, manifested by dinners like the one for me after *The Sleeping Beauty*, or by kind words (after partnering Mary Jago in her first *Giselle*, for which she had to wait quite a few years, he beamed with pleasure and said, "About bloody time!"). Most obviously, it could be seen in the way he gave his time and encouragement to any dancer with a quick mind and a passion to learn. On the rare occasions when one of us received a greater ovation than he did – as I did at a London gala in 1973 – he would be delighted with our success, happily basking in reflected glory, as good teachers do when their protégés excel.

Given our love for Rudolf and our strong appreciation of all that he'd done for us, we were uniformly shocked when an article by John Fraser appeared in the New York *Times* on July 27, 1975, under the headline, "Nureyev, Leave Canadian Ballet Alone." Blaming Rudolf for putting the company's men (namely principals Tomas Schramek, Sergiu Stefanschi, and Frank Augustyn) in his shadow, John attacked Rudolf for his temper tantrums and the notorious *Sleeping Beauty* budget, calling his association with us "a hindrance" and urging him to "pack up and move somewhere else."

Despite John's intentions, which had the best interests of the company at heart but were misguided, this article upset everyone – including the allegedly slighted male principals – far more than anything Rudolf himself ever did. To set the record straight, in my view our international exposure would still be severely limited if it hadn't been for Rudolf, and without his inspiration and training, and the opportunity to perfect our repertoire by giving so many

performances, we wouldn't have been dancing as well as we were. Frank, Tommy, and Sergiu wouldn't have had the chance to dance many of the ballets in which they excelled and developed, including all the contemporary ballets listed above. A week later, heartfelt letters from the company appeared in the New York *Times*. I. H. MacLeod, chairman of the National's board, accurately described the "enormous debt our company owes to him [Rudolf]," and all ten principal dancers signed a letter protesting John's reliance on "rumour and gossip" in arriving at his conclusions. It's true that Frank, a natural mimic who bears some physical resemblance to Rudolf, probably modelled himself too much on Rudolf in his early years, but young dancers exposed to great ones have always done that, and it's a small price to pay for everything Rudolf gave us.

One point in John's article, easily overlooked among the more outrageous charges, was particularly rankling, "Chintzy numbers like 'Flower Festival in Genzano' started appearing in programs as an easy sop Nureyev could throw to any audience." Denmark's Bournonville repertoire, with its easy jumps and precise footwork, is one of the glories of dance, and the "Flower Festival" pas de deux is one of the glories of this tradition. Bournonville technique, vastly different from the grand Russian style, didn't come easily to Rudolf. But perhaps because it was so hard for him, Rudolf adored Bournonville dancing, and he always attempted to do it well, even though he knew he could have looked far more impressive dancing something else. Far from being an "easy sop," "Flower Festival" was yet another example of Rudolf's determined quest for excellence and his generosity to us – for National Ballet ballerinas looked terrific in it.

⅋ꙮ

Throughout this period, and for some years thereafter, Rudolf frequently invited me to appear with him as a guest artist all over the world, even though we weren't physically suited to each other (I was definitely too tall). But he found this discrepancy challenging: working with taller ballerinas forced him to use bigger, more-expansive movements and to stand taller. The only concession he asked me to make was to do a long, stretched-out arabesque in *Swan Lake*, so I wouldn't hide him completely.

As much as I learned from him in those early years, today I appreciate his insights even more. In every classical role I've ever danced, I've heard his voice reminding me of the need for clarity, attack, power, precision. He hated it when anyone coached his productions in an overly lyrical style; he

Les Sylphides.
(*Right*) Giselle.

insisted on a fresher, purer, more-contemporary approach. Personally, I agree that the time for the old style is past, and that classics must be done boldly if they're to be done at all. Rudolf emphasized this style of dancing later as director of the Paris Opéra Ballet, which offers some of the highest-calibre dancing anywhere in the world.

Through Rudolf, I had some memorable encounters with the Russian dance world, both past and present. One evening in San Francisco, a plump sixtyish woman appeared in Rudolf's dressing room to invoke the spirit of her dead father. It was Kyra Nijinska, eccentric daughter of an eccentric father, Vaslav Nijinsky, who in his time was a dancer as renowned as Rudolf and perhaps the most extraordinarily innovative choreographer of this century (he astonished Paris with the sexually scandalous *Afternoon of a Faun* [1912] and the first *Rite of Spring* [1913] before going mad). Apparently as demented as her father, Nijinska flung herself on her knees, choking and gurgling, her eyes rolling wildly. Heaving her large frame upright, she moved around the small dressing room with the convulsive, angular gestures – and the dark, darting eyes – I recognized at once from old photographs of Nijinsky. Rudolf watched with affection and respect as she completed her impassioned solo. Ending as suddenly as she began, she nodded and quietly left the room. She had indeed called forth her father's spirit.

Among Rudolf's many Russian friends in San Francisco was the ballerina Natalia Makarova, who would herself invoke spirits in our shared dressing room years later. After seeing the last of our five gruelling *Swan Lake*s, she expressed her horror in heavily accented English, "It's not possible you dance so many! I always need week to recover after just one!" At a dinner she gave for us, I was my usual quiet self, listening happily to reminiscences of school life in Leningrad. But halfway through the meal, I was forced to make an exhibition of myself, when I felt an intense charley horse in the back of my leg and nearly toppled the dinner table in my haste to stand up. As tears came to my eyes and everybody else tried not to laugh, Natasha slipped me a little vodka, the unofficial Russian cure for any aches or pains.

In the summer of 1974, I met Baryshnikov again while he was performing in Toronto with a small group of Soviet dancers. Rudolf organized a dinner party to which Gelsey Kirkland and Peter Martins, from Balanchine's New York City Ballet, had come. Peter told Baryshnikov that he was wasting his career in the Soviet Union, and Gelsey promised, "If you leave Russia, I'll leave Balanchine to dance with you." I had a feeling that plans were already in motion, and, sure enough, just a few days later Baryshnikov defected, fleeing the KGB with help from lawyer Jim Peterson and journalist John Fraser. Gelsey

*Curtain calls with Margot Fonteyn for* The Moor's Pavane.

kept her promise, and she and Baryshnikov danced for a few amazing but stormy years at the American Ballet Theatre.

From the start, Rudolf wanted me to have an international career, so he secured invitations for me to dance with him in Vienna, London, and Australia, negotiating the engagements through his agent, S. A. Gorlinsky. That early in my career, I didn't even know what an agent was, but I dutifully went along to the meeting Rudolf had arranged. Gorlinsky turned out to be quite an elderly gentleman, and, between his thick accent and my shyness and naïveté, I felt extremely uncomfortable. At one point, Gorlinsky turned to Rudolf and said, "Well, what should she make for the Australian engagement? Three, four thousand?" Rudolf dismissed the suggestion abruptly, "No, no, that's far too much. This is just the beginning. We don't want to spoil her. Get her $1,200 for the two performances." We all laughed – in my case, because $600 was a lot more than I'd ever been paid for a performance. No doubt, if I had followed Rudolf's advice faithfully, I would eventually have made a handsome living, but money has never been my motivation for dancing, and to this day I'm uneasy talking about fees. I care much more about what and with whom I dance than about how much I'm paid.

The greatest benefit of my guest engagements with Rudolf, apart from the pleasure of his company and guidance, was meeting and working with the woman we both saw as the ideal ballerina: Dame Margot Fonteyn. Rudolf had invited me to join Fonteyn, Paolo Bortoluzzi (from Béjart's Ballet of the 20th

Century and American Ballet Theatre), and several members of the Royal Ballet in the "Nureyev and Friends" tour in Washington, D.C., in 1975. The repertoire included *Marguerite and Armand* (Ashton's version of the *La Dame aux Camélias/La Traviata* story, created for Fonteyn and Nureyev; I'm still proud of having been listed in the program as Fonteyn's understudy); the *Corsaire* pas de deux; Béjart's *Songs of a Wayfarer*; and *The Moor's Pavane*, José Limón's interpretation of *Othello*.

I was overcome by shyness the day I met Fonteyn, but she immediately put me at ease by laughing at the alliteration of "Karen Kain from Canada" when Rudolf introduced us, and I saw right away that the warm glow she radiated on stage was genuine. It was hard to believe that this vital, elegant woman was old enough to have been dancing in 1949, when she dazzled New York as Aurora during the Royal Ballet's first American tour. But it was easy to see why her beautiful proportions, lovely face, and great musicality had inspired Ashton to create ballets like *Symphonic Variations*, *Daphnis and Chloë*, and *Ondine*, works through which she and Ashton virtually defined the British style.

Completely without pretension or ego, she treated me as an equal, a comrade in arms. She invited me to her dressing room, and, as we chatted about make-up tips and traded Rudolf stories, she darned some silk tights that she'd owned since before the Second World War. She wouldn't dance in anything else, and, because they were no longer available, she was constantly mending her old ones. One evening after rehearsal, she invited me back to her hotel to meet her husband, former Panamanian politician Dr. Roberto "Tito" Arias. An assassination attempt more than ten years earlier had left him a quadriplegic, able to speak only through a special device in his throat. I couldn't decipher a word, but Margot translated happily as she fed him his dinner. All in all, we had a pleasant picnic on her bed in the infamous Watergate Hotel.

Experiencing Margot's graciousness and kindness only intensified my admiration for the woman whom Rudolf had constantly held up to me as an example of perfection in *The Sleeping Beauty* and *Swan Lake*. Every step he had taught me was accompanied by comments like, "Margot did this way, so you do it, too!" I was enchanted when Rudolf asked Margot if she'd coach me in these roles – we'd be dancing them with the National in New York in a few weeks – and she generously agreed, despite the fact that she was then in her fifties, dancing two ballets every night, and tending her paralysed husband. I began to understand why Rudolf claimed, quite seriously, that she was the only saint he knew.

These rehearsals with Margot and Rudolf were one of the high points of my life, but they were also the most confusing – and amusing – I've ever had. The disagreements I'd come to expect in ballet became a civilized art form, for

Swan Lake.

*With Rudolf in* Le Corsaire *pas de deux, wearing my homemade head-dress.*

Rudolf and Margot disagreed about everything. When he assured me that *Swan Lake* was her greatest ballet, she responded that her personality was far better expressed in *The Sleeping Beauty* and *Ondine*, and the rehearsal continued with each of them approaching the roles from completely different viewpoints.

We began with the Swan Queen's first meeting with the Prince. Rudolf was analytical and technical: "The swan is a large, regal bird, with great dignity. The line must be clear, it must be proud." So I concentrated on my turnout, stretched out my line, and held my arabesque as long as possible. Rudolf was delighted, but Margot said he had got it all wrong: I had to focus on the story, the feeling of the moment. "Imagine yourself alone in your bedroom at night," she said. "You're brushing your hair – or grooming your feathers as the Swan Queen would do – when all of a sudden a stranger intrudes. Imagine the gentle calm you feel in the beginning, and then, when you're startled, feel the intense pounding of your heart." I hear her words whenever I dance this section of *Swan Lake*; this is just the kind of dramatic motivation I need, but few coaches ever give it to you.

Rudolf and Margot also argued good-naturedly but constantly about how she had danced almost every step in *The Sleeping Beauty*. "You danced this step with the power of a little soldier, very correct," he'd say, and she'd protest that she very much hoped she hadn't danced it that way *at all*! This was a fascinating demonstration of the difference between how a dancer feels she's dancing and what her partner and the audience see. It's very likely that both Margot and Rudolf were right. However, after this, I sometimes took Rudolf's assertions about how Margot had danced with a tiny grain of salt.

Rudolf had warned me that at some point during the two-week season I would dance the pas de deux from *Le Corsaire* with him – he planned to add it when he felt he needed an extra challenge – so I ordered a tutu that was an exact replica of the one I had seen Margot wearing in photographs. The day we opened, Rudolf decided to put *Le Corsaire* in that night. I had never danced his version, or any other version, for that matter, and I had seen it only once or twice, so both the steps and the music were completely unfamiliar. As diplomatically as I could, I suggested that I might not be able to learn it in time. "Of course you learn!" he insisted, running through the basics with me for an hour. "Now we are ready," he assured me. When I was still worried, he invited me to his room during his massage. While a burly masseur pounded Rudolf's knotted muscles into submission, I furiously scribbled his last-minute instructions in my notebook, but I didn't feel noticeably more confident.

Meanwhile, I had no head-dress to go with the costume, so Margot, with her typical generosity, came to my rescue and helped me make one. We strung pearl beads on thread, whipped them together with some masking tape, and wound the result around my bun. Listening to the cascade of harp cadenzas before my solo, I suddenly realized that I had no idea when to go on. Again, Margot saved me: "Ready, steady, GO!" she whispered, gently pushing me onstage. The performance went remarkably well, but in retrospect I can hardly believe I had the courage to attempt it with so little preparation. It must have been the ignorance of youth.

I also danced Emilia, Iago's wife, in *The Moor's Pavane*, with Rudolf as Othello, Margot as Desdemona, and Paolo Bortoluzzi as Iago. We had rehearsed this adequately, but that didn't keep me out of trouble. Once, as Margot and I posed together near the back of the stage, she said something so funny about Rudolf's mood that we both began to giggle. When the choreography sent Paolo in our direction, he started snickering too. Afterwards, Rudolf glared at us with fire in his eyes, "Here I am, killing myself out there, and you all laugh!" He was absolutely right, of course, and although Margot could usually jolly him out of his moods, this time he took longer than usual to thaw.

Normally, Rudolf's stage behaviour was impeccable, but occasionally he surprised me. Sometimes he would make quiet comments that were quite disconcerting. During a supported arabesque, he might ask, "Who is that cute guy in the wings?" Or, barely moving his lips, he'd complain, "That ballerina is such a cow." I'd have to nod and smile as if he'd said something charming and princely.

He also had some other little quirks. Every Aurora knew that, if she used lip gloss, there'd be no kiss in the Awakening Scene, and if we wore perfume, he'd accuse us of trying to asphyxiate him. Occasionally, he'd show his distaste for some of the company's tackier props. He particularly hated the tulle lilies that Giselle drops at his feet in one of the most moving moments of Act II; he called them dirty Kleenexes on popsicle sticks. Once, after I'd scattered them at his feet before disappearing into my grave, he tenderly gathered up the detestable lilies, swivelled on his knees, and turned his back on the audience. This wasn't part of the choreography, so we all watched from the wings with unusually rapt attention. He gazed at the flowers lovingly and, just as I was thinking what a great acting job he was doing, he furiously tore off bits and crammed them into his mouth. When the company still didn't get the hint, I replaced the props with some beautiful silk flowers.

*Congratulations from Rudolf and Erik Bruhn after a performance in London.*

The only major temper tantrum I remember – and the only one that was truly unprofessional – was at our last *Sleeping Beauty* at the New York State Theater in the summer of 1979. Late in Act II, there's a blackout just before the Prince enters the palace to find the sleeping Princess. Normally in our production, a spotlight picks him up on the staircase as he makes his way through the sleeping courtiers, but if the cue was late or the man on the spotlight couldn't find Rudolf right away, Rudolf would snap his fingers and bring the spotlight to heel. But this night that strategy didn't work. The technician completely missed the cue, and as I lay on my bed I heard Rudolf swear and stomp off the stage. He kicked a lighting boom in his fury, and the commotion and clatter of falling lighting gels could easily be heard in the auditorium. With growing rage, Rudolf tried to slap the stage-manager across the face, and then stalked into the corridor, where he attacked a bulletin board.

There I lay, eyes closed, my friends standing around with their mandolins and pretending to be in a deep slumber themselves. Then, first one costume and then another started to rustle nervously, and finally the whispers started, "He's not coming, Karen." I suddenly realized I might have to wake myself up and react with delighted surprise to a stage full of sleeping people, like some madwoman. I thought longingly of my Groucho glasses – the ballet was on the verge of becoming sheer farce, and we might as well really give the audience something to talk about – but I hung on a little longer, listening to more commotion and increasingly urgent whispers, "Karen, he's *still* not com-ing!" Suddenly, the thrashing and cursing was quite close by; Rudolf had re-emerged from a totally unexpected direction. He made a loud, impatient kissing sound, barely bending down at all, and I "awoke" to two eyes blazing like laser beams. He was so furious about the spotlight that he didn't realize he had missed his own cue and had "kissed" me far too early.

My worries that I'd never be awakened at all were superseded by the prob-lem of being awakened too soon. I stretched, yawned visibly, rubbed my eyes, and rolled around the bed in one awakening posture after another to fill endless bars of music. Finally, my cue came, and I sat up and smiled, but Rudolf, in no mood to play "Prince Charming," just scowled at me. As the curtain fell on this happy scene, Rudolf announced that he would not appear in Act III, because he'd hurt his foot. I wasn't surprised; lighting booms aren't the softest things in the world. But since Frank Augustyn and Tomas Schramek had gone off to a movie, it would have to be Rudolf or nobody. After extending the intermission to forty-five minutes, which cost thousands of dollars in overtime, he finally agreed to finish, but with ill grace and wilfully indifferent dancing.

What I found unforgivable was not so much Rudolf's initial anger as his failure to dance Act III in character and give the audience the performance it had paid handsomely to see. They knew they'd been cheated, and instead of the customary twenty-minute ovation at the final curtain, there was almost no applause at all. Rudolf's lack professionalism shocked me to the core, and it was a long time before I forgave it. Despite my lasting admiration and love for this most glorious of Russian dancers, I was still a product of English train-ing, and my sense of good manners and professional responsibility had been violated profoundly.

We continued to dance together, but during the eighties our careers took different directions. After a good deal of soul-searching, I decided to remain a full member of the National Ballet in a city and country that were not consid-ered major centres of the dance world. Hurt when I turned down the opportu-nities for a truly international career that he himself had so carefully cultivated for me, disappointed that I wasn't always available for guest engagements with him, and distressed that the National Ballet never invited him back for more than an occasional gala performance, Rudolf occasionally had bitter thoughts about what he perceived as our ingratitude. Once he lashed out at me in the press, saying that I was wasting my time "schlepping around the provinces." But I had made my choice, and although he never learned to like it, at least he accepted it. His first question to me was always, "Karen, are you happy?" And I knew that he genuinely hoped that my answer would be yes.

*With Rudolf after a performance of* Alice *in London. Rex Harrington looks on.*

Dancing was the most important thing in Rudolf's life – except once, when he was very young and very much in love with Erik Bruhn. At that time, he told me, dancing lost its power over him and his dearest wish was to be with Erik. But Erik had told him that he was a fool, because "work is the only thing that matters." Rudolf later claimed that that was the best advice he'd ever received, and that from then on he had dedicated himself exclusively to his art. Although I wasn't prepared to make the same commitment, we remained friends, and he knew that I revered him as the dancer and coach who had influenced me more deeply than anyone else.

We danced together for the last time – fittingly, it was the grand pas de deux from *The Sleeping Beauty* – at a 1984 televised performance from New York celebrating the Met's hundredth birthday. What I remember most was chatting with Sir Frederick Ashton for the last time and watching Rudolf, flamboyant in one of his weird snakeskin outfits, embracing the always-elegant Margot as they stood in the wings listening to Placido Domingo, and, no doubt, remembering all of the other times they'd been in each other's arms on stage.

Four years later, for Rudolf's fiftieth birthday, I stood with him again at the Met, touched to have been invited as one of his favourite partners. I somehow suspected even then that neither his career nor his life would continue very much longer, and my joy at seeing him was tinged with sadness at the thought of a world without Rudolf. At that time, however, Margot's visible frailty was of more immediate concern. I had had no idea that she was ill.

After Rudolf and I stopped dancing together, I followed his career as he branched out in his insatiable quest for new kinds of excellence: his directorship of the Paris Opéra Ballet through the eighties, his appearance in the musical *The King and I*, and even his forays into conducting symphony orchestras. I remembered his passion for Bach and for Glenn Gould, the only artist he admired as much as he did Margot and Fred Astaire. Rudolf had once tried to explain to me that a pas de chat had five distinct counts, and I was frequently bemused by his almost mathematical fascination with musical intricacies. He might well have become a good conductor if he had been given the time. To this day, I often recall the wonder of his dancing and marvel at the energy and joy with which he consistently sought out new challenges and inspired others to do the same.

I saw him dance on those last few "Nureyev and Friends" tours. It was painful, partly because he'd lost so much of his technique, and partly because I sensed, long before I knew for sure, that he was sick. I couldn't reconcile the magnificent, powerful creature that Rudolf was in his prime – and will always be in my mind – with the less-commanding dancer, and finally the fragile shadow, that he became.

The devastation AIDS has caused in the dance world is overwhelming – and I speak only of the dance world, because that's what I know. The cloud of AIDS is a dark and continuing presence in our daily lives, and the brilliance that we've lost – the dancers, choreographers, and musicians – can never be replaced. Our beloved art is irreparably diminished. We organize benefits to raise money for research and the relief of suffering, but it seems such a pittance in comparison to the needs. On a personal level, so many friends have died that we can hardly count them all. Among those who have touched my own life most closely are American Ballet Theatre's Clark Tippett, who collapsed with AIDS-related pneumonia just before we were to dance *Le Corsaire* and the *Sleeping Beauty* pas de deux together; Kelvin Coe, of the Australian Ballet, whom I remembered fondly from Moscow in 1973; John Aubrey, Alistair Munroe, and Howard Meadows, my former comrades at the National Ballet; choreographer-dancer Constantin Patsalas, a close friend who had created numerous roles for me over the years; and, early in 1994, principal dancer Gregory Osborne, to whose memory the company's winter season was dedicated. Of these and all the other brave and gifted people we've lost and continue to lose almost daily, there were none whom I treasured more than Rudolf. His courage in his own battle with the disease didn't surprise me; many times I'd seen the force of his will and determination make him almost superhuman. But I still can't quite believe that this was his last battle, and that he lost.

Rudolf was immensely important to me both professionally and personally. I saw depths of generosity in him as a partner and as a man that will always inspire me, and he drew from me levels of determination and commitment that I might never have known I had without him. I stopped being afraid of him many years ago, but my love and respect for him as a man, and my sense of awe at his genius, will always remain.

Branching Out

*"My candle burns at both ends;*
*It will not last the night;*
*But ah, my foes, and oh, my friends –*
*It gives a lovely light!"*
– Edna St. Vincent Millay, American poet

The events of 1973 had marked for me the start of the kind of life a young girl dreams about when she wants to be a ballerina: excitement, exotic places, glamorous partners, the most wonderful roles, applause, and fame. At least that's what it looked like from the outside; to me, looking back, it was the start of an almost-schizophrenic decade. I was the anything-but-calm centre of a whirlwind of activity. Fresh from success in Moscow, I was developing both a partnership and a personal relationship with Frank Augustyn at the same time as I was becoming one of Nureyev's favourite partners. There aren't many twenty-two-year-olds who can be intensely involved with two men at once, even if one of those relationships is purely professional. I was constantly challenged by geographical dislocation as well: not only were National Ballet tours a constant strain, but I was also appearing in guest engagements with Rudolf from New York to Vienna and Australia. To make matters worse, the National Ballet would undergo major changes in artistic direction – from Celia Franca to David Haber to a year with no director to Alexander Grant. As well, the repertoire was changing constantly. At home, Ann Ditchburn and Constantin Patsalas were creating ballets for me while I was struggling to satisfy Rudolf's classical standards, master the delightful complexities of our new Ashton ballets, and tackle the more-contemporary works brought in for the Hurok tours. To top it off, choreographers like Eliot Feld and Roland Petit wanted me for their works, and I was learning yet another

*(Previous page)*
*Roland Petit's*
*Coppélia with*
*Rudy Bryans.*

repertoire for "Nureyev and Friends." And then there were the demands from Canadians for films and television specials involving their newest stars, Frank and Karen. I had everything I had ever thought I wanted, and I was beginning to understand the old warning, "Be careful what you wish for. You might get it." All these opportunities, wonderful in themselves, would prove to be far too much for me to handle – so much so that, by the end of this glittering decade, I'd be forced to reassess my life completely, both on- and off-stage. When Frank and I returned from Moscow, however, I was thrilled that my career was surpassing my wildest dreams – and with astonishing speed.

*Rehearsing Nana with Roland and Cyril Atanassoff.*

In Moscow, I had met a man who would become very important in my life over the coming decade. This was Roland Petit, the French choreographer who'd seen me in rehearsal and insisted, to Celia's chagrin, "I must have her in Marseilles!" He meant it: for the next six months, he was constantly on the phone until I agreed to dance *Le Loup* with his company, Le Ballet National de Marseille, in May 1974.

Roland had been France's best-known choreographer since the forties. Having joined the Paris Opéra Ballet at sixteen, this dynamo of a dancer-choreographer founded the Ballets des Champs-Elysées at twenty-one and then, at twenty-four, the Ballets de Paris, for which he created dazzlingly chic contemporary works like *Carmen* for his wife, noted ballerina Zizi Jeanmaire. Trendy long before the word existed, he also choreographed films like *Hans Christian Andersen*, *Daddy Long Legs*, and *Anything Goes*. He created *Kraanerg*, in which I made my professional debut, for the National Ballet of Canada in 1969, and, in 1972, he founded the Ballet de Marseille. Later I would learn that one reason Erik Bruhn left Denmark was to dance in Petit's ballets, which sizzled with sex and theatricality.

But there was a big problem. In those days, National Ballet dancers didn't become guest artists with other companies; it was considered a kind of defection. I knew that I'd never get permission to go to Marseilles unless it was during company holidays, so that's exactly what I did.

This was the first time I had been a guest artist, and the contrast with the National was fascinating. To start with, Marseilles – a rough, smoky, colourful town, with sections as much like Morocco as France – wasn't Toronto, even the seedier side of Toronto that I had seen in my school days. And, as I noticed on my very first day, the Ballet de Marseille was not the National Ballet of Canada. For one thing, although there were only thirty-five dancers, they were

a far more diverse crew, both in nationality and training. The company studio –
a stately, elegant building that had once been the library of Marseilles – was as
beautiful as the National Ballet School's Quaker meeting house, but at least
three times larger. I appreciated its extra-high ceilings; in the company's
cramped studio at the St. Lawrence Hall, I had learned to restrain myself in
big lifts after poking my foot through the ceiling.

The composition of the Ballet de Marseille was also quite different to what
I was used to. Whereas the National cultivated its female ballerinas carefully,
Roland's permanent roster of principals was often exclusively male. Fascinated
by the personalities of different women and impatient to work with anyone
who caught his eye on the international scene, he imported guests for the leading female roles, as he did with me. Bringing to his artistic life a dichotomy that
some men practise in earnest, he saw female dancers as goddesses or whores; his
"*étoiles*" – the imports and his wife, Zizi – were the former, treated with exceptional kindness, while corps women tended to be second-class citizens. Roland's
artistic fickleness suited his choreographic needs and fostered big takings at the
box office.

The most glaring difference between the companies was the contrast
between their artistic directors. Reserved and restrained, Celia was tough but
fair; as a former dancer, she saw the benefits of running a dancer-focused company. Roland was primarily a choreographer, and he put his need for inspiration
first. A flamboyant, dictatorial, highly-strung man, he had a peculiar obsession
with sexual banter that took some getting used to. Although happily married to
Zizi, Roland was usually in mad pursuit of various men in the company, and he
was always discussing human anatomy in ways that were somehow funny and
naughty rather than obscene. The sexual titillation in some of his ballets
reflected the realities of company life. Eccentric, even bizarre, he was one of the
most fascinating men I had ever met. He was completely charming, he made
me laugh uproariously, and I can't imagine anyone ever finding him boring.

On my first visit, I gave only a few performances of *Le Loup*, but they went
well, and I took special delight in my partner, Denys Ganio, with whom I would
have the pleasure of dancing for many years. Consequently, I was eager to
accept Roland's invitation to return in the fall of 1974, particularly because
Roland intended to create a new ballet, *Les Intermittences du Coeur*, based on
Marcel Proust's *Remembrance of Things Past*, in which I was to dance the role of
Albertine. The dates conflicted slightly with the National's season, but it was
important to me to find a way to do both. Being involved in the creation of a
full-length ballet was such a rare experience – in my whole career, it has never
happened at the National – that I was determined to take part.

*Dancing
Albertine
in* Les
Intermittences
du Coeur *at
Le théâtre du
Champs-
Elysées
in Paris.*

I loved Proust's novel, but was somewhat surprised to discover that my scene was based on a single paragraph, describing the author's thoughts on seeing Albertine asleep. Completely obsessed by her and jealous of any life she leads apart from him, he begins to imagine her dreams as a way of possessing them, and her, to the fullest. My pas de deux, one of the loveliest scenes in the ballet, enacts that dream. One example from the creation of this scene is representative of the way Roland always worked with me as a choreographer. Having got me from the bed to the floor, Roland thought for a moment about where to go from there. Suddenly an idea came: "You're just like a dog," he said to Denys, who was again my partner. "You're sniffing out clues as to where she's been, whom she's met, who's been touching her." The image caught our imaginations, and we quickly created the next section together; while Denys doesn't move remotely like a dog in the finished product, the idea behind the metaphor comes through clearly.

*Les Intermittences du Coeur*, a series of isolated tableaux, was a major success. It's still in the repertoire, and Natalia Makarova, among others, has danced Albertine. The dream sequence, one of my favourite pas de deux, was included in my twentieth-anniversary performance at the National in 1988, with Denys as my partner.

While preparing for the ballet's première in September 1974, I realized another major difference between companies: where they spend their money. While Canadians often put their money into their homes, the French happily lived in tiny apartments so they could afford more sensual pleasures, such as fine clothing and excellent food and wine. Roland shared these priorities, so that, although neither I nor his permanent company were particularly well paid, there was an air of glamour in working with him that I'd never experienced before. Sets and costumes for Petit ballets were lavish beyond belief, even to someone who had seen Rudolf's extravagant *Sleeping Beauty*. We were always running up to Paris for special costume fittings to get the details just right. I wouldn't classify Roland as a great choreographer, but he is certainly a great magician, who assembles movement, sets, costumes, and music into a spectacular package that often works brilliantly on-stage.

Our longest runs were in Paris, where I usually stayed in the apartment of Elizabeth Cooper, the flamboyant red-headed company pianist that we called Babette. She lived near the Paris Opéra, and her neighbourhood was a revelation. Looking like the quiet little "bunhead" I was, on my way to rehearsal at eight in the morning, I would pass an extraordinary buffet of women slouching against lampposts and wearing the most outrageous combinations of marabou, sequins, and hotpants. The display went on for blocks, and out of the corner of my eye I'd try to guess which of these gorgeous creatures were men, so artfully disguised that I wanted to ask them for make-up tips. Walking by the Bois de Boulogne one afternoon around half past five, I innocently asked why there were so many empty cars parked on the grass. Babette smiled and said, "It's the businessmen on their way home, visiting the working girls." The casual attitude to sex, fidelity, and prostitution in Paris never ceased to amazed me, and the caricatures of voluptuousness I saw daily on the streets provided a context for some of the more grotesque representations of women in Roland's works.

I was equally amazed by the glamorous life of the principal dancers. In Paris, Roland's company performed at the Théatre des Champs-Elysées or the Théatre de la Porte St.-Martin, where we would be visited backstage by Yves St. Laurent, Marcel Marceau, or some film star. Often our productions opened in Monte Carlo's jewel-like opera house in the presence of Prince Rainier and Princess Grace. We would take the overnight train from Paris, and, just before we arrived in Monte Carlo, a porter would wake us with tea or coffee. Because we usually did the same ballet night after night, we rarely rehearsed once performances had started, so our days were free for shopping and seeing friends – though not as free as one might think, thanks to the nightlife. Instead of going home after performances, as in Canada, I would join Roland and the dancers at an elegant restaurant to celebrate; then we would go on to a discothèque called Jimmy's, where we would dance until the sun rose over the sea. Or we would board someone's yacht – once it was film director Sam Peckinpah's, a close friend of Petit's – for a lavish moonlight dinner.

It was terribly exciting, and I loved every moment. With Rudolf, everything was work; Roland turned almost everything into play. But I didn't keep going back to work with Roland for the glamour and fun; they were simply incidentals. What I really treasured was that, more than anyone else, Roland offered me the freedom to create full-blooded characters. He'd give me a quick character description – it could be something as simple and striking as the dog metaphor in *Intermittences* – and then let me have my head, treating me as an important part of the creative process. This was a rare and exhilarating example of trust, and I quickly understood why most great dancers crave, above everything else, the opportunity to work with a choreographer who lets them participate in the alchemy of creation.

I returned to Marseilles in the fall of 1975 to create the role of Swanilda in a new production of *Coppélia* that was very different from Erik Bruhn's version for the National, with its frankly tragic interpretation of Dr. Coppélius, the dollmaker who falls in love with his creation. In Petit's *Coppélia*, the first and most successful of his send-ups of classical ballet, Dr. Coppélius (like Erik,

*Coppélia.*

Roland took this role himself) was a high-energy vaudevillian who did a wild pas de deux, half apache dance and half Fred Astaire, with a life-sized doll attached to his shoes. Like many Petit ballets, *Coppélia* had the lightness of operetta; sprinkled with allusions to other dance forms from the cancan to the Charleston, it also had a touch of cabaret, including a great deal of tutu-wiggling at the audience.

One aspect of Dr. Coppélius's obsession with Coppélia was that he made all the dolls in his workshop to look just like her (and, consequently, like me). This prop detail ensured that I'd be asked to dance the ballet frequently over the next few years. Fortunately, the ballet was a big hit, and our film for French television has been aired successfully for years in Europe, though it's never been aired in Canada. The critics were kind, comparing me to a former member of Petit's company, the dance-actress Leslie Caron. Claude Baignères of *Le Figaro* was flattering in a review in which he said I was "sparkling. . . . the heart of the feast."

My next Petit ballet was completely different. Choreographed for Zizi Jeanmaire in 1949, *Carmen* was a classic, and in 1975 it was being remounted for the first time in fifteen years. Roland was very nervous, because he wasn't sure the ballet would stand up to the passage of time. Just as Nureyev had wanted to recreate me in Fonteyn's image, so Petit tried at first to turn me into the young Zizi, but he couldn't have found an unlikelier candidate. Even at fifty, Zizi was a tiny, small-featured woman with enormous allure. She was a fine dancer, who took her ballet training very seriously, despite her equal success as director and star from 1974 to 1980 of the cabaret Casino de Paris, in which she spent a lot of time singing while huge men in loincloths carried her about the stage. Her extravagant personality was her greatest asset, and her saucy, gamine quality in *Carmen*, in which she wore a very chic close-cropped haircut, had given dance a completely fresh image.

Carmen, *with Denys Ganio.*

If she felt threatened by my dancing one of her greatest roles, she certainly didn't show it; I found her consistently generous and funny. We both knew I'd be a very different kind of Carmen. Zizi's petite build allowed her to dance with a tight, crisp style and very precise footwork, highlighted by the choreography, but for a tall, lyrical dancer like me, it was almost impossible to dance the steps at the same speed – especially because, as Zizi kept telling me, Roland was making the choreography even harder than it was to begin with.

There was another obvious challenge as well. I was still a very young and relatively innocent woman, and I had to become an experienced vamp. I'd done nothing like this in Canada – sexpots aren't called for in *Swan Lake* or *The Sleeping Beauty* – and, as a television documentary would illustrate, Roland had to teach me how to bump and grind. When we rehearsed the bedroom pas de deux, he directed me as if we were doing a striptease, "You take your stockings off. Yes, like that! And now you are stretching your body to show yourself to him. . . ." *Carmen* caused a sensation in 1949 and had been banned in Quebec, and I was beginning to see why.

Although some critics find it dated, and it certainly has a forties air about it, *Carmen* remains a highly effective piece of theatre. Liking the ballet as much as I did, I was pleased to get good reviews at the Paris opening, with Baignères in *Le Figaro* writing that I was "a Carmen of steel and fire, a marvel of technique and temperament."

Having changed my stage temperament for *Carmen*, in my next collaboration with Roland I completely changed my appearance. In the spring of 1976, he created *Nana*, an hour-long ballet, at the Paris Opéra Ballet, with me in the leading role. Based on Émile Zola's novel, the story tells of the adventures of a completely amoral woman. In Roland's interpretation, Nana is the symbol of evil decadence, but her manner is so innocent that her actions seem like child's play. There's an extravagant series of sensational encounters. In one pas de deux, Nana makes a besotted banker beg and heel like a little dog at her side

*Carmen persuades Don José to kill for her.*

as she laughs at his voluntary degradation. There's a lesbian affair, and then Nana tempts, torments, and rejects a young boy, who kills himself in despair. Wreaking havoc everywhere, she reacts with no more than slightly careless surprise, like someone who's accidentally knocked a vase off a table. In short, she's not a particularly nice person, and she fascinated me. I'd never had a crack at this sort of character before Carmen, though Ann Ditchburn would very soon give me something almost as seamy in Louise, the Mother in *Mad Shadows*. Obviously, Nana would draw on both my youth and the new sophistication I had acquired in *Carmen*, and I was determined to give my all.

*A red-haired Nana.*

Roland loved radical changes in appearance, often through hair colour, and since Zola's Nana was a redhead, I had to be one, too. A wig would have satisfied him, but four days before we opened, I decided I would never get an opportunity to experiment like this again, so I went to the nearest hairdresser. I'd confidently taken a little swatch of fabric for them to match, since I had the impression that French coiffeurs could do anything. "*Impossible, mademoiselle!*" they cried. "*Vous êtes trop brunette!*" Distraught, I insisted that it was *absolument nécessaire* to have precisely that colour, and, after some huddled, whispered conferences and much shrugging of shoulders, they agreed to try.

It's not clear who felt most nervous. I knew nothing at all about hair colouring, and when they'd bleached me to a bright canary yellow, I began to perspire. By the time they'd finished muttering among themselves, mixing a vile orange potion and slathering it onto my head, I was trembling. The hour I had to wait to see the result of all these incantations and concoctions was probably the longest hour of my life.

The result was a pleasant surprise. I was a strawberry blonde, and my fair skin and green eyes made my new hair seem natural. I was a little embarrassed when Erik Bruhn and Constantin Patsalas came to the opening and saw my new persona, but they thought it was quite fetching, and for the next six weeks I looked like a would-be Rita Hayworth. To this day, many of my acquaintances at the Opéra think of me as a redhead, although I switched back to my original colour soon after.

I wish the ballet had been as great a success as my hair. Roland hadn't choreographed for the Paris Opéra Ballet in years, and he had been dreading it – not a good recipe for inspiration. The Opéra is renowned for having strikes at the most inopportune moments, and, sure enough, we had them too, involving both dancers and stagehands. My unease deepened when I heard the music – by Marius Constant – played by the orchestra for the first time. The nuances we

*A costume fitting for* Nana, *before I became a redhead.*

had heard in the four-instrument version to which we had rehearsed were lost in the lush orchestration, and we barely recognized the score, let alone our cues.

Reviews were mixed, but I emerged relatively unscathed; one critic said that the Paris Opéra Ballet didn't have any other dancers who could do the role at all, which I took as praise. Ezio Frigerio's costumes, which included some judicious padding to make me more voluptuous, were warmly received, but the ballet's conclusion – a procession, with Nana leading hundreds of men to their deaths – was accompanied by a German march too closely associated with the Second World War for many in the audience. Boos easily outnumbered bravos for Roland, and probably most of them were genuine, but I knew that Belgian choreographer Maurice Béjart, disdaining Petit and his works, retained a claque for Petit's openings, and Roland returned the compliment, perhaps by hiring the same claque. It was part of the game, a time-honoured European tradition.

I managed to avoid an equally unpleasant tradition. Everyone warned me to expect great resentment from the Opéra dancers and "glass in the pointe shoes" (ballet's equivalent of a stab in the back), but instead I was treated with the greatest kindness, receiving flowers and small cards wishing me good luck before the première.

It may have helped that I had quickly become friends with a young soloist, a kind, handsome man who drove me around Paris on his motorcycle. We fell deeply in love and spoke of marriage. I couldn't envisage living permanently in France, so the next year he came to Canada, and we discussed whether he would be happy here. But we were both intensely committed to our dancing, and, when we realized that marriage and a move to Canada would mean that he'd have to give up his citizenship, his pension with the company, and quite possibly his career as a dancer, we reluctantly decided that marriage wasn't in the cards. We've kept in touch over the years, and he is now choreographing and teaching in Paris.

ॐ

I continued to dance with Petit's company well into the eighties, creating several new roles along the way, and in the fall of 1976, I would join him for a Canadian tour that should have shown me just how dangerously I was flirting with personal catastrophe. But those stories are best told a little later; for the moment I'd like to reflect on what I learned in those first few years with Roland.

First and foremost, Roland gave me self-confidence. Like Rudolf, he thought I was so special that he persuaded me to believe it, too. However, where Rudolf enhanced my conviction that I could do the classics well, Roland greatly broadened my dramatic range in contemporary works. He did this partly by giving me the chance to dance in modern classics like *Carmen* and partly by offering the greatest gift of all: new roles that I could shape from the beginning.

While story ballets with strong characters were (and remain) a staple of the National's repertoire, we had received no dramatic training at all, for acting was considered of minimal importance in comparison to good technique. In my early years, I felt painfully inept as an actor. I had no idea how to overcome my inhibitions and become someone quite different on-stage, or how to develop a character, or how to show characterization by the way I danced the traditional steps. If I had some success in roles that demanded acting, like Juliet, it was probably because my honest response to the music and my ability to react spontaneously on-stage somehow conveyed the right feeling.

Roland didn't teach me how to act, but he did the next best thing: he threw me into heavy dramatic roles and encouraged me to express aspects of my personality that I may well have hidden, even from myself, and that had certainly never been tapped before in dance. I was allowed to be histrionic, sensuous, angry, even eccentric. Over time, the differences between what was expected of me in Canada and England as opposed to France led to a kind of schizophrenia in my image. In North America and London, I was known primarily as a lyrical dancer, an *ingénue* with a fresh, pure style and well-balanced technical skills. But in France, in roles like Carmen and Nana, I was a dramatic dancer who could be funny, coquettish, immoral, and seductive from one night to the next. I was allowed to be a bad girl, and it amused and delighted me when one critic compared me to Brigitte Bardot. Roland let me explore the darker sides of life on-stage, even if I wasn't yet ready to explore the darkness hidden within me in private life.

As my 1976 tour of Canada with the Ballet de Marseille would show, Canadian fans and critics were distressed whenever I stopped being the Sugar Plum Fairy. It would be years before I'd be cast in a dark, or even a complex, role at the National Ballet, with one exception: my old friend Ann Ditchburn's *Mad Shadows* (1977), based on Marie-Claire Blais's neo-Gothic novel, in which I would play a sexually enslaved, abusive mother.

Unfortunately, I'd been in Europe and Russia for much of the time that Ann was creating the ballet; when I returned, there were only a few days left before the première, and I never felt completely comfortable in the role. To make matters worse, *Mad Shadows* made the transition from studio to stage rather badly, in part because it had been choreographed to André Gagnon's piano score but was performed to a fully orchestrated version, with many of the same problems that befell *Nana*.

ℰ

By the summer of 1976, thanks to a steady stream of glowing notices from Europe and my continuing partnerships with both Rudolf and Frank, I had become a star, Canadian-style. Recognitions came thick and fast; there were honorary degrees from Trent, York, and McMaster universities and from the University of British Columbia; I was made an Officer of the Order of Canada; there were invitations to 24 Sussex Drive and Government House, where my memories include admiring Trudeau's patience as he trotted off to the bathroom with one of his young sons, who was just being toilet-trained, and the good humour of Prince Charles when he inadvertently broke the ice one evening by spilling all the peas on his plate onto the tablecloth.

My new celebrity also brought offers to explore other media. Vancouver filmmaker Jack Darcus proposed a film called *The Falcon and the Ballerina*, to be directed (depending on what month it was) by everyone from Silvio Narrizano to Eric Till. It was to be about a musician who falls in love with a burnt-out dancer at the end of her rope. By the time the money and directorship problems had been solved, the time slot when I was available had come and gone – so no falcon and no ballerina, and that may have been just as well, since the story came a little close to the bone. I had already had an intermittent "pop" television career: two CBC specials in 1974 with Quebec composer-pianist André Gagnon and choreographer Brian Macdonald. (In 1979, I would also have my own CBC Superspecial – the somewhat embarrassing term they used at the time – with Frank, Jeff Hyslop, a multi-talented dancer who became a good friend, actor Douglas Campbell, and singer Maureen Forrester, who claimed that she lost five pounds with all the dancing.) My serious television career was a bit more extensive. In 1976, Frank and I made a television version of *Giselle*, directed by Norman Campbell, and in 1979, we would tape *La Fille Mal Gardée*. In the eighties, Norman would direct me in television versions of Ronald Hynd's *The Merry Widow* and Glen Tetley's *Alice* and *La Ronde*. In France, there was Roland Petit's *Coppélia*. There would also be three television documentaries: *Karen Kain: Ballerina* (1976), *Karen Kain: Prima Ballerina* (1989), and *Karen Kain: In Her Own Words* (1994), all produced by Pat Ferns.

I have mixed feelings about dance for television. Performance conditions are usually far from ideal, so you're not preserving the best for posterity. In *Giselle*, I had to do the Mad Scene cold at ten in the morning. If I had been an experienced actress, I might have known how to prepare for early-morning hysterics, but I wasn't, and if the scene worked, it may have been because I was in a panic about doing it at all. Moreover, we danced on a concrete floor, which

*Ann Ditchburn's Mad Shadows, with Laszlo Surmeyan.*

was so painful that I got a serious kink in my neck and shooting pains up my legs. For *Fille*, we had a non-negotiable demand: a sprung floor. We got it, but because the surface was painted to make it more photogenic, paint came off on our shoes and made the floor treacherously slippery. But what makes filming for television a true ordeal is the endless waiting around, which makes it almost impossible to stay warmed up. Somehow the most difficult dancing always came at the end of an exhausting day; with no audience, very little adrenalin, and taped music that was often at the wrong tempo, it was difficult to do your best.

When you see the results, you wonder whether it was worth the trouble. Much of the vitality of dance is lost in the transfer onto video, which somehow bleeds all the energy and shading away. You dance your legs off, but on TV you look slow, anaemic. Film has more depth of field and picks up three-dimensional movement better, but that costlier medium is seldom used, and even when it is, there's only a fraction of the excitement of a live performance. On balance, however, films and tapes are important because they provide pleasure to thousands who never get to see live theatre; think of the impact of the Moira Shearer film *The Red Shoes*, which persuaded many young people to become dancers. As I get older, as I watch tapes of Fonteyn, Nureyev, and Bruhn in their prime, I appreciate the tremendous value of having some record of ballets and performers.

ʃə

I reached what many people might consider the peak of celebrity in 1980 when Toronto lawyer William Hechter commissioned Andy Warhol to paint my portrait. The Factory, Warhol's studio, was a huge loft with enough desks for a newsroom and an overall feeling of chaos. "Andy wants your hair up tight in a bun," said one assistant, while another added, "He wants white make-up with dark red lipstick." Suddenly, I realized there was someone else in the room: Warhol was clicking away with a Polaroid, and, as they applied the make-up, he kept muttering to himself unintelligibly. I began to wonder if I had some special attraction for people given to strange incantations. I was asked to strike several poses, and then, abruptly, it was over.

The results, a series of silkscreens unveiled at a huge reception at the Sutton Place Hotel, were greeted with a deathly silence. I hated the portrait myself: my lyrical self-image seemed unrecognizably distorted by Warhol's garish colours – sea-foam green, orange, purple, and puce. For years, I kept my copy in the basement, as did my parents. Their cat, Jeffrey, habitually marked

*My first dubious encounter with myself by Warhol.*

his territory on it, as if expressing the views of the better-mannered human component of the Kain household. Over the years, however, I've come to see Warhol's portrait as bold and striking, and at my husband's urging, my copy now hangs in our dining room.

While my extracurricular career was busier than I had imagined possible during the seventies, and my guest appearances with Rudolf and Roland brought me joy and confidence, significant changes that would have a profound effect on me were occurring at the National Ballet.

In 1974, Celia Franca retired as artistic director, partly because she thought the board was interfering unduly in artistic matters. Her departure marked the end of an era for the company; as founder of the company, for twenty-three years she wielded complete authority and demanded unquestioning obedience, but her successors would have to establish an appropriate balance between artistic control and a more collegial relationship with dancers.

The Dream. *(Above) with Jacques Gorrissen as Bottom;*
*(right) with Luc Amyot as Oberon.*

I've always admired Celia's vision and discipline, and I'm deeply grateful to her for having given me so many opportunities early in my career. She was capable of great gentleness, as I remember from the time I singlehandedly blew an important performance of Sir Kenneth MacMillan's *Solitaire* in Japan in 1970. It was my big break – I was one of only six girls in the small corps – and I was so nervous that I couldn't even hear the music; I panicked, lost my concentration, forgot every single step, and wandered across the stage in an agony of embarrassment and guilt. Celia found me sobbing in the dressing room. Instead of bawling me out for ruining the performance, she asked, with obvious concern, "Karen, what happened?" And she went on to give me more important roles.

She was also a magnificent coach when she chose to be. I'll never forget a rehearsal for my first *Giselle* when she, Mary McDonald, and I were alone in the studio. Instead of drilling me in the steps and interrupting every other beat as Mary played – normal rehearsal routine in those days – Celia spoke quietly and magically of the moonlight in the forest and the eerie wind as the Wilis entered, talking me through Act II and giving me a subtext for the whole performance. A master class from a brilliant Giselle, this was as memorable as my rehearsals with Fonteyn.

But I was also pathologically afraid of Celia, partly because I was afraid of many people then, but also because I thought I could never meet her high standards. I respond better to the carrot than the stick. Celia normally didn't have to use the stick, because we'd been so well conditioned that we felt it without a word from her. But she didn't offer many carrots, and I needed them to develop the confidence to give a good performance. As director, compliments weren't her style, but since her retirement she's been very generous with praise, and it's deeply appreciated. Unfortunately, old habits die hard: even now, when I hear she is coming to a performance, I get nervous.

After she left, David Haber – my first agent, and a man I liked – took over briefly, but then he was fired, and for over a year David Scott and Joanne Nisbet had to run the company as well as rehearsing and coaching. Then, out of the blue, in the spring of 1976, the word came down from the board: our new artistic director was Alexander Grant.

Few of us had seen Alexander Grant dance, but we certainly knew who he was. Short, with large, expressive facial features, he had been an exceptional demi-caractère dancer, particularly in comic roles. He'd created characters in many of Sir Frederick Ashton's ballets, most notably the idiot boy Alain in *La Fille Mal Gardée*, and his close friendship with Ashton helped him acquire that marvellous ballet for the National. An injury Alexander sustained as Alain ended his active dancing career, and he has a pronounced limp to this day, but he continued to perform straight character roles and for a time ran the Royal Ballet's educational "Ballet for All" program. These seemed excellent credentials, and, as a member of the Royal Ballet, Alexander was almost one of the family already.

We liked him immediately; he had a great sense of humour, he was completely approachable, and he wanted to be liked – something that would later prove to be his undoing as artistic director. His first few years were terrific, partly because of Ashton acquisitions like *Fille* and *The Dream*. We were thrilled when Alexander persuaded the great man himself to come and oversee his work.

*More of* The Dream, *with Jacques Gorrissen as Bottom.*

Slow-moving, with a long, creased, hound-dog face, Sir Fred was the best advertisement for alcohol and cigarettes you could imagine. Well over seventy, he spent his days in the studio and partied all night, nursing his scotch, his serpentine fingers delicately balancing a cigarette as he told stories of Margot, Bobby (Sir Robert Helpmann), and the old days with the panache of a professional showman. He was a one-man history of British ballet, and we adored him.

But somehow he and I kept having bizarre misunderstandings in the studio. During one arduous rehearsal, Sir Fred sighed, "I'm longing for a drink!" As usual, I was painfully self-conscious about my height, so what I heard was, "I'm longing for you to shrink." Taken aback, but relieved that the issue was out in the open, I plaintively replied, "I'm sorry, but there's nothing I can do about that!"

Later, practising a very painful step he'd borrowed from Georgian folk-dancing, I ran across the stage on pointe, drilling my toes into the floor.

"Don't crucify yourself," he urged. I thought he was considerately telling me to take it easy on my feet, so I stopped. Unfortunately, he meant that my arms were stretched out so stiffly I looked like a crucifixion scene. That may have been the only time in my life I interpreted a criticism more positively than it was intended.

The joy of working with Sir Fred every now and then was great, but not enough to sustain us. After a few years, I realized that the company was losing ground; standards were slipping, including my own. The double loss of morale and momentum that had started with a few dancers had spread through the company like a virus. My frustration sparked my first and only experience as co-founder of a ballet troupe.

During a tour of western Canada in 1978, my malaise boiled over. One morning, Frank, soloist David Roxander (a good friend of ours), and I were sitting in a greasy spoon in Regina, and I said casually, "This is so tedious that we should put together our own tour." After a few minutes' discussion, the wild idea looked like a real possibility, and Ballet Revue was born.

Seven of us took part: three real-life couples (Frank and me, Ann Ditchburn and Tomas Schramek, Cynthia Lucas and David Roxander) and another soloist, Karyn Tessmer. Peter Sever, who had worked with the National and was now running Great Artists Management Inc., set up a five-week tour for our annual vacation.

Ballet Revue was an artistic commune, perhaps the most loosely structured touring group ever assembled. We all had an equal voice in every decision, from repertoire to casting, and the operating principle was that everyone could do anything he or she wanted. Ann created a new ballet, *Truth and Variations*, with music by Elizabeth Swados, and after that we threw in everything but the kitchen sink. With generous sponsorship from Imperial Oil, we made our debut in April 1979 in Niagara-on-the-Lake, but not before handling our first crisis.

Frank had had one memorable panic in Moscow, and he chose our opening night to have another. Convinced we'd flop, he got in his car at the Oban Inn, rolled up the windows, locked the doors, and started the engine. We put our bodies on the line, circling the car and shouting all the persuasive arguments we could muster to get him to stay. Finally, he gave in and the show went on – and on, for more than three hours. We had enough sense to make drastic cuts before the next show, but one item we kept in turned my height into an intentional joke. After Karyn and Tommy danced the grand pas de deux from *The Sleeping Beauty* straight, David and I entered as "Couple No. 26" in a send-up of the Moscow competition, with Frank as a very strange Russian judge with a clipboard, fake moustache, tights, a ratty fur coat, and ballet shoes. Because David is about a foot shorter than I am when I'm on pointe, our straight-faced attempt to do the pas de deux was funnier than any satire. The audience loved it.

In some ways, Ballet Revue was smooth sailing. We sold out every night, and requests for bookings poured in from as far away as California and Australia. We had created a project for ourselves, and we even made a little money, with Tommy establishing himself as a crackerjack accountant. But, to Ann's disappointment, we never repeated the experiment. She had hoped that Ballet Revue would become a permanent workshop for new choreography, and she left the National shortly thereafter to pursue choreography, writing, editing, and film. However, the rest of us were committed to making the National our top priority, and we didn't think that that could be combined with a commitment to Ballet Revue. We saw what a strain it was to replace holidays with hard work, as I ought to have learned years earlier; most of us wound up with very short fuses on the tour. Once David Roxander and I started an argument in the morning and continued squabbling straight through the performance, ignoring our colleagues' urgent orders to cool it.

While Ballet Revue had given us a breather, the National continued to drift, uninspired, and, although I liked him very much as a friend, I thought the problem was Alexander. An artistic director must provide artistic guidance in the studio. I watched Alexander teaching roles he'd made famous, and it seemed that he wanted the other dancers to be carbon copies of himself. I began to wonder whether he had ever observed other artists analytically, or whether he was interested in discovering what individual dancers in the National were capable of doing. I saw that he was particularly uncomfortable coaching ballerinas; he didn't seem to know what to say to us at all. Finally, and very reluctantly, I concluded that, despite his charm as a man and his genius as a dancer, he lacked the ability to give just the right hint or correction that would make us better versions of ourselves. When he started coming late to rehearsals and falling asleep once he was there, my discouragement was complete – and I wasn't alone in my assessment. Other dancers agreed, and after four years under Alexander, it was painfully apparent that both the public and the critics knew our performances weren't good enough. The box office was beginning to suffer.

Dancers at the National had been trained to be obedient and keep their opinions to themselves, but I screwed up my courage and asked to speak to the president of the board. When I explained my concerns about the company's

*The cast of Ballet Revue: (left to right) Ann Ditchburn, Tomas Schramek, Cynthia Lucas,
David Roxander, me, and Frank. Karyn Tessmer is missing.*

well-being, he listened politely, but I didn't feel my comments were really being heard. Shortly thereafter, a three-year extension of Alexander's contract was announced.

By now, negativity had become a company characteristic. Having acquired one British ballet after another, we started calling ourselves "The Sadler's Wells of Canada." *Fille* and *The Dream* had been wonderful, but we took a dimmer view of works like *Les Patineurs* (1937) and *Two Pigeons* (1961), which seemed dated. Despite the fact that Alexander had encouraged our talented troika of home-grown choreographers, Ann Ditchburn and James Kudelka left the company, seeking the opportunity to choreograph major ballets more frequently, so only Constantin Patsalas remained as an in-house choreographer. We weren't developing a clear artistic identity of our own. We kept reading mediocre reviews and depressing box-office figures, and we wondered whether the board was ever going to notice.

A major reason for our mediocrity was Alexander's casting policy, a reflection of his personality and his chosen style as artistic director. As a person, he wanted to be loved (and he's one of the most lovable people I know); as a director, he genuinely wanted to make his dancers happy. Principals automatically danced every principal role, and talented younger dancers who asked for major roles were often given them as well. This might not have been disastrous if we had been performing almost every day and had enough ballet masters and mistresses and rehearsal studios to guarantee everyone adequate preparation and performance time. But we didn't have those resources. In any case, proper preparation wouldn't have been enough even if we could have afforded it; it's a hard truth that no dancer is suited to every role, and no amount of dedication and hard work can change that. So dancers who could have been brilliant in a role suffered from inadequate rehearsal and performance time, and dancers who shouldn't have been cast had the double disadvantage of miscasting and poor preparation. This was a sure prescription for loss of morale and of quality. It all boiled down to a problem of leadership. Alexander's easy-going nature, so great a contrast to Celia's, made him well-loved, but it didn't permit him to take the tough decisions, without which any artistic director will fail.

My own frustration was the greater, because I knew I could have been dancing almost every night if I had accepted all the invitations that came my way from Rudolf and Roland, whereas in the company I was lucky to get a performance a week in our short seasons. The crisis came in May 1982, just after I'd returned from dancing Giuletta, a role created for me in Roland's new ballet *The Tales of Hoffmann*.

A reporter asked Alexander why he had allowed me to miss the Toronto spring season. "Perhaps Karen is a little more special," Alexander replied. "She has more leverage. We have to cope without her." Then came the kicker, "What can we do? Sue her? We don't believe in settling differences like that." Alexander may have been exaggerating with humorous intent, but I was hurt and angry. My contract with the National required me to do a certain number of performances a year, and I had already exceeded that figure by at least ten. His public suggestion that I had broken my contract and opened myself up to legal action was so insulting that I couldn't let it pass. When Stephen Godfrey called to ask whether I would comment on the situation for the *Globe and Mail*, I remembered Karen Bowes's bravery in my first year with the company and agreed. I'd spoken quietly to the president of the board with no response, so it was finally time to go on record publicly.

In the interview, I spoke frankly about Alexander and his role in the deterioration of the company. I commented on Alexander's casting policies and the deficiencies I perceived in his exercise of the directorship. For once, I also took the opportunity to defend myself. Noting that I felt I had been punished in subtle ways for having undertaken any guest engagements, I said, "I've been timid too long. I've been made to feel incredibly guilty when I shouldn't. I love the National, but I've got to speak up for myself when it's clear that the company won't stand up for me." I explained that, while I remained fully committed to performing in Canada, a dancer's life was short, and, if I wasn't getting the chance to dance regularly here, then I had to go where better opportunities existed. (For the record, our subsequent artistic directors, Erik Bruhn and Reid

Anderson, understood this principle perfectly and always encouraged National Ballet dancers to perform elsewhere when good chances came along.)

This interview brought the situation to a head; as if in response to my concerns, just two weeks later the board announced that Alexander would be asked to leave a year before his contract expired. While I agreed with this course of action, I was shocked at the cruel way in which it was implemented: the decision was made public while Alexander was in Jackson, Mississippi, judging a ballet competition. Justifiably outraged, Alexander told reporters that the board's behaviour was "nasty, shabby, and back-stabbing." That was undeniably true. What wasn't true was everyone's assumption that I was responsible for the stabbing.

As I later found out, my interview was just a convenient occasion for an action that the board had been contemplating for some time. These days, I might have been aware of the situation: dancers' representatives now sit on the board, and I'm one of them. But in the early eighties, communications between the board and the dancers were poor. If someone had just once taken me aside to say that the concerns I had expressed to the president were being seriously discussed, I would never have spoken publicly. Without that knowledge, I felt I had no choice but to speak out.

Piecing the situation together from the outside, I suspect that Betty Oliphant had a strong influence on the board's decision. There was little affection between Betty and Alexander; things had gone so far that they'd had a war in the press. Alexander had said that he was accepting dancers from schools other than the National Ballet School because "It is not our job to teach technique. I must take the very best that is available." Betty, not about to let him get away with that insinuation, responded that "The National is still a very fine company, but the things that used to be its strengths just aren't there anymore. . . . The technique is generally much more careless." Personally, I think there was some truth on both sides.

Naturally, Alexander was deeply hurt by the board's decision, and I regretted having played such a public role in causing him pain. I appreciated his generous words to the *Toronto Sun* six months later: "I do not blame Karen in any way. It was unfortunate that her absence in May coincided with a very bad box office." But it would take years for him to forgive the National, if indeed he's been able to forgive it yet. Wanting to show my personal regard for him in a public way, on the occasion of my twentieth anniversary with the company in November 1988, I wrote him a letter asking him to join me. I said that there had been a lot of water under the bridge, and that I valued much of what he had done for the company. He wrote a lovely letter back, wished me well, and said that he couldn't attend only because he was already committed to perform elsewhere.

The next time that there was such unhappiness and dissatisfaction within the company, we were all far better equipped to address it. The dance world was changing. Speaking out in criticism of Alexander was one of the hardest things I've ever had to do, and I was able to do it only because I cared so much for the National and felt that I was probably the only dancer in a strong enough position to be able to do so without tremendous fear of the possible consequences. But now a new generation of dancers has more confidence in their right to speak up; they're no longer the perpetual boys and girls of the ballet, but fully-grown adults, and they know it.

In 1982, I was thirty-one, and in many ways I had only just – very belatedly – grown up. In this chapter, as in two previous ones, I've described the highlights of my public life in the seventies. But as my career progressed, my emotional life steadily deteriorated – a fact that I concealed even from myself, in the process wasting a good deal of time and energy. In retrospect, I wish I'd been able to read the signs of imminent burn-out when they first appeared with utter clarity: fall 1976. Those signs are obvious in interview after interview: to Lawrence O'Toole of the *Globe and Mail* (September 11, 1976), I said, "I've tried to bite off more than I can chew. I'm running around guest-appearing with everybody. It's been like that for two years now, and I just can't keep it up." But I was a good little girl, and a responsible eldest daughter as well; of course I kept it up. Even if I had recognized how deeply I was in trouble, however, I wouldn't have known where to turn.

My European successes with Roland Petit had aroused so much interest at home that a fourteen-city Canadian tour, with me as guest artist, was arranged for the fall of 1976. For me, it would be a personal disaster on almost every level.

As usual, I had overbooked myself. While the Ballet de Marseille was traversing the country from east to west, the National Ballet of Canada was touring in the opposite direction. I had never learned to say no to any request, even if it meant worrying myself sick, so, eager to accommodate everyone, despite my full understanding of the rigours of even a single tour, I agreed to criss-cross the country by plane and dance in two simultaneous tours.

The tour with the Ballet de Marseille started badly. In Ottawa, the French press loved the troupe's theatricality and vigour, but the English papers thought the choreography shallow and trite. It was the classic conflict of two cultures, two legitimate tastes, but I was mortified. My colleagues from Marseilles had been so excited about performing in Canada, partly because of my own enthusiasm for my country and partly because they wanted me to be appreciated here for the works in which I had established my reputation in France. I felt somehow responsible for what I saw as the shabby treatment Roland and his company were receiving, and I was so distraught about this on the phone with my parents that they immediately jumped in the car and drove to Ottawa to console me for a few days.

Throughout the tour, reviews for me were also mixed, partly because the Canadian public had never seen me dance dark or sultry roles outside the tasteful classical confines of *Swan Lake*, and they didn't know what to do with *Carmen*. I'm still not sure whether in my depression I danced badly or whether Canadians stubbornly refused to acknowledge what they saw – and the reception I'd received in Europe inclines me towards the latter explanation. William Littler (*Toronto Star*) said I danced the role of Carmen "as naughtily as Doris Day," while McKenzie Porter (*Toronto Sun*) opined that "unlike Jeanmaire, Karen Kain is not built for strumpet roles. . . . She just cannot be coarse." Reviewers in Winnipeg said they'd rather see me in almost anything else.

I was soon past caring. Zig-zagging across the country, I was near collapse. I felt so under-rehearsed in a new ballet, *Notre Dame de Paris* (Roland's version of *The Hunchback of Notre-Dame*), that I knew I couldn't do it credibly, if I could do it at all. Racked with guilt in this lose-lose situation, I bowed out of my scheduled appearance in Montreal, something I rarely do.

On one particularly awful occasion, I was to take a flight from Toronto to St. John's, Newfoundland, to dance *Coppélia* with the National and then fly straight to Calgary to rejoin the Marseille troupe. But I stopped to buy a magazine in the Toronto airport and missed my seven-in-the-morning-flight to St. John's. The next flight was at noon, and I phoned my parents in hysterics, asking them to come to the airport to keep me company. Then fog prevented my flight from landing in St. John's, and we were forced to land at Gander instead. After a five-hour cab ride from Gander to St. John's in the middle of the night – with four businessmen, none of us saying a word – I finally arrived at three in the morning. I barely got through the performance and onto my Calgary flight, which was also delayed by fog, arriving ninety minutes before the next performance.

By then I was so frazzled that I begged the Marseille staff to allow Elisabetta Terabust, my alternate, to replace me. "But we can't," they said. "The theatre is sold out for you." Wretched, absolutely at the end of my tether, I wept uncontrollably as I tried to put on my make-up. Then – and this is one of those amazing, unpredictable things about the theatre – I gave one of my best performances in *Carmen*. Perhaps the only escape from my misery was to be on-stage in a role I knew well, too exhausted emotionally to be able to think about what I was doing so that my instincts took over and carried me through.

All through these years, the demon driving me was my desire to satisfy everyone, to let nobody down, to balance Canadian tours and seasons with TV specials and official dinners in Ottawa and new creations in Paris and guest engagements with Rudolf in London and Vienna. My life was so schizophrenic that I felt I was living multiple lives all at once. Even now, I've had to break the story of those years into four separate chapters to make some sense out of it, find some cohesiveness in the chaos so that a reader can understand what was going on. I tried so hard to do what everybody wanted me to do, and, of course, there were so many conflicting demands that I was sure to fail.

My first loyalty was always to the National Ballet, even though my greatest need as a dancer was to perform in a context that gave me confidence – and increasingly that meant with Rudolf or Roland, men who believed in me and whose cultural heritage allowed them to show that belief openly. I quickly learned that nobody at the National Ballet of Canada wanted to hear about my exploits or my problems. My absences were resented. Why was I being invited to all these places when dancers who worked equally hard at home were not? The administration went out of its way to remind me that I was going to be treated exactly like anyone else – that's fair, that's the Canadian way – so I often found my rehearsals scheduled at particularly inconvenient times. If I was exhausted or frenzied or put a foot wrong in any performance, that was my own fault, and therefore I deserved no sympathy. My problems served me right.

Perhaps I sound a little paranoid; perhaps I *was* a little paranoid. But the people in the wardrobe department confirmed that it wasn't just my imagination. "You wouldn't believe what so and so said about you," they would say as they were fitting a costume. I heard so many second-hand complaints that I was just a product of the publicity department, and that it spent so much time on me that it didn't have time to promote anybody else, that I hired my own publicist, Gino Empry, to show that I had no intention of monopolizing our staff. Unfortunately, the plan backfired, since a few people thought I was trying to get even more publicity, so after a while I stopped the arrangement.

Initially my response to all the accusations and talk was a good cry. What hurt most was that I often missed the company terribly when I was away, but when I came back it seemed that nobody had missed me at all, that in fact most people would have preferred me to stay away.

But you can cry only so long. You get tougher after a while; you develop a thicker skin. I gradually came to understand how difficult it was for people to accept the wonderful things that were happening to me – especially because I had so carefully concealed the price I was paying. My colleagues wouldn't have been human if they hadn't sometimes resented the attention I was getting.

However bad it was sometimes, I also recall moments of generous and unexpected support and affection from my fellow dancers. After five performances of *Swan Lake* in a row on tour, my infected corns hurt so much that I couldn't break in a new pair of shoes, so, unasked, Mary Jago broke them in for me. When my feet ached so badly I almost wished they'd fall off, Nadia Potts bought Epsom salts and prepared a hot foot-bath. After I'd done particularly well in a performance in New York, Vanessa Harwood complimented me so spontaneously and generously that I almost cried. There may have been tensions, but underneath we cared deeply about each other.

In the Prologue to *The Sleeping Beauty*, the principals and soloists dancing the Fairies have to support each other as each one in turn lifts her leg in an attitude on pointe, until all stand together triumphant. Later, we have to keep formation perfectly in a tight, moving circle. When we did well, we were elated at the success we had had together, as an ensemble. For me, those choreographic moments now symbolize something deep and lasting within the company itself, something to rely on even in the darkest times.

But during the seventies, I was so caught up in my own whirlwind that every difficulty – the conflicting requests and obligations, the less-than-perfect performances, the sleepless nights and tears, the rumours, the real or perceived slights – fuelled my own deep insecurity, and I felt mounting waves of panic. There was pressure everywhere I turned. My life was a full-blown Canadian fairy tale, yet I couldn't cope with it; I felt guilty that I wasn't happy, that I was falling apart more and more often. A private and work-driven person by nature, I had neither the time to develop the inner resources I needed to deal with my public life nor the ability to admit that I was in trouble. I'd reached a turning point and the most painful period of my life.

*The Private Cost of a Public Life*

*"Failure is not the falling down but the staying down."* –
Actress Mary Pickford

Most people discover fairly quickly that you can't immerse yourself in your work and neglect your personal life completely without serious consequences. I had always taken pride in overwork; in a *Globe and Mail* interview in 1971, just before my first Toronto *Swan Lake*, I told Barbara Gail Rowes, "I enjoy working. Just working. Killing myself until I'm nearly sick. That's when it feels good." With workaholics like Rudolf Nureyev and Erik Bruhn as my idols, it would take me far too long to realize that my total commitment to dancing had left me incomplete and vulnerable.

As early as May 1974, I had a premonition that I wasn't ideally suited to the lifestyle of the career-first-and-always ballerina. Right after my very first performances as a guest artist with Roland Petit, I had flown straight to Vienna to appear with Nureyev in *Swan Lake* at the Vienna State Opera. The performance had gone well, Rudolf was proud of me, and the audience had leapt to their feet for a twenty-minute ovation. But as I sat in my small hotel room, surrounded by bouquets of flowers, I thought, "Why am I so unhappy?" I suddenly realized that this was going to be my life: jetting from one city to another, packing and unpacking in impersonal, nondescript hotel rooms. It was a life Rudolf, who lived only for his work, could embrace completely, but I missed my friends and family, my colleagues at the National.

Sensing my loneliness and feelings of displacement, on our day off Rudolf distracted me with visits to the Vienna Woods and various palaces and museums.

He insisted on taking me to the Sacher Hotel for my first authentic *Sachertorte*, and he proudly exhibited the famous Viennese wrought-iron gates that had inspired part of his *Nutcracker* set at the Royal Ballet in London. His continual kindnesses, and the joy and challenge of dancing with him, cured this bout of malaise, and the inspiration each of us gave the other on-stage was a constant incentive for me. I kept up the pace and put everything I had into my dancing. Ballet is a profession where total emotional commitment is essential – but no less dangerous for its necessity.

Choreographer Antony Tudor said, "Man moves more truthfully than he speaks," a perception that modern-dance pioneer Martha Graham phrased slightly differently, "Movement never lies." Honest dancing reveals one's true character: the warmth of a Fonteyn, the impulsiveness of a Seymour. Every movement mirrors the interior life, regardless of the overlays that inspired acting may superimpose. It is the ability of great dancers to mirror both the characters' emotions and their own inner lives that makes their art true and moving and that forges the emotional bond with the audience that – in rare performances – becomes unforgettably powerful.

My joy in dancing has always been transparent. In fact, it's one of the things that has made me a good dancer. But a less-happy side began to emerge during the late seventies. As my professional life became more crowded, and I grew less able to juggle my own obligations and satisfy other people's expectations, the physical and emotional toll grew ever heavier. I was constantly exhausted, depressed, anxious, and full of vague guilt. Everywhere I looked, I saw my own failures, and if no one else saw them, that was even worse: I was convinced that, one of these days, I would be found out, exposed, and even more humiliated. I couldn't believe that my inner turmoil wasn't already completely mirrored in my dancing – and indeed sometimes it was, though just as often I could escape into my roles, use immersion in them to gain temporary relief from my own pain, and give what people would tell me was an inspired performance.

Ever since my days at the school, I had had periods – sometimes very long ones – of dark moods. But from the mid-seventies on, the bleakness grew worse, most likely because of the impossible agenda I had set for myself. There would be good and bad patches, moments of triumph and of agony, but gradually the bleak periods expanded into weeks and months, while the good ones shrank to days or hours. If I was dancing with Rudolf or Roland, it was different; they still believed in me, and they could still make me believe in myself – when they were around. But when they weren't, I became despondent.

I now recognize that what I experienced was a typical clinical depression. All I wanted to do was sleep, for hour after hour if at all possible. When I wasn't sleeping, I was crying, for no definable reason. Anything or nothing at all would set me off on a crying jag, and that was one of the most frightening aspects of my condition. As a dramatic artist I had to ferret out the linkage between emotional cause and effect as part of my daily work. How could I *not* know why I suddenly burst into tears? My not knowing was yet another proof to me of my inadequacy.

I was falling apart, and I couldn't bear the thought of anyone seeing me. I still had some pride. I had been drilled in the niceties of professional behaviour at the school since I was eleven, and one of the rods with which I beat myself was the self-accusation that my tears, my emotional instability, were completely unprofessional.

If my days were full of shame and embarrassing, inexplicable outbursts of tears, my performances were exercises in sheer terror. Just as, throughout my career, I'd heard and remembered only the negative things people said about me, so now I could think only negative things about myself. Early in my depression, I could forget about my inadequacies on-stage if I managed to throw myself completely into the role, but later even that escape was usually denied me. Instead, as I began each step, no matter how easy, I would think, "I can't do this. I've never been able to do . . . a fouetté, an arabesque, a simple *glissade*, whatever it might be. I'm bound to fall over." And sometimes I did. I was full of negative images: I actually *saw* myself losing my balance, falling down. I felt I had nothing to offer: no talent, no technique, no musicality, no acting ability, and no smile.

Some days it would be even worse. I had always been nervous in the wings, but on the really bad days I would work myself into a full-scale panic attack. In retrospect, I've learned to admire my courage in going on at all at those times, for I did go on, always, even though I expected disaster. I was a professional, and my performances were still – usually – selling out. The company was depending on me.

Sometimes my lacklustre performance would be evident, and the applause would be muted, merely polite. But at other times – and these were even worse for a perfectionist like me – people would give me a warm reception, perhaps even stand and applaud, when I knew I'd been dreadful, and I would interpret their enthusiasm as proof positive that I'd never been any good. I had always danced badly, and somehow nobody had ever noticed.

Looking back, I think most of my performances during that period were acceptable, and maybe a few were good. But some of them were truly bad. "Movement never lies." My performances mirrored my emotional turmoil and my utter lack of self-confidence. I'd lost touch with whatever had been instinctual in my dancing, which is what carried me in my early years, and I was in no condition either to replace it with calculation or to recover it. I've never asked her, but I wonder whether Celia had noticed something when, several years after she retired, she returned to remount *Les Sylphides*. She quietly cautioned me about burn-out when she learned that I was spending all my vacations guesting somewhere or other. I dismissed her warning at the time as yet another piece of criticism, but now I see her concern as perceptive and touching.

*With Frank, meeting Princess Margaret on a tour to London.*

My reviews in the late seventies confirmed that I had slipped. In the company's July 1979 New York engagement with Rudolf, I was in comparatively good emotional shape because, after all, Rudolf was there (though that was also the season when he had his temper tantrum in *The Sleeping Beauty*). But critics who had previously admired my dancing spotted something lifeless and flat in my work. Anna Kisselgoff noted in the New York *Times* that "Miss Kain, once so radiant as Aurora, now offered a sedate princess." Clive Barnes, in the *New York Post*, was harsher, "Miss Kain, a dancer of great promise, has not really developed much as a classical ballerina. She is polite, correct and muted. . . . Here she lacks nothing so much as excitement."

By August, when the company appeared for the first and last time at London's Covent Garden, home of the Royal Ballet, I knew I was in serious trouble. Alexander was taking us back to show us off to his own company, and we all wanted to do well for his sake. On opening night, in front of London's

*Conversation with Prince Charles in Ottawa.*

critics and the most glittering audience we had ever had in that city, I gave one of the worst performances of my career. I was sick with fear, and, naturally, it showed in my dancing.

After the Covent Garden season, I made the decision to stop dancing altogether. I told Alexander, "That's it. I'm quitting; there's no joy for me in this any more." He was very kind and very understanding. I wanted to disappear forever; he suggested that I take a few months off and return before the fall season.

I went to Europe to visit old friends and try to heal myself, and I spent some time in Paris with choreographer Molly Molloy. When I saw her recently, she told me how worried she had been about me in 1979, and how, after much thought, she had decided to give me a present to cheer me up: she would create a solo for me. We had begun working on it, but she soon realized that it wasn't going to work. "It was beyond your strength even to shift your weight from one foot to another," she said.

As it happened, a few months wasn't enough. I needed more time, but, true to form, I came back to Toronto as promised. I still couldn't bear to let people down, but my misery continued unabated.

It was Betty Oliphant who finally got me back on track when she paid me a backstage visit after a less-than-glorious performance of *Giselle* in early 1980. Betty herself has always been very open about her own emotional difficulties at a particularly impossible time in her life, and, characteristically, she was very direct with me. "I can tell you're seriously depressed, and I think you should get some help," she said bluntly. She arranged for me to see a psychiatrist whom she thought would be right for me, and this time I was ready. For the next two years, I was in therapy almost every week.

I didn't find it easy; I spent much of the time in tears, but they were cathartic and a measure of the effectiveness of the therapy, and in any case it was a lot better than crying in the washroom. Through those weeks and months, my therapist led me to examine areas of my life I'd never explored before and to face them head on, and I came to understand both how I'd got into this mess and how I could find my way out.

Like many dancers, I'd always been a perfectionist. While perfectionist tendencies are imperative for any artist, and perhaps particularly for dancers, I began to understand the origins and the dark side of my perfectionism. My family had been loving and supportive, but also – inevitably, given their background – critical, with very high expectations for all of their children. As the eldest child, I probably felt the weight of these expectations most. My accomplishments were praised, but very temperately, and even then what I heard – or invented – was not my parents' pride in me but rather how far I fell short, how far I still had to go.

*Teaching class and stage make-up to young ballet students in China as part of a cultural exchange, arranged by journalist John Fraser, 1979.*

The critical atmosphere of the ballet school added fuel to the fire of my insecurity. I was desperate to please my teachers, but, in the context of mastering so arduous a craft, the overwhelming emphasis was placed on what was wrong. Some of these problems could be corrected with hard work, but some could not – my turnout, for example, or my height. I struggled to make the best of my physique, but in some areas failure was assured, so I laboured all the more strenuously to compensate. One of the reasons Daniel Seillier had been so good for me was that he believed in my talent, gave me hope that it really existed, and helped me see that my good qualities might do much more than compensate for my faults, and that's why I worked for him with joy, while for some others I worked in terror. He was the first of those beloved mentors for whom I would do anything, simply because they thought I could. Yet all this time, from most of the people around me, I was learning that praise was awarded only on the basis of what I did, not who I was or how hard I was trying. I always felt I had to accomplish more and more to stay in the same place, to prevent my shortcomings from conquering me. Looking back, I appreciate the paradox of ballet training: too little perfectionism makes a lazy dancer, and too much kills the human spirit. The only solution is to adjust the blend of criticism and praise with exquisite sensitivity to the emotional make-up of each individual, to provide the kind of psychological support systems that the school now has in place, and, wherever possible, to give every child the sense that he or she is valued no matter how well a class or performance has gone.

I was a classic workaholic, and my dedication was the more destructive because, for most of my early career, I had no outside interests, no social skills, and a narrow social life that included only dancers. I now think that I threw myself into developing the demanding physical aspects of dancing to avoid developing anything else, including inner strength. One of the reasons I danced straight through my vacations was that I believed I wasn't accomplishing anything – indeed, had no excuse for being alive – unless I was working in the studio or performing. Only through therapy did I begin to see that I had been following an irrational process; my workaholism was fuelled by the need to feel deserving of praise, yet I didn't trust that praise when I received it.

Some people have natural self-confidence; I don't, yet I'd chosen a profession in which you can't succeed without an aura of confidence. Oddly enough, as much as I loved being visible on-stage, I was extremely uneasy with any visibility off-stage. I hated being the centre of attention unless I was on-stage, and then I felt that people were looking at Juliet, not at Karen. In the company, as at home and in school, I felt intense pressure from myself and from others to excel, yet I rarely felt pleasure in any success; no matter how loud the bravos, I would remember the one miffed pirouette in an otherwise glorious *Swan Lake*, feel physically ill that I had let the audience down, plunge into depression, and vow to work extra hard for the next time.

It was time for me to shift from depending on having other people believe in me to learning to believe in myself – to dance for myself, to judge for myself how I'd done, to praise myself when I'd done well, to forgive myself when I'd done badly. In retrospect, I agree that the company shouldn't have treated me differently from anyone else. But the focus of their democratic principles should be quite different: instead of making us all feel ordinary and lucky to be there at all, they should have found a way to make every dancer feel special.

Through my therapy, I also discovered that I had a pathological sense of responsibility. This had started at home, where as eldest daughter I'd assumed responsibility for anything that went wrong in the lives of the people I loved, and it had continued into my career. If any partner put a foot wrong, I felt it was my fault; if the box office or reviews weren't good, that was because of me. I think I've finally learned to distinguish between good and irrational senses of responsibility. When I tried to do something about the company's deterioration in Alexander's later years, or now when I sit on the board as a dancers' representative, that's something to be proud of; when I start to fret because my partner did a poor variation, I've learned to short-circuit the instantaneous guilt by telling myself, "Karen, that's not your fault!" I've also learned to cope with the sense of guilt that plagued me for years as I contrasted my sudden success with the struggle of others – in the company or in my family – to gain recognition and respect for who they were. I still feel sharp twinges when I think about how it must have affected my sisters and brother to have a "star" in the family, but I'm trying to discriminate between feeling sorrow that my success has inevitably had some negative impact on people I love and feeling paralysing guilt.

My depression and my years in therapy also taught me that I had to change a number of things in my life. Most importantly, I needed to find some balance. I learned that, even though I didn't always feel like it, I had to open up myself and my life to the world beyond dance. I made more time for friends and family, I sought out relationships that would nurture my self-confidence without undermining the new independence towards which I aspired, and I ended relationships – both personal and professional – that were draining my strength and harming my emotional well-being. I started to develop a more realistic sense of what I could and couldn't do. There were no more double tours like the one in 1976 and no more avoidance of vacations, and I learned to organize my time better. At last I was taking control of my own life. Gradually, I learned to recognize and acknowledge my own legitimate needs, and to try not to feel guilty when I couldn't help everyone or accept all the demands on my time and goodwill. I finally realized that I could, and must, establish my priorities myself.

I strongly recommend psychotherapy to anyone who has felt distress like mine – and I know there are a lot of them, in the dance world and everywhere else. Simply knowing that it's there for me if I should need it has increased my own confidence and security: if I'm in trouble again, I know where to turn. It helped me unscramble much of my confusion and recognize and express much of the anger I'd stored up over the years as a good little girl.

One of the things that would help me most in my bid to become a healthier, happier person would be friendships outside the dance world. The stage for this expansion of my world had been set at a New Year's party in 1974, where I had met a woman named Marlaina Sniderman, and as we talked, I was drawn to her intelligence, her vivacity, her astonishing ability to make me feel at ease in a situation I normally found intensely uncomfortable – a large party. Even then, I knew she had a generosity of spirit that reached out to embrace others. Instantaneously, I trusted her and felt that I could open up to her as I could to no one else. I invited her to lunch a few times, and, although we had great fun, I was always the one who initiated our outings. For the first year of our friendship, she never called me once, and I began to worry that I was being too pushy. Then she started phoning, and our friendship grew much closer. Years later, she told me that the reason she had avoided calling was because she had thought I would be inundated with invitations and she didn't want to pester me. She finally called me only when her husband suggested that I might be beginning to assume the friendship was pretty one-sided. Instinctively, she had done just the right thing: there were indeed many people who were absolutely determined to be my Best Friend, and I had run from them. One of the reasons Marley is indeed my best friend is that she let me come to her and had the sense to know when it was time to reciprocate.

Early in our friendship I was a single woman. Marley's husband, Robert Sniderman, had dreams of opening a restaurant, and every Sunday Bobby and a friend would try out recipes, and Marley and I would sample the results. All the experimentation and calories paid off: in 1984, Bobby opened a very successful restaurant called The Senator; he's gone on to open several more, and must be one of the few people in Toronto to have expanded in the restaurant business in recessionary years.

Filled with laughter and fun, their house became my second home, and those Sunday afternoons are among my happiest memories. At a time when I was experiencing profound difficulties, Marley was a shining example of emotional health – and my lifeline. Over the years, she has taught me what friendship is. Warm, funny, and incredibly intuitive, she understands what I'm thinking or feeling even if I can only manage to put three words together to express it. It probably helps that she's a psychotherapist by profession. In many ways, we're opposites; she jokes that she can make small talk to a door-knob (and she can), while I can go for weeks without saying a full sentence when I'm preoccupied by a role. But Marley can always draw me out; she has taught me to express my feelings in ways I never could before, and the shared memories we've developed over the years have strengthened our bond.

Gradually, I developed other relationships outside the dance world as well. In the fall of 1979, I met Lee Majors, an American actor best known for his TV series "The Six Million Dollar Man." He had read about me in the paper when he was in Toronto shooting a film with Burgess Meredith, and he decided to come to *The Sleeping Beauty*. Afterwards, he came backstage and invited me for a drink; since he seemed a sensitive, quiet, gentle man, I accepted, and for almost two years we saw each other off and on during breaks in our busy schedules.

Over time, I came to see how unhappy Lee was. He and Farrah Fawcett had been divorced a few years earlier, and for a while he dealt with his unhappiness by turning to alcohol. He called me "coach," because he could control his drinking when I was around. Like me, he was intensely shy, something that showed in the caution and limited range of his acting. He wasn't enjoying his career much at that time, and he shied away from the attention that went with it. Neither of us liked large social events.

Meanwhile, I was learning to enjoy life, thanks in part to my therapy. Lee flew to New Orleans, where I was guesting, to celebrate my thirtieth birthday with me in March 1981, and I remember thinking, "I feel happier now than I ever have in my life." That was ironic, given the company I had that evening. In addition to Lee, who had his problems, we were dining with a young dancer whose problems would prove fatal: Patrick Bissell, who, like Lee, had the attractive vulnerability of a child.

Patrick was a stunningly handsome dancer, who had quickly risen to the top at American Ballet Theatre, and he had appeared with the National as a guest for several years. We were physically and temperamentally well suited as partners, and his passion and commitment on-stage were contagious. Audiences and critics loved to see us together, but our partnership would never have a chance to develop. Patrick was a walking time bomb. When he told me once that he had to take ten Valium at night to sleep, I knew something was wrong. This was an enormous amount – on the few occasions that Valium was prescribed for me, one was enough to make me sleep for a day – but I didn't realize that he was using Valium to counteract the effects of cocaine.

Despite his drug problems, Patrick could work under pressure. On one occasion he flew into Toronto in the evening to dance in *Romeo and Juliet* with Vanessa Harwood on the next day. But Frank, who was to dance with me that

*Dancing the Black Swan pas de deux with Patrick Bissell.*

very night, had just been injured, and the company manager greeted Patrick with the news that he would be dancing with me in two hours. Patrick had had a little vodka on the plane, and he hadn't danced our version of the ballet for a year. Nonetheless, the staff threw him in the shower, gave him a coffee, and, after a quick consultation with me, he was on-stage. I talked him through each act, and he was such a stage creature that the only time the audience might have suspected he was completely unprepared was when he would do a *tour en l'air*, realize that he didn't know which leg to land on, and end up on both knees. That was Patrick: impulsive, sometimes ungainly, but always enthusiastic.

I had invited Patrick to be my partner in New Orleans, so I was embarrassed when he arrived under the influence of both drugs and alcohol. He missed his first rehearsal, and Ivan Nagy, a leading dancer with American Ballet Theatre, who was coaching the production, started teaching him the role in his hotel room. It was a rocky few days; in a dreadful mood, Patrick slapped the Lilac Fairy at the dress rehearsal, but he was a complete professional at the performance.

This was one of the last times I saw Patrick, but Gelsey Kirkland's book *Dancing on My Grave* describes how their brilliant partnership and individual careers were cut short by cocaine. They were fired from American Ballet Theatre, and, in 1984, after repeated attempts at rehabilitation, Patrick was found in his apartment, dead from an overdose. At my birthday dinner, however, Patrick's death was unthinkable; he was just a mixed-up kid who had chosen a far-more-dangerous way to deal with his confusion than I had.

By that dinner in 1981, however, I knew what I wanted in my own life. Through therapy I was beginning to understand what I needed in a relationship, and, reluctantly, I had realized that Lee and I wouldn't be good for each other in the long term. He must have sensed that I was drifting away, for he asked me to marry him. I cared about him, but I couldn't accept. We had had wonderful times, but just as I had known I couldn't live full time in the glamorous world of Roland Petit, so I knew that I didn't want to get lost in the unreal world of celebrity, Hollywood-style.

I calmly accepted that I would live my life alone, and I realized with some delight that I loved my life the way it was. With good friends, I didn't need romantic entanglements. Most of the time, I was happy. Just at this moment, Ross Petty came into my life.

ℒℬ

The National Ballet of Canada celebrates its own birthdays with fund-raising galas, and for its thirtieth birthday, in 1981, Frank and I were dancing *Diary*, choreographed by Lynne Taylor-Corbett to music by singer-songwriter Judith Lander. Judy and Ross had been friends since they had performed in *Jacques Brel Is Alive and Well and Living in Paris* in 1972 in their home town, Winnipeg. Since Ross was in Toronto making a movie, Judy invited him to a rehearsal. It was the day before the gala, and I was in my usual preoccupied state; Ross and I were introduced, but I don't remember it at all. So that was that – once again, so much for love at first sight – and he flew back to New York, where he'd lived for the previous seven years.

A year later, the not-so-memorable Mr. Petty was back in Toronto at the Royal Alexandra Theatre, performing the title role in the musical *Sweeney Todd*, written by Stephen Sondheim and directed by Harold Prince. It was July 1982, and happily Ross's memory was better than mine. Howard Meadows, an ex-dancer from the National who was then our wardrobe master, was working at the Royal Alex while we were on summer vacation, so Ross asked him whether I was in town. He wanted to invite me to a performance.

When Howard delivered Ross's message, I could think of many reasons not to accept. First and foremost, I had no idea who he was. I'd already seen the show on Broadway (with Len Cariou and Angela Lansbury), and while it was terrific, I wasn't sure I wanted to see it again, especially when I was flying to Italy in two days to dance in the Spoleto festival with Peter Ottmann and Ann Ditchburn. I picked up the phone, intending to decline the invitation. I'm generally uncomfortable returning calls; if there's no answer, I don't make a second attempt, and I certainly wouldn't have called back on this occasion. If there'd been an answering machine, I'd have left a polite refusal. But fate was on my side: Ross picked up the phone. His mellifluous baritone poured into my ear, and even though I had supposedly learned to say "no" in therapy, my defences began to melt. My "No, I really can't" turned into a "Well . . ." and finally a "What time is the curtain?"

Ross left only one ticket at the box office, so obviously my bringing a date was not part of the scenario, but by the time I arrived, I had forgotten his name. I looked for it on the program, where I also learned a little about Ross.

He was born in Winnipeg, and he made his first professional appearance at the age of fifteen in the chorus of *The Student Prince* at Winnipeg's Rainbow Stage. After a degree in English at the University of Manitoba, he headed for Europe, where he appeared in the musical *Belle Starr* with Betty Grable in London's West End. In France, he sang at the Lido in Paris and the Palm Beach Casino in Cannes, before returning to North America to try his luck in New York. In the United States, Ross co-starred with Ginger Rogers and Sid Caesar in Cole Porter's *Anything Goes*, toured with the national company of the Alan Ayckbourn hit *Bedroom Farce*, and made his Broadway debut as Constance Cummings's doctor in Arthur Kopit's *Wings*. Obviously, his career was taking off, and *Sweeney Todd* was a major stepping-stone.

This Sondheim milestone was not your typical Broadway hit, and when I heard two ladies behind me saying, "You know, dear, it's a musical, like *South Pacific*," I knew they were in for a shock. Sweeney, "the demon barber of Fleet

*On my father's sailboat the day after our first date.*

Street," wields a blood-stained razor, ruthlessly transforming his clients into the main ingredient of meat pies. Certainly a far cry from "Some Enchanted Evening." I'd been nervous about what to say if I didn't like the performance, but my fears quickly evaporated. Ross was brilliant: passionate, dangerous, totally convincing, with mesmerizing eyes that devoured the audience. Even now, more than twelve years later, people stop Ross on the street to tell him how vividly they remember his performance.

As I watched, I kept trying to recall what he had looked like when we met, hoping that the wild-haired, white-faced madman on stage was the product of make-up. After the show, I went back to Ross's dressing room to congratulate him and was surprised when a petite, elegant, silver-haired woman opened the door and said, "He'll be with you as soon as he's finished washing the blood from his hands." Ross's mother had come from Winnipeg to see her only child (his father, Victor, died in 1969), and her presence that night worked in his favour. I figured that, if he didn't feel awkward bringing his mother along for a drink, he must be a special man. I found Violet adorable, and we were joined at Joe Allen's by Gino Empry, who was then working as publicist for the Royal Alex. It was an unusual foursome, but I enjoyed myself and found Ross very attractive. I was sorry I had to leave for Spoleto the next morning.

When I returned from Italy, *Sweeney Todd* had ended its run, and I expected Ross to be back in New York. But on my answering machine was a beautiful baritone voice, "I'm still in town, and for one reason only." At dinner

169

that night Ross was charming, funny, and warm, and I was smitten. The next day I took him to meet my parents, and we went sailing in my father's boat. Although our careers separated us almost immediately – Ross was starring in *Carnival* and *Brigadoon* with the Pittsburgh Civic Light Opera and I was off to Scandinavia with Roland Petit's company – we were already serious about each other and planning when and where we could meet again.

I think I fell in love with Ross because he openly expressed the emotional, sensitive side of himself that most men keep hidden. He listened to me; he understood what I was saying and what I had left unsaid, and his support gave me a peace and security that I never thought I would find. It was a bonus that I didn't have to explain the demands of an artist's life – the strange hours, the intense moods – because he already knew.

In October, just four months after we had first gone out, we were sitting in the kitchen of Ross's Greenwich Village apartment after a beautifully crisp New York fall day and a romantic dinner at the neighbourhood Italian restaurant. Taking courage from the red wine, my heart pounding, I asked Ross to marry me.

He paled slightly, clearly a little stunned, but recovered quickly and said, "I'll never let you eat the mussels in that restaurant again!" I was serious, and he knew it, even if the prospect of marriage was a shock for both of us. Ross was thirty-six and I was thirty-two; veterans of the romantic wars, neither of us had thought that marriage would be an option in our lives. And then we fell, head over heels. There were so many things about him that were right for me, and the thought of not being with him was unimaginable.

I was surprised by how much attention our engagement received in the press when we finally announced it in December 1982. And, of course, there was a lot of suspicious curiosity about Ross: who was this man entering my life? Nothing could have prepared him for the proprietary interest that Canadian ballet fans were taking in me. Since he had lived in New York for most of the years that I had been in the company, he had barely known who I was when he came to rehearsal with Judy Lander. He certainly had no idea of the media circus that would surround him once we started seeing each other – which is probably a good thing, or he might have had second thoughts. On our wedding day, the *Globe and Mail* published John Fraser's article, "A Toast to the Bride from One of the Unchosen," in which he referred to me as "She" and warned "What's-His-Name" that he'd "better treat her good. Or else." This was neither the first nor the last time that Ross would good-naturedly endure the slights and jokes that came his way as the man who had dared to marry Our Karen.

For eight months, we planned every detail of our wedding, and, in what seemed like a wonderful omen, we were to be married at St. Clement's Church

*Our official engagement photo by David Street.*

by the Reverend Terence Finlay, Jr., whose father had married my parents in Winnipeg more than thirty years earlier. The rehearsal was rushed and haphazard; relatives and friends floated in late, chatting and joking as they wandered down the aisle. I found this totally unacceptable. This was a rehearsal, and Celia had shown me how they should be run.

*The family: (left to right) Sandra, Kevin, Violet, Ross and I, my mother, my father, and Susan.*

As I took charge and ordered people to their positions, I caught my husband-to-be looking at me with a bemused expression. But the show must go on: I turned to Ross and John Goss, a dear friend who was a conductor at the National Ballet, and announced, "You kiss me now, Ross. Okay, hit it on the organ, John!" In his wedding speech the next day, Ross joked that he hadn't known how bossy I was until that moment, and he felt great sympathy for what Frank Augustyn had had to endure.

The wedding took place on May 28, 1983. Marley was my matron of honour, and Ross's best man was Paul Hecht, another Canadian actor living in New York. My sisters, Sandy and Susan, were my bridesmaids, and my brother, Kevin, was one of the ushers. I had agreed to let the *Toronto Star* photograph all the preparations at the Windsor Arms Hotel, and my sisters were a little upset when the *Star* ran a huge photograph of all three of us, in curlers and without make-up, toasting the day with champagne and gorging on scones and clotted cream. The preparations had continued through a hectic afternoon, and nobody seemed immune to the chaos. Even my father, an oasis of calm as he sat quietly in the corner reading his newspaper, had discovered when we were leaving for the church that he had forgotten his cufflinks. A messenger was dispatched to find them.

Our wedding day was the fairy-tale event of every bride's dreams, starting with the exquisite dress, designed by Maggie Reeves. More romantic than anything I'd ever worn on stage, made of hand-embroidered silk, it had a high

*As the sun finally broke through, we greeted well-wishers outside the church.*

neckline in front but plunged to the waist in the back, where a large silk flower was placed as an accent.

I was concerned that Ross and I wouldn't be able to slip the rings on during the ceremony – I had witnessed that struggle between brides and grooms before – so Marley and I smeared Vaseline on my finger just before I marched down the aisle. Unfortunately, Ross and Paul, who had both the rings for our double-ring ceremony, had been thinking along the same lines, and slathered them with Vaseline. We could hardly hold on to them, much less put them on each other.

I had felt intensely nervous when my father and I walked down the aisle in front of our two hundred guests, but both Ross and I were moved by the intimacy of the ceremony itself, and taking my new husband's warm hand in mine gave me a sense of calm for the first time that day. Outside, a crowd of well-wishers cheered us on, and although the day had started with a light drizzle, the setting sun had the decency to peek through the clouds just as we left the church for our reception at the Courtyard Café. We enjoyed a three-week honeymoon – by far the longest holiday I'd ever allowed myself – in Puerto Vallarta, Mexico, in a villa high above Mismaloya Beach.

Some time later, I received a lovely handwritten note from Dame Margot Fonteyn. She had heard of my marriage belatedly, and she wanted to offer her best wishes that I would find in my marriage as much satisfaction and joy as she had in hers. I was deeply touched. I would soon discover that my marriage, like Margot's, would encounter difficult times, but would gain in strength from our facing adversity constructively when it came.

Before the marriage, whenever we had discussed our future life together, we anticipated splitting our time equally between New York, where Ross had his career, and Toronto, where I had mine. Yet what sounded fair in discussion turned out to be impossible in practice; as many performers know, the only winners in the struggle to maintain a long-distance relationship are the phone company and the airlines. Although I seriously explored the possibility of dancing in New York, I was feeling particularly positive about the National Ballet at that time, since Erik Bruhn had just arrived as our new artistic director. I began to realize how important the relative safety and comfort of Toronto were to my happiness and peace of mind compared to the mean streets of New York, and since Ross was more flexible as a freelance actor, he agreed to move to Toronto.

This was certainly the right resolution for me, and it seemed reasonable in the circumstances, but it was very hard on Ross – far more difficult than I understood at the time, and quite possibly harder than I realize to this day. He'd been making great strides in his career in the United States, and for him to move back to Toronto was probably even more disrupting than it would have been for me to move to New York. Returning to the small pond of Toronto after having braved the vaster waters of London, Paris, and New York was a disappointment; he missed the challenge and satisfaction of making it in New York, and was understandably perplexed when his experience and success in larger theatrical centres counted for very little here.

The fact that he was married to "Canada's Sweetheart" made matters still worse. The career demands placed on me, all the media and public attention, the constant barbed comments about how lucky he was to be married to me – all these were difficult to handle. Over the next few years, Ross was buffeted by unsolicited attention, not because of his own considerable talents but simply because he was married to me – and my energies were directed towards a career that was flourishing. Not surprisingly, he was somewhat resentful of the degree of my involvement in my career. He'd made career sacrifices to move to Toronto, and the support that he was consequently able to provide for me was, ironically, making me even busier, less available to him, at a time when the pressures on him were mounting, in large part because of me. Instead of the sweet ballerina who obviously adored him, he found himself living with a driven woman.

*The madcap cast of* Aladdin: *(left to right) Scherazade (Me), Widow Twankee (Bruno Gerussi), the evil Abanazar (Ross), and Aladdin himself (Jeff Hyslop).*

When Ross formed his own production company in 1986, his spirits improved immeasurably. He'd had so little control over his life as an actor, which consists largely of waiting for the capricious decisions of casting agents and directors, that he relished the chance to create his own projects and see them through. His first productions were the Canadian tours of the English pantomimes *Cinderella, Snow White,* and *Aladdin,* in which we both performed. In 1987 and 1989, he engineered successful television specials of *Cinderella* and *Aladdin* for the CTV network. But he still had mixed feelings about his move back to Canada.

Just prior to the *Aladdin* tour, in November 1988, the National Ballet gave me a twentieth-anniversary gala. I had put a great deal of effort into planning the evening over the previous months; I had to decide which had been my favourite works, select from this list the items that would make the most balanced program, cajole my favourite partners from the past into coming to perform with me, and then find just the right running order for the show. Afterwards, there was to be a black-tie dinner at the Royal York Hotel, with a "roast," traditionally a biting, no-holds-barred event at which the guest of honour may do a little basking in the limelight, but also gets skewered in the process. We finally settled on the list of speakers who would savage me, presumably in a light-hearted and fairly

affectionate manner: choreographer Brian Macdonald, journalist John Fraser, Frank Augustyn, broadcaster (and dear friend) Brian Linehan, and Ross.

Having seen how much work I had put into all the planning and determined to make me proud of him, Ross set to work on his speech. Familiar with roasts of the Dean Martin–Don Rickles variety, Ross prepared his remarks accordingly, and for days he scribbled furiously at his desk. The effort he was putting into his presentation touched me, and I was terribly curious about what he would say every time I heard him chuckle with delight when he had perfected a particularly choice line. But since his "roast" was to be a present to me, he insisted on keeping the text a surprise, rehearsing his delivery only when I was out of earshot. It turned out to be one of the biggest surprises of my life – both at the time I first heard it and then, almost five years later, when I was working on this book.

As always, I was apprehensive about the performance at the O'Keefe Centre, the more so because I had planned so much of it myself and felt responsible for its success. To my great relief, it was wonderful; I'd been inspired by my partners and delighted at the chance to dance so many works I loved and to thank so many people who had been responsible for my success. It had been such a special evening, and for once I myself felt very special, well and truly celebrated. I was emotionally exhausted, and I looked forward to unwinding at the dinner – for I certainly needed to unwind. When the time came for the speeches, I was deeply moved by the first four speakers, who gave a series of gentle, affectionate tributes, even though we'd all been told this was to be a "roast." Glowing with happiness, I sat expectantly as the fifth and final speaker rose. Surely my joy would now be crowned by loving words from my husband.

Ross started off well, but then he made a joke about one of my past relationships. Hardly anyone laughed, and I felt my mother and father, sitting on either side of me, stiffen. Several jokes followed in the same vein, and I realized right away that his attempt to roast me had a very hard edge to it, and his sardonic, self-deprecating humour was not being understood. As I listened to him struggle to turn the situation around – and it turned out that he was editing desperately as he sensed the audience's muted reaction – I was embarrassed for him and for myself. Worst of all, I was shocked by the depth of his anger, for that was all I could see in his speech at the time, and indeed for years after in my memory of it.

For the first time I realized just how hard it had been for him. Ross was expressing long-suppressed resentments of the career sacrifices he'd made in moving to Toronto and the media circus in which he was now forced to live. I felt a sense of responsibility for his pain, and guilt that I'd been thriving on his

*Camping it up with Ross.*

*Ross and I with the legendary Jeffrey in my parents' garden.*

sacrifices without fully comprehending their extent. I was angry with him for not having told me in a way that I could really hear; I was angry at myself for not having seen. I wondered if I'd completely misjudged our relationship; I wondered if we could ever forgive each other.

I had to speak as soon as he'd finished, and speaking in public has always been exceptionally hard for me. On this occasion, I scrambled to think of something I could say to turn things around and restore the light-hearted mood with which the evening had begun, but I don't have a quick verbal wit at the best of times, and this was hardly the best of times. I looked at Ross; he was white, stricken. Distracted and disoriented, I pulled out the notes I'd prepared and rushed through them, thanking Ross for his speech and for having put up with me for five years.

The event was a complete nightmare for both of us, the most difficult thing we have ever had to deal with. Well aware that comedy has a dark side, and alarmed that he might harbour buried reservoirs of anger that had unconsciously been expressed in his speech, Ross went into two years of therapy, in which I also participated, and I'm still profoundly moved by this gesture of love and commitment on his part. We began to make a concerted effort to define our expectations and roles within our marriage and work towards a balance that was fair and liveable for us both.

The result has been a more secure, supportive, and happy relationship than we've ever had before. Ross gives me a perspective, a calm, and a strength that remind me not only of who I am, but what I am capable of. He has accomplished what neither Rudolf nor Roland ever could: their belief in me served as a substitute for my belief in myself, but Ross's love for and belief in me have helped me maintain and continue to develop my own inner strength, nourishing my own belief in myself.

There's an afterword to this story. In the summer of 1993, revisiting this painful territory in order to present it fairly and honestly in this book, we recreated the event on the spur of the moment in our living room when Penelope Doob asked if she might see a copy of Ross's speech. Somehow, in the emotional turmoil, I'd never seen the unedited text of the talk Ross had intended to give – and would have given if the event had gone differently. He dug it out of the basement and, at my request, agreed to perform it once again. I started by explaining my mood and expectations on that evening in 1988, and Ross delivered a very touching, very funny address. He began by saying that he hadn't been sure whether to give a roast, as requested, or a toast, so he'd do both, with the roast first, because it was "the end of a long evening, so perhaps a little spice and titillation should be the order of the hour." Now, five years after the actual event, his jokes were witty, occasionally hilarious, and his tone, though dry, clearly reflected his love for me. After what now seems a fairly gentle "roast," the speech became an eloquent "toast," describing his feelings on watching me perform ("one of the rare times my heart is ever in my throat"). The text ended, "My darling, may your artistry live on for as long as you desire. May your love and humanity be with you forever."

It's now very clear that he had laboured long and lovingly to craft a worthy gift, which was misunderstood in what can now be seen as an example of the best intentions gone disastrously awry.

Ross and I had hoped to enhance our marriage in another way. We'd never been able to decide on the right moment to think about having a family, and in early 1988, when I was almost thirty-seven, I had been thrilled to discover I was pregnant. I knew I would have to cancel my announced performances and the media would want to know why, so for everyone's sake I had to make a public announcement far earlier than I would have liked.

At three and a half months, I miscarried. Ross and I were devastated. He was producing Heath Lamberts' one-man show in Vancouver, and I flew out immediately to be with him.

But I couldn't stay for long, since I had agreed to be a master of ceremonies with Glen Tetley at the first Erik Bruhn Dance Competition, which took place in Toronto five days after the miscarriage. I had loved and admired Erik very deeply, and I wanted to be there. Before we went on, Glen took me aside for a few moments. I can't remember exactly what he said, though I've often tried – I remember hardly anything about that week – but somehow he found just the right words to quiet my grief and ease my torment. Even if he had done nothing else for me in my whole life – and he's done a great deal – I would love him forever for the comfort he gave me then. With his warm support, I stepped onto the O'Keefe Centre stage, but it was one of the most difficult things I have ever done.

The question of having children is still unresolved, but as the years go by, I find that my nephews, Dylan and Taylor (my brother Kevin's twin sons), and my god-children, Zachary (Marley and Bobby's son) and Julia (Tomas Schramek and Deborah Todd's daughter), and Julia's brother, Milan, provide me with all the pitter-patter of tiny feet I need, and a vast amount of joy and love as well.

My real life was turning out to be richer and more complex and unpredictable than the fairy-tale life perceived by the outside world. The intense emotions I experienced during these years – from the crashing lows of burn-out, depression, and miscarriage to the highs of a great career and marriage – taught me an unexpectedly positive lesson: I had more strength than I had realized to cope with whatever fate had in store for me. From that knowledge grew a new and treasured self-confidence.

# The Bruhn Years: A New Maturity

*"Go as far as you possibly can – and then I'll tell you what more I want."*

*"Dance every performance as if it was your last."*
– Erik Bruhn

Once I was in my thirties and feeling more peaceful in my personal life, I realized that I would have to decide whether to make a real break from the National Ballet of Canada and commit myself fully elsewhere. Despite my dissatisfaction with Alexander and my disappointment that I wasn't getting to create many new roles, the National was home. Was it cowardly to feel uncomfortable at the prospect of abandoning the comforts of home to seek new challenges and opportunities elsewhere? Or, from a different perspective, was it disloyal and ungrateful even to consider leaving? After Moscow and my early successes with Roland and Rudolf, Canadian critics had openly speculated about when I'd leave for greener pastures and what the National would have to do to keep me. They urged the company to give me the ballets and choreographers I needed, and to treat me well or risk losing me. But the company remained unshakeably democratic; even if they had had the financial resources, they wouldn't have given me my pick of new ballets.

Nevertheless, I had stayed. In retrospect, I realize that, while I was always excited by the opportunity to appear in new works around the world, I wasn't ambitious about building my career. I didn't like the life of the homeless guest artist, the nagging feeling of being always unprepared, and the loneliness. I had stayed because, on balance, it suited me to stay. It had probably been wise to turn down many of the opportunities I'd been offered, and I've almost never regretted having done it. Some I refused because I didn't think the working

*(Previous page)*
*Eliot Feld's*
At Midnight.

conditions would give me the confidence to do well; others I rejected out of loyalty to the National.

After some very successful London appearances with Rudolf, for instance, the Royal Ballet invited me to appear in its 1977 spring season in any role I chose, and the following year Roland Petit asked me to star with Baryshnikov in *The Legend of Joseph* in Vienna. But both seasons conflicted with National Ballet seasons, so I turned them down. Of these, I regret only the former: might I have danced Manon? MacMillan's Juliet?

The only other opportunity I regret having had to refuse was dancing the role of Kitri in Nureyev's version of *Don Quixote* in Vienna in the late seventies, when I was at the right point in my career to have done justice to the role. Rudolf's version is the best I've seen, and I would have loved a chance to tackle it. But Alexander refused to let me miss a season at the O'Keefe Centre.

When Lucia Chase was director of American Ballet Theatre, she invited me to dance *Giselle* and *Swan Lake*; since I didn't feel comfortable with the partners she had suggested, I declined, knowing I wouldn't be at my best. But when Ross and I were married and contemplating whether to live in New York or Toronto, I decided to find out if American Ballet Theatre was still interested in me. An ideal opportunity to explore that possibility came up in the summer of 1983 when I was dancing Cranko's *Onegin* with the Stuttgart Ballet in Spoleto. Mikhail Baryshnikov, ABT's new director, and I were both performing at a gala at the Festival of Two Worlds in Spoleto, and we were all staying at the same hotel.

One day a group of dancers was relaxing around the pool, and, spotting Misha, I decided to see if he was interested in me. It turned out that he was — but not as a dancer. We'd become better acquainted since I'd seen him, gloomy but dazzling, in the studios and cafeteria of the Kirov School when Frank and I were there in 1973. The next summer he had used my apartment as a neutral zone for strategic discussions with Sergiu Stefanschi (whom he had known at the Kirov School), Dina Makarova (a photographer-translator who had ties with American Ballet Theatre), and his then-girlfriend, Christina Berlin, to plan his imminent defection. A little later, he'd danced a few times with the National, although never with me, because we were poorly matched in height. He had kindly said that this was as disappointing to him as it was to me, but he put this a little less elegantly to John Fraser: if somebody chopped my legs off at the knees, Misha said, I'd be perfect for him! For all these reasons, I hoped he would seriously consider the possibility of my joining ABT. But when I approached him by the pool to ask if we could discuss it, he said, "Sure, Karen, we talk about it tonight. We talk about it before dinner, after dinner, and tomorrow morning, when we wake up, we talk about it again." I knew his reputation for breaking hearts in the corps de ballet (the film *The Turning Point* had more than a grain of truth to it), yet I thought that in his new position he would be more professional. Since he wasn't, and I knew I could never work with someone with that attitude, this was the extent of my pursuit of a career at ABT.

I've always been awed by Baryshnikov's talent as a performer, and when I saw him dance with Twyla Tharp in Toronto in 1993, I was highly impressed to see that, at the age of forty-six, he was still in tremendous physical condition, still devoted to his profession. But I might still have had only bad memories of him as a person if I hadn't run into him a few years ago in New York. I was getting out of a taxi near ABT just as he was leaving, and he greeted me with courteous warmth. He was a changed man. I sensed that he'd gone through some rough patches himself, and there was an air of decency and respect for women that I'd never seen before. Although by that time I had realized that Toronto gave me more of what I needed than New York, perhaps I would have considered ABT more seriously if he had shown the same attitude in Spoleto.

In the early eighties, there was still one option that combined the advantages of being a guest artist and having a home company. Roland Petit had realized that I wouldn't join his company full time, but he still wanted me to consider spending six months of the year in Europe, with Marseilles as a base, which would allow me to guest with Rudolf more frequently as well. At the time, I considered it seriously; Roland saw me as a muse, and was eager to create as many new ballets for me as I could wish, and dancing with Rudolf was always a challenge and a joy.

At this point, Alexander Grant was just about to join the National as artistic director, and I wrote to ask his advice. He urged me "not to get lost in the world of the wandering guest artist. . . . Your life as a dancer could be shortened without a true home." Citing "the everlasting challenge of the classics to conquer," he mentioned Fonteyn as a dancer who had stayed with one company all her career and had blossomed. While I appreciated his concern, I noticed that he didn't mention that Fonteyn had had Ashton to create ballets for her whole career, whereas most of the ballets created for me were coming from France, not Canada. As well, for the last years of her career, Fonteyn had assumed permanent guest-artist status with the Royal Ballet so she could dance around the world with Rudolf.

I'd been dancing with Roland's company every year since 1974, and its August-September 1980 season in New York demonstrated what a role that is created for you can do. Anna Kisselgoff wrote a rave review of Petit's *Coppélia* in the New York *Times*, announcing that I was "simply the best female dancer on stage all season." Those words were a wake-up call to Canada: suddenly I was no longer yesterday's news, a dancer who wasn't living up to her reputation. After Canadian Press picked up the review and sent it across the country, the *Toronto Star* sent Gina Mallet to write about my success in New York. It's amazing what a few words in the right places can do.

But Roland was getting impatient. Was I going to give him more than a few weeks at a time so he could create more ballets around me? I considered it seriously, but my experience with *The Tales of Hoffmann* in April 1982 gave me my answer. My own role, Giulietta, was uninspired, as I had expected; it's common knowledge in Roland's company that the first parts of a ballet Roland creates are the best, as if he has a fixed quantity of inventiveness that is depleted as the choreography progresses, and, because of my other commitments, my part in *Tales* had been choreographed last of all. But this time there was little to admire anywhere in the ballet, and we were all struggling to make something out of it. The dress rehearsal was chaos. The costumes – beautifully made in Paris, as always – arrived at the last minute, and there were technical problems with the lavish sets, which included a huge wine barrel that opened up to provide the dancing space for the last act.

Normally, I don't judge a work before it has opened. It's not unusual for the dress rehearsal to be a shambles and then, amazingly, everything comes together for the opening. But this was the only time in my whole career when I knew we were in a major flop before the curtain went up. My instincts told me that there wasn't a shred of choreography on which to hang the ballet. Roland had been totally unimaginative, counting on us to save it in performance. This time, I didn't think we could. All the principals gathered in my dressing room, shaking their heads and saying, "*Oh la la, quel cauchemar!*"

What a nightmare, indeed. But we could understand what had happened. In exchange for munificent funding from the city of Marseilles, Roland had to come up with a full-length ballet almost every season, and this time he hadn't found the inspiration to make it work. It made me realize once and for all that, although Roland had been wonderful to me, I had become disenchanted with the lack of real substance in much of his work. His stagecraft was magical, but he didn't have the gift of the truly great, an Ashton or a Balanchine: being able to build a choreographic structure so beautiful that no dancer could ruin it. I found myself wanting to go to Marseilles less often. For instance, after *The Tales of Hoffmann* Roland offered me the role of Cathy in a full-length ballet based on *Wuthering Heights* – a role I would have loved – but I had to refuse: it was planned for Christmas 1982, and having just fallen in love with Ross, I didn't

*Erik Bruhn's* Coppélia, *with Jacques Gorrissen on my left and Tomas Schramek on the couch.*

want to be away that long. Roland thought that was a pretty feeble excuse, but he got the message that I was concentrating on my life in Canada.

ð

My forays away from home continually reminded me what a roller-coaster-ride the life of a guest artist can be. In 1980, the New York season that began in September as a personal triumph with Roland's *Coppélia* ended dismally in October with the first – and only – season of a new group, Makarova and Company. I've always admired Natalia Makarova enormously, so I had been flattered when she asked me to be one of the stars for a month of performances at the Uris Theatre in New York just after *Coppélia*, and especially so because of the calibre of the other leading dancers involved: Cynthia Gregory, Elisabetta Terabust, Fernando Bujones, Peter Schaufuss, and Anthony Dowell – quite a line-up. I was scheduled to dance Balanchine's *Raymonda* pas de dix and Petipa's *Paquita* in two of three alternating programs.

At the initial *Paquita* rehearsals, I felt a little uneasy watching very talented but very young and inexperienced corps women attempting difficult solo variations that required true ballerinas. They didn't quite have the technique, the grand Russian style was completely foreign to them, and they had only three weeks to unlearn everything they'd been taught until then and rise like phoenixes from the ashes as Kirov ballerinas. Many reviewers noted the very discernible gap between ambition and execution.

There were other problems as well. Makarova had just had knee surgery and was understandably exhausted as ballerina, ballet mistress, and producer all in one. Nevertheless, she seemed keen to add the title of choreographer to the list. She'd commissioned a new work from Lorca Massine, a young choreographer and the son of the great Léonide Massine, who'd worked for years with Diaghilev and who became even better known as dancer-choreographer in the film *The Red Shoes*. On opening night, I watched Lorca tear his hair out while Makarova danced his new ballet. She began and ended with the music, but in between she was making rather imaginative changes to his choreography. Anthony Dowell, her partner in the work, later told me that he didn't know why he had spent weeks in rehearsal if she was going to improvise the entire pas de deux. In numerous interviews during her long and glorious career, Makarova lamented that, "I have excited so many men in my life, but never a choreographer." I think I know why.

The bad reviews, the inexperienced corps, the poor attendance, and the chaotic rehearsal schedule threw us all into a slump. Denys Ganio, my long-time partner from Petit's company, was so disgusted and depressed that he abruptly left the theatre one day and flew back to France. Anthony Dowell rose above it all – he'd been dancing with Makarova for years – but he used to tease us by standing in the wings during performances and waving his airline ticket as we danced. "Just a few more days, and then I'm home," he'd say. "Just a few more days." We were all counting the days; the whole season felt like a jail sentence.

Despite the strides I had made with therapy, I was still quite vulnerable and very sensitive to the general lack of morale. My confidence ebbed daily, and I began to panic when Makarova, on short notice, said she wanted me to dance a variation in the final performance of *Paquita*. There wasn't enough time left to rehearse adequately, so I refused. Determined to have all of her stars on-stage for the final performance and convinced she could bolster my confidence by being firm, Makarova kept rehearsing me right up to curtain time. It was a fierce battle of wills, and mine had grown stronger thanks to my therapy; I was not about to dance something I didn't think I could do well. "I'll rehearse till I drop, but I will *not* dance tonight," I insisted, and I stuck to my guns. Natasha was annoyed with me for quite some time.

⟡

Meanwhile, the dancers at the National were surviving the years of low morale and flagging energy under Alexander, and soon there was a compelling reason for optimism. Late in 1982, just after Alexander's cruelly public humiliation, the search committee convened and announced the news we had all hoped to hear: Erik Bruhn had agreed to become our new artistic director. Unlike Alexander, Erik was no stranger to the company or the school. An old friend of Celia's from their Metropolitan Ballet days, he'd been choreographing and dancing with us since the early sixties; he'd taught many of us during his brilliant and eagerly awaited guest-teaching engagements at the school; and over the years he'd come to regard the National as his family. We celebrated. One of the greatest dancers of the century, a man we all knew and idolized, had agreed to cast his lot with us and be our leader. We were going to be on the artistic fast track again. So, while Alexander was serving out his contract until the summer of 1983, Erik was working feverishly to establish a new artistic order.

The epitome of the *danseur noble*, the most romantic of princes, the man with the cleanest sense of line and the most elegant manner of any dancer in the world, Erik began his career with the Royal Danish Ballet in his native Copenhagen in 1946, almost immediately took leave to dance with the Metropolitan Ballet, and was a star by the age of twenty. But, seeking new

*Erik in rehearsal.*

dancing challenges and unable to find them within the context of the Royal Danish Ballet, he decided to leave. His international career included legendary performances with American Ballet Theatre from the early fifties to the sixties, through which he established glorious partnerships with Dame Alicia Markova, Maria Tallchief, Carla Fracci, and Natalia Makarova.

He was still in his prime in 1971 when, because of intense pain from ulcers that weren't properly diagnosed for several years, he announced his retirement. For those of us who knew him well, the diagnosis was no surprise. Despite his calm exterior, Erik was one of the most highly-strung, nervous performers I've ever met. After treatment, he believed he had lost the ability to tackle major classical roles, but he graced the stage for some time in character roles that called more on his extraordinary acting abilities than on his technique: Petrushka, in the renowned Fokine–Stravinsky ballet; Madge in *La Sylphide*; the Moor in *The Moor's Pavane*; and Dr. Coppélius in his own staging of *Coppélia*. He even branched out into straight dramatic acting in his native Denmark, and, during a holiday I spent with Erik and Constantin Patsalas in Copenhagen, I saw him in *Rashomon*; with his acting talents and his beautiful baritone voice, he could have had a bright future in the legitimate theatre.

He'd been appointed artistic adviser to the National Ballet of Canada in 1964, staging imaginative versions of *Swan Lake*, *Coppélia*, and *La Sylphide* that remain in our repertoire. During the seventies, he became a regular guest teacher at the National Ballet School; Betty Oliphant adored him and constantly held him up to us all as the ideal *danseur noble*. All the while, he had observed us with his keen analytical intelligence; he knew exactly where our weaknesses lay and what he could do about them.

He'd been second only to Nureyev in my childhood pantheon of dance heroes. When we were about thirteen, Linda Maybarduk and I went to see him dance James in *La Sylphide* at the O'Keefe Centre. As usual, we were in the school seats in the last row of the top balcony, so I brought along my trusty field binoculars for a closer look. The first thing I spotted was two empty seats in front row centre, and Linda and I made a dash for them at intermission.

It was sheer ecstasy seeing him that close, although I still used my binoculars – and not just to focus on his technique or his noble manner. We were groupies as well as ballet students, and we waited breathlessly for his kilt to fly up during a spin or jump so we could get a good flash of his splendid thighs. At the end, we shrieked and squealed our approval when he took an "opera call" in front of the curtain. Erik, probably very much amused at this demonstration, looked in our direction and smiled, and for weeks afterwards Linda and I argued about which of us he'd acknowledged.

At that age, Erik excited us because he was one of the greatest – and best-looking – male dancers of all time. But when he became artistic director in 1983, we were to become even more inspired by his guidance in the rehearsal studio. In almost every respect, he was the ideal director; he had all of what I'd come to recognize as Celia's virtues, and while we loved him (most of us, anyway, and most of the time), he wasn't dependent on being loved, so he was well prepared to take the hard decisions that had troubled Alexander so much.

First and foremost, Erik treated dancers as intelligent, creative adults who deserved – and got, from him – the freedom and encouragement to take risks. He told us more than once that he never trusted a dancer who didn't fall over in class and rehearsal. Even if you failed when you took chances, he knew that that was usually more interesting and rewarding than playing it safe. He gave dancers in principal and soloist roles unaccustomed artistic freedom; in the past, company coaches and teachers tended to give precise instructions on how to do the steps and fit them to the music, but Erik took a quite different approach. He knew that individuality was a major part of the dancer's art, and he loved to see our different senses of musicality and interpretation expressed. We learned to experiment, to ask questions, and he'd say, "I don't mind if you start the phrase on that note, or that accent, or if you use this arm. Just show me what you can do with it." He'd pause, then add, in slightly ironic tones, "Surprise me!" Not that he gave us *carte blanche*; he'd gently eliminate anything that didn't work. But he made us think and dare, giving us a freedom to find our own way that was completely unheard of before his arrival. He made us develop our own creativity, stifled for so long. He knew that our besetting artistic sin as a company was excessive restraint, so he had no fear that we'd go over the top with excessive self-indulgence if we were given our heads – and even if we did, he'd be there to pull us back if he had to.

To challenge us, in class he'd create exercises that were almost impossible. Then, once we'd struggled to master the steps and had achieved a little success, he'd instantly reverse the whole sequence. It was as stimulating mentally as it was physically.

But this didn't mean that company life was going to be all upbeat; it was part of Erik's philosophy and style to keep everyone just a little off balance. He certainly started as he meant to go on. His first act as director was to announce that it was time to clean house. He met with each department to give us all an ultimatum: every member of the company, in every department, had one year to prove that he or she deserved to be there. In his meeting with the principal dancers, he turned to me and said, "Your beautiful smile isn't always enough." I got the message: he was warning me – and, through me, all of us – not to rest on our reputations.

The possibility of losing our jobs at the end of the year was terrifying and demoralizing for a few of us. I was frightened too, but I knew Erik was right: we needed shock treatment. There was a lot of dead wood in the company; we'd been coasting for years, and for years I had said as much to anyone who would listen – and to a few, like certain members of the board, who wouldn't. I took Erik's ultimatum as a challenge, and I love challenges. Like most of the other dancers, I was determined to get myself out of the doldrums and become a better dancer.

In this renewed quest for excellence, I was helped enormously by our new principal ballet mistress, Magdalena Popa, who ironically had been given her first exposure to Canadian dancers as a member of the jury for the 1973 Moscow International Ballet Competition, where Frank and I had won the award for best pas de deux. A native of Bucharest, Romania, Magdalena had studied at Leningrad's Vaganova Choreographic Institute, the official school of the Kirov Ballet, where she showed such exceptional talent that she was the first student since the great Galina Ulanova to be invited to dance principal roles for the Kirov (in her case, the leads in *Swan Lake* and *The Nutcracker*) while still in the school.

Upon her return to Bucharest, she quickly became prima ballerina with the Bucharest State Opera Ballet, but, thanks to frequent guest engagements, her reputation spread throughout Europe, especially after she won a silver medal at the Varna competition in 1964 at the age of twenty-three, and her interpretation of Giselle earned a gold medal at a dance festival in Paris in 1965. In 1982, when she was director of the Bucharest company as well as its prima ballerina, Magdalena sacrificed her own position for the interests of her young daughter, whom she wanted to grow up in the west; she defected. Betty Oliphant admired Magdalena – they had served together as jurors for several ballet competitions – and Betty strongly recommended that Alexander hire her as a ballet mistress. He did, and that was one of his last and greatest legacies to us.

It took me a while to learn to trust her – it's very hard to change when you're a dancer in your thirties – but Magdalena slowly proved her value by telling me her theories and giving me time to digest them. Suddenly, I realized that she was changing my whole approach to classical technique, helping me correct weaknesses in my training, and giving me new insights that led to improvements in areas where I'd thought I'd reached my limits long ago. The older you get, the harder it becomes to find someone who knows more than you do and has the gift of teaching you in ways you can accept, but when you're lucky enough to find such a person, you thrive. Equally important, Magdalena was the first person who didn't encourage my workaholic tendencies to rehearse to the point of exhaustion. Knowing that too much practice makes injuries, not perfection, she helped me learn to sense when I had reached the physical – or emotional – limits beyond which my dancing would only deteriorate. My only regret is that I didn't work with her much earlier in my career. She gave me some of the tools I needed to meet Erik's challenge and raised the classical standards of the whole company.

Slowly but surely, the company began to come out of its collective slump, but not everyone made it. Some of us weren't invited back; others decided it was time to retire and move on to new challenges. Over the next two years, there were many changes at the top. Principal dancers Vanessa Harwood, Nadia Potts, and Mary Jago, having reached the age when all but the hardiest ballerinas retire, left the company; George Crum, conductor and music director since the company's founding in 1951, retired, and long-time ballet master David Scott accepted an offer from the London Festival Ballet in England. Suddenly, Veronica Tennant and I were the only veterans still performing leading classical roles. Later Erik told me that he regretted his handling of the dismissal of senior dancers and staff. He realized that, in his eagerness to have a fresh start and give the company a new look, he had set a bad example by failing to treat the people who had built the company and devoted their lives to it with more dignity.

I passed the test and stayed, but that didn't mean I needed no improvement. Erik gave me two pieces of advice, short and pointed: "Don't be anyone's good girl" and "Give your own performance," don't allow anyone or anything to throw you off balance. He saw that I still cared a lot – too much, he thought – about pleasing other people and avoiding conflict if at all possible; he knew that I still tended to feel responsible when other people did less than their best, and that, as a result, my own performances sometimes suffered. When I failed to mend my ways quickly enough, he went even further: "Karen, you're not enough of a bitch." Erik loved to play mind games. He'd make some sharp or enigmatic comment and leave you to lose sleep trying to figure out exactly what he meant. Finally, I concluded that he thought I backed off too soon when my partner didn't give me what I wanted or needed. I did, indeed, find those times frustrating, and I did back off at a certain point; but I think I was right to do so, especially when I was working – as I did, increasingly – with younger, less-experienced partners. I've watched some ballerinas, determined to make themselves look good, belittle their partners, and I've seen how demoralizing that can be to the men, especially when they're trying their hardest. I also know how I personally respond to dismissiveness and negativity in the rehearsal studio, and it seems to me that you achieve more by not being temperamental. The era of prima donna ballerinas has passed, and thank goodness. For every time I might justifiably have stamped my feet and stormed out in a huff, there are dozens when people have responded generously and constructively when I've tried to be generous and constructive with them.

Despite his reservations about my lack of assertiveness, Erik obviously respected me, and on our European tour in 1985, he said so. Our first stop was Luxembourg, where our performance of *Don Quixote* was a complete disaster. Scene changes didn't work, spotlights came on when the stage was supposed to be dark, cues were missed, and I was so jet-lagged that I kept falling asleep during intermissions, reviving just long enough to resume my spunky characterization of Kitri. Using the best side of my professionalism, I stayed calm enough to give a decent performance. When the curtain fell, Erik seized me by the arms and said, "All I did was thank God that you were on the stage. I was humiliated by almost every aspect of this evening except you."

I'd been pleased to pass my exams at the end of his first year, but these words meant far more to me. They made me realize that I was successfully learning to assume a new role, to take on the proper responsibilities of a senior dancer: I hadn't been distracted by the disasters and I hadn't felt guilty that others had messed up. Instead, I'd taken responsibility for myself. Erik always said that you should dance every performance as if it were your last, and I've tried never to forget it.

With that philosophy, and having enriched his own career tremendously by judicious guest appearances, Erik was sensitive to the needs of artists to perform

*Kitri in* Don Quixote.

away from their home companies, especially when that would give them the chance to create roles in new ballets. So strongly did he believe in the artistic necessity for broad exposure that he established a program for excellent young National dancers to spend time with other companies when they were still in a formative stage. After everything I'd gone through, I could only rejoice – and wish Erik had been there when I was a very young dancer. But I would soon take advantage of Erik's support for guest appearances.

With Erik's leadership and encouragement, my confidence increased to the point where, after years of refusing invitations from Eliot Feld in New York, I was ready to take the plunge. As I've mentioned, when Eliot had staged *Intermezzo* for us in 1971, I had found the experience terrifying but exhilarating. He had attacked us all brutally in the studio to get the best out of us – and we had succeeded. Even then, I had felt we were friends – at least, outside the studio. Now, more than a decade later, we were determined to work together again. In my first season with him (1984), he reworked *Impromptu* for me; this solo, originally created for Birgit Keil of the Stuttgart Ballet, suited me so beautifully that I would dance it at the National's thirty-fifth-anniversary gala. Eliot and I worked so well together, now that he had mellowed a bit and I had gained confidence, that I went back for succeeding seasons, dancing in works including *Straw Hearts, Adieu, At Midnight,* and an amazing seventeen-minute solo to music by Steve Reich called *Echo.*

Working with Eliot has been a revelation; he expertly guided me back to recognizing my own gifts, and I trust his taste more than anyone else's. Eliot has helped me come out of myself, trust my instincts more, and, as he puts it, "find the dancer within." I've had many doors opened to my "mind's ear," as Eliot calls it, by learning to hear the music through his choreographic interpretation of it. Because he discovers a new dance vocabulary for every ballet he creates, his works often look as if they were created by different choreographers, which makes them even more interesting and challenging to dancers. When I see Eliot's company now, I'm struck by the level of perfection he inspires through his ability to draw extraordinary performances from dancers who, without his influence, might look quite ordinary.

*With Rex Harrington.*

Meanwhile, Erik was commissioning exciting new works for the company; he wanted us to have our own created repertoire, instead of continually borrowing established works from elsewhere. After living for so long in New York, where the contemporary dance scene is so rich, even eccentric, and after performing with the José Limón company in *The Moor's Pavane*, and after seeing many works by contemporary choreographers in Toronto over the years, Erik decided to kill two birds with one stone: to broaden the minds and talents of National dancers by inviting the greatest Canadian contemporary choreographers to create some of these distinctive new works. Even before taking over as director, he was gauging the interest of well-known Toronto choreographers Danny Grossman, Robert Desrosiers, and David Earle. Erik's first season included Danny's *Endangered Species*, an anti-war piece to the music of Krzysztof Penderecki (not a new work, but one on which the company could cut its modern-dance teeth), as well as John McFall's serene *Components* (to a John Adams score) and three new in-house works: Constantin Patsalas's ethereal *L'Île Inconnue* (to Hector Berlioz's "Nuits d'Été"); his somewhat rowdier *Oiseaux Exotiques* (to a score by Harry Freedman); and David Allan's *Khachaturian Pas de Deux*. I was in only one of these new works – *Oiseaux Exotiques* – in which I had both a very romantic pas de deux and a Carmen Miranda number (Constantin called it "The Black Widow") that let me be overtly sexy and that Roland would probably have adored. This was the first time I had ever danced with Rex Harrington, who would become my frequent partner from then on. Rightly convinced that we'd work well together, Constantin talked me into it, and it took only a few minutes in the studio for me to appreciate Rex's great talent as that rarest of male dancers, a sensitive natural partner.

The next season there were two new contemporary works, Robert Desrosiers's *Blue Snake*, so bizarre that nothing remotely like it had ever been seen in our company, and David Earle's *Realm*, far more serene in nature. Again, there was an in-house work: Constantin Patsalas's *Concerto for the Elements: Piano Concerto*, a reworking of a ballet that had won him first prize in the 1979 Boston Ballet Choreographic Competition. Erik's final season, 1985-86, brought a new jazz-inspired work by Danny Grossman (*Hot House: Thriving on a Riff*); our first-ever piece by the Czech artistic director of Nederlands Dans Theater, Jirí Kylián – the magnificent *Transfigured Night*, to Arnold Schönberg's score, and widely heralded as a modern masterpiece; and the incorporation into the repertoire of a very long solo to Vivaldi that Constantin had done for me, *Sinfonia* (the music was actually called "Concerto Grosso," which made us laugh – and eventually decide to change the title).

Erik also brought in many other more classical works, from Cranko's *Onegin* to Petipa's *Raymonda: Act III* to Balanchine's *Symphony in C* for the company's first all-Balanchine evening. The company was very excited about all of this, and so was I. It didn't matter that not all the new works were great successes; we learned from all of them, we grew as performers, we stretched our creative wings, and the sense of artistic ferment was intoxicating. Thanks to the contributions of Grossman, Earle, and Desrosiers, for the first time we no longer felt separated from the rest of the dance community in Toronto, and we were also acquiring excellent works from contemporary choreographers working within the tradition of ballet. This sense of community remains strong, and I for one see it as one of Erik's greatest gifts to us. Ballet has always been much better funded than contemporary dance, and that fact has caused some resentment over the years. But whether we dance in pointe shoes, running shoes, or bare feet, we're all dancers; we have the same goals, the same passion for our art, the same compulsion to excel; we serve the same demanding mistress. The tradition Erik began of having us all dance at each other's fund-raising performances continues, and it gives me great personal pleasure.

For me, the high point of Erik's tragically short tenure as director was his commissioning of *Alice*, Glen Tetley's insightful commingling of Lewis Carroll's story and life, set to American David Del Tredici's powerfully dramatic, richly textured score for soprano and orchestra. During Alexander's directorship, I had loved working with Glen on *Sphinx*, a striking work originally created for Martine Van Hamel and American Ballet Theatre. An American choreographer who has worked in modern dance as well as ballet, a student of both Hanya Holm and Antony Tudor, Glen performed with both American Ballet Theatre and the Martha Graham Company before becoming a freelance

Romeo and Juliet with Rex.

*My first pas de deux with Rex Harrington in* Oiseaux Exotiques.

*"The Black Widow" in Patsalas's* Oiseaux Exotiques.

*The final scene in* Alice, *with Kimberley Glasco and Owen Montague.*

choreographer and artistic director. His style demands a fluid, expressive torso, which poses a great challenge to classically trained dancers.

When Glen decided to base his ballet on both the fictional and the historical characters involved in *Alice in Wonderland*, he told me that he didn't think I would be suitable for the young Alice. I accepted that easily; I'm pretty realistic, and I know the importance of casting a new work accurately. But, through Erik, Glen asked if I had any interest in a cameo role as Alice Liddell Hargreaves – for whom the book had been written – as a grown-up, and I responded that I would love to take part in any way I could. But somehow this "cameo" role grew like Alice when she ate the wrong thing in Wonderland: when Glen arrived, he had changed the concept entirely. Now there would be two Alices: Child Alice, the Alice who inspired, and is the heroine of, the book, who would be danced by Kimberly Glasco, and Alice Hargreaves, the historical Victorian child, grown into maturity and, finally, old age, whose nostalgia for her past gives the ballet such depth.

Creating a role is every dancer's dream, and, when the dancer shares actively in the creative process, making a new ballet is the greatest delight. Glen was always fully prepared for rehearsals and knew roughly what he wanted to see, but he let us share the adventure of creation. Some choreographers illustrate the steps they want very precisely, finding the movement in their own bodies and then expecting the dancers to recreate it exactly, whether it fits their bodies or not. For the dancer, this process can feel little different from learning any existing role, except that the movement style may well be novel, and sometimes you feel more like a handy body than an artist. With Glen, we were co-creators; he'd sketch the movement and then ask us to expand it, flesh it out, and adapt his idea as closely as possible to our own bodies. This is a very-demanding-but-intensely-satisfying way of working; you're like a painter in the workshop of Raphael or Michelangelo, taking the outline given to you by a master and adding detail and colour under his watchful eye. You know the master's style, and that's the idiom you use to create the movement in your body; you show the steps, experiment with them, find alternatives to get the effect the choreographer wants, in an intimate, consuming dialogue of creativity. If you've done your work well, the role can fit you like a glove. Every day with Glen was a joy; we worked with great concentration, but also with humour and warmth. Glen was never threatened by our contributions: he suggested, we experimented, and he edited. This was the best rehearsal period I'd ever experienced, and it was a marvellous bonus when the ballet turned out to be a great success.

Because I put so much of myself into the role of Alice Hargreaves, it began to feel a true part of me. Like Alice Hargreaves, I felt I was looking into my own past, seeing – and also protecting and loving – my younger self in the Child Alice. I was almost thirty-five, and while Kim isn't decades younger, I was well aware of some of the particularly painful aspects of the contrasts Glen established between the perpetually young fictional Alice and the real Alice, an adult who grows older and wiser during the course of the ballet. A sense of the inevitable passage of time, an awareness of the physical changes that come with maturity, a nostalgia for lost youth, all these emotions are the very core of the ballet, and the person in whom they're centred is Alice Hargreaves. Often Glen would have Kim and me do the same steps, but they would look and feel very different. As the Child Alice, Kim approached these shared passages with a fresh innocence, but as Alice Hargreaves, I was asked to bring greater maturity and wider experience to my interpretation. The differences an audience sees on-stage between the two Alices aren't acting; they're heightened reality. Feelings of both detachment and identification were intensely poignant to me in Alice, and in 1993, John Neumeier would evoke them again in his nostalgic ballet *Now and Then*, in which I am also an older dancer looking back at my younger self.

It was clear from the start what I would find the most difficult section of *Alice*: the end, when I become the elderly Alice, and the contrast between the frozen immortality of art and the mutability of life is at its greatest. Glen showed me a picture of the real Alice Hargreaves as an old woman; she was incredibly fragile, and her clothes hung loosely on a body that seemed to have shrunk within them over the years. I imagined my own joints stiffening with arthritis, my bones growing brittle and slowly turning to dust. I remembered hearing older women say that, even though they could barely move, inside they felt like young girls of sixteen.

Glen was worried that it would hurt my vanity to appear as the elderly Alice, shuffling across the stage in heavy shoes and an old dress, even her mem-

*As Alice Liddell Hargreaves.*

ories fading, and it's true that this part of the ballet is very painful to perform. But the pain has nothing to do with vanity and everything to do with the reluctance we all have to see our powers diminish and our bodies weaken. Neither as a dancer nor as a woman have I ever seen myself as a perpetual Aurora who simply can't afford to be associated with an image of aging and decline, and I don't intend to make a career out of facelifts.

But even if I were terrified of aging, I would still have done the role gladly. In narrative ballets it's the character that matters, and I was totally committed to creating a moving portrait of Alice Hargreaves. I think I succeeded, at least in Glen's eyes: when I rehearsed that stumbling, hesitant final walk in the studio for the first time, without benefit of costume or lighting, I saw tears in his eyes.

Precisely because I was older than the other dancers, *Alice* was very special to me – not only because I knew more than they of what is gained and what is lost as one grows older, but also because I knew how rare this kind of rewarding collaboration is in the dance world. *Alice* was new and fine, and for once, it was all ours. A great success both in Canada and New York, *Alice* gave us our entrée back to the Metropolitan Opera House in July 1986 – without Rudolf or Hurok. Janice Berman of *Newsday* called it "a work of magic," and Bill Zakariasen of the *New York Daily News* hailed it as "sheer, unadulterated enchantment." Clive Barnes of the *Post* said I had "never been seen to better advantage," and Anna Kisselgoff of the New York *Times*, who pronounced *Alice* "a rare and beautiful ballet," said that I showed "previously unrevealed complex artistry. Passionate, sensuous, dancing with force and plush new quality, Miss Kain is the catalyst for the choreography."

Kisselgoff had come to Toronto for the February première, and I showed her first review to Erik the next morning. When he read that commissioning Tetley was "a stroke of genius on the part of Erik Bruhn," his face filled with joy; Erik felt that this was his ballet, too, because he had contributed a great deal by providing Glen with the moral support he needed to tackle something so different from the ballets he had done before. That memory of Erik's face is precious, because that was the last time I saw him alive.

When Erik conducted rehearsals or class, he was absolutely in command and everyone felt – and welcomed – his authority. But occasionally he'd be away for two or three days at a time, and rehearsals he was scheduled to take had to be postponed. At the time, we assumed that his absences were due to his drinking, something we forgave easily, knowing the pressures he was under and aware that one rehearsal with Erik was often worth many with anyone else. Sometimes he joked that the only reason he worked so hard was to sweat all the alcohol out of his system. I've observed that Russian and Scandinavian dancers drink a lot more and are often much moodier than their North American counterparts. Baryshnikov was famous for polishing off a bottle of vodka by himself at parties and then playing soulful Russian songs on his guitar, and, after performances, Makarova would often skip dinner in favour of one cigarette after another and a significant number of glasses of Smirnoff's.

Years before Erik was artistic director, I had given a party for the company at my house in Cabbagetown, and Erik, having drunk more than usual, was in a very strange mood, grabbing amorously at anything that walked by, male or female. Unfortunately, one person who crossed his path was my mother. Erik grabbed her and gave her one long, lingering kiss. My mother is quite conservative, so she screamed bloody murder, and we all rushed to the kitchen to see what was wrong. Erik was barely aware of what he'd done and remembered nothing the morning after, but my mother could never look him in the eye again.

In any case, there had always been periods when Erik drank a lot, and that may have prevented us from seeing that he was sick, not simply recovering from a hangover, for some of those missed rehearsals. Although he was always incredibly handsome, under his elegant, loose-fitting clothes, his legs and arms were stick-thin; he ate very little and was very fussy about what he would try. His long-time companion, Constantin Patsalas, who was for many years resident choreographer with the company, told me that one doctor who examined Erik was shocked: it was the first case of adult malnutrition he had seen in Canada.

Certainly, Erik had looked ghastly for about a year; everyone knew he was working much too hard, and friends would try to lure him out for at least a meal a day. Constantin, who was a wonderful cook and made a point of preparing meals that Erik could eat, had been away in Asia and Australia for months on a Canada Council Senior Artists' grant. But Erik was determined to do everything he could to make *Alice* a success, and he was seldom away from his duties even for a rest or a meal. He refused to see a doctor when friends urged him to go; instead, he made jokes about being so old that he looked like an iguana. In retrospect, he probably knew he was very sick; comments to some close friends indicated that he was putting some of his affairs in order.

Erik was admitted to hospital in March 1986. He'd always been a heavy smoker, and his father had died of lung cancer at an early age; by the time they discovered the tumour on his lung, nothing could be done. He wrote the company an open letter from his hospital bed on March 19. Among other things, he said:

> My illness comes now at a most unfortunate time, but then illnesses always do. However, I have come to realize in the last year that my nearly three years with you as a director have been the most fulfilling and rewarding experience in my entire professional life. Coming from a former first-class egomaniac, this is not a small thing to admit!
>
> Let's go on from here, spirits up, with confidence, belief, and mutual respect for each other – not only go on, but go on inspiring each other. This way, you will really help me through this difficult time of mine, knowing that the outcome will be something we can share forever.

On April 1, 1986, at only fifty-seven, Erik Bruhn died. The company was informed that same day by Valerie Wilder, the company's artistic administrator, and Lynn Wallis, the artistic coordinator. There were seventy of us in the room, and most of us were in shock. Veronica was inconsolable; I was too stunned to cry. My first reaction was anger – not at him, but at life, and at all of us for not having seen how sick he was. His presence had galvanized us; I'd never felt the company filled with such potential. He taught us to have more faith in ourselves. That a man of his stature would agree to be our artistic director had made us value ourselves infinitely more. He made us feel worthy of his presence – and then it felt like he abandoned us. He had shown us what it could be like when a company had inspiration, motivation, and momentum; we had tasted it, and then it was gone. No wonder I railed at the fates.

For years after his death, I dreamt about him so vividly that waking life paled in comparison. Even now, the dreams come in waves, and Erik seems so real I could touch him. I hear that exquisitely deep voice, the low laugh that followed some joke. Sometimes after a performance, I hear him saying what he often said on such occasions, of my own or other dancers' performances: he'd come up and say slowly, with great emphasis, "That was un-be-*liev*-able!" It was typically Erik: unless you asked, or he voluntarily went on after a sufficiently impressive pause, you'd never know whether he meant unbelievably good or unbelievably bad.

He made you think, and guess, and come up with your own solution. That was Erik's way: he inspired you to find the best dancer within you, and in three short years, he brought a company that was in decline to new heights. If he had lived for even a few more years, who knows what we might have achieved? Like his beloved friend Nureyev, but in a very different way, he made us in demand around the world. There are two ways for a company to tour internationally in all the best places. In the past, and in the classics, you needed a superstar like Nureyev. The more contemporary way – Erik's way – is to have so fine and original a repertoire, with ballets like *Alice*, that everyone wants to see you. Erik did that for us, and I'm sure he would have gone on doing it.

Erik was simply irreplaceable, and no one would have had an easy time taking over after his death. But when the board announced two weeks later that Valerie Wilder, Lynn Wallis, and Constantin Patsalas (then on leave) would jointly direct the company, the dancers were shocked. This was Erik's express wish, in order to provide some continuity and to ensure that his immediate plans would be carried out, but we felt strongly that this was the wrong team for all sorts of reasons.

We were also told that Erik had dictated a letter expressing his desire that Constantin, our resident choreographer, be part of the artistic team; he'd known Erik for many years, and Erik admired his work, much of which was in the company's repertoire. But Constantin had been away from the company for many months on his Canada Council grant, returning shortly before Erik's illness and death. Moreover, Constantin was as highly-strung as Erik, he was suffering from extreme grief at Erik's death, and, as the difficulties increased, that grief turned to unpredictable anger. We had always been friends, but I found it impossible to support him as things grew worse. Within a few months he was dismissed, and he launched one lawsuit for wrongful dismissal and another challenging the company's rights to perform his works without his supervision. (Constantin would die of AIDS in May 1989, leaving Amalia Schelhorn, a former soloist with the company and Constantin's good friend, the rights to his ballets.)

Valerie, who had danced in the corps for some years before going into artistic management, was a brilliant woman in many ways, with superb administrative qualities and a razor-sharp, highly logical mind. She knew how to spot quality in dance, but instilling and inspiring it were not her strong points, and she was not easily accepted in the studio. However, she has proven herself to be a perfect support to someone with real artistic vision, like Erik

*Tatiana in* Onegin.

or Reid Anderson. Unfortunately, Lynn Wallis, a longtime *repetiteur*, or "rehearsal mistress," for the Royal Ballet, was not an Erik or a Reid. She could reproduce the Ashton ballets with great accuracy, and she could be warm and generous, but she conveyed a sense of hostility and negativity toward many dancers. Erik had originally brought these women to the company as part of a collaborative artistic management team, and while this worked very well when he was alive, we quickly realized they were not what we wanted as artistic directors.

Empowered by the events surrounding Alexander's departure, we made our very strong feelings known, but privately; we didn't want to see a repeat of the hurtful press coverage. Quietly but forcefully, we extracted a promise from the board of directors that there would be a serious review if the arrangement wasn't working within six months. In my view, the board thought they'd heard the last of us at that point; we'd settle down and forget our complaints once we'd presented them. But after six months, when the situation was worse, we felt even more strongly. It seemed that the only way to make our protests heard would be to strike during the lucrative *Nutcracker* season.

Realizing we meant business, the board hastily proposed a research and review committee for long-range planning, and Veronica and I were elected as the dancers' representatives. But since Valerie and Lynn sat on the committee as well, the situation was extremely awkward. The committee kept steering the discussions to long-range planning, instead of to the crisis at hand. At one point, Veronica, one of the most controlled and positive people I've ever known, stood up and shouted, "You aren't listening to us!" And they weren't. We had to tell the dancers that we weren't being taken seriously and that the committee didn't believe that we really represented the dancers' views. So then the dancers wrote supporting letters directly to the committee, which Veronica and I presented to the chairman. At this point, to her credit, the new president of the board, Judy Cohen, decided that we deserved a full hearing. Dancer after dancer – some of them in tears of frustration – described their artistic frustration, and the board finally realized that, although the company was being very well managed, artistically we needed a change. To this day, I'm proud that we as dancers made a difference, and that, no matter how long it took, we were heard and heeded. This was a milestone in the quest of dancers to become, and to be seen to be, intelligent adults and artists, not the boys and girls of the ballet.

*With artistic director Reid Anderson.*

When the board agreed to seek a new artistic director, Veronica and I were asked to comment on the final short list of candidates and to define the ideal artistic director. It was hard to say just what I meant by terms like "inspiration" and "soul," but I gave it my best try: an artistic director must have a vision that he or she can communicate to the whole company, so that everyone is inspired to share that vision and knows their role in achieving it. I had experienced such inspiration, such mobilization, under Celia Franca, Rudolf Nureyev, Eliot Feld, and Erik. And I said we needed it again as soon as possible.

Finally, the choice lay between a respected American dancer and a Canadian dancer who had spent most of his career at the Stuttgart Ballet, Reid Anderson. In 1984, he'd taught us John Cranko's *Onegin*, and I'd been impressed by how much he was able to get out of us. He explained every role, from the principals down to the small character roles, articulately and persuasively, and he built a production with depth and feeling. I was pleased when the board announced his appointment as artistic director, and we all agreed that it was an excellent decision to invite Valerie Wilder to continue as associate director, where she is as great an asset as she was to Erik.

Reid has been with us since 1988, and despite very difficult economic times, he's kept us busy, happily challenged with new works and important tours. Morale is high, we're dancing well, and we're treated with the respect we deserve. Because of his intimate connections with Stuttgart and the European dance scene, he's been able to acquire more works by Jirí Kylián, and William Forsythe and John Neumeier have created new ballets especially for us. Reid strongly supported the innovative work of resident choreographer John Alleyne, and he managed to lure James Kudelka back to the company, a circumstance that gives me particular joy. Personally, I've found Reid very considerate; he's made it clear that he wants me to dance as long as I feel comfortable. He knows that dancers of all ages have something of value to offer on-stage, and he keeps an eye out for works that will suit me, to be sure I keep the motivation to go on dancing. He maintains the company's democratic tradition with a difference: instead of making us all feel the same, he has the gift of making us all feel special.

Erik Bruhn confirmed once and for all that I'd been wise to make the National Ballet of Canada my home base. Working with Erik was, to use his own favourite word in a completely laudatory sense, "Unbelievable!" He was our artistic director and our inspiration for less than three years, but in that short time we all became much more creative and mature dancers. And, in my case, he helped me move with grace into the next stage of my life as the company's senior ballerina.

# Putting It All Together: A Dancer's Life

*"But when the moment arrives for me to dance on-stage I want to throw away all those thoughts that I have collected and touch the desires that are inside me as completely as possible, in a simple presence and spirit of life. I hope that I can in some way answer all the people who have helped me in life."*
– Kazuo Ohno (A pioneer of the Japanese Butoh movement, still dancing in his seventies)

Preparing a role is never easy, and it doesn't get much easier even when you've been a principal dancer for twenty years. For an example, let's revisit a typical rehearsal for the most recent full-length role I've learned, Kate in John Cranko's *The Taming of the Shrew*. It's January 1992, and "the dungeon" – the poorly lit downstairs studio with its low ceilings – is freezing. This is a critical rehearsal for *Shrew* and I'm very anxious, not least because the company première is a few weeks away and I have no idea if I'll be dancing opening night. To leave the casting this late is highly unusual, but I know the reason: Shakespeare's Kate, the shrew, is a "fiend of hell," an "irksome brawling scold," and Reid Anderson doubts that I can pull off the tricky combination of anger, bitchiness, and broad humour. He may be right: I'm not tough and I don't often get mad, so Kate is a real stretch for me dramatically.

I've wanted to dance Kate, one of the best comic roles in ballet, ever since I first saw Marcia Haydée and Richard Cragun perform Cranko's ballet over fifteen years ago, so it's unbearably frustrating that I can't find the key to the character. I'm painfully aware that this may well be the last full-length role I'll learn, partly because of my age, but mostly because the National Ballet's budget won't allow any more big ballets in the foreseeable future. That extra pressure doesn't help, nor does my wondering how I'll cope with the humiliation if, at this stage of my career, I'm not chosen (or not worthy of being chosen) for the first cast.

I'm struggling to understand Kate's rage and find the right motivation for the steps, but Reid isn't giving me much help; he just keeps telling me my facial expressions are wrong. It seems to me that all my instinctual suggestions from the beginning of rehearsals have been rejected, and my confidence is pretty much non-existent by now.

In the famous first-act fight pas de deux, I have to walk away from Petruchio three times, and I don't know why. I can't find the natural, intelligible motivation that I need to justify the choreography. First, I stride away triumphantly, but instantly Reid corrects me: I have to look confused. It's better the next time, but then I can't get the right grimace when Serge Lavoie has me in a kind of half-nelson. All Reid tells me is, "Make a funny face," but not why, or how. Finally, we discover that, if Serge pins my arms really tightly, the grimace comes naturally. So it goes, with one frustration after another. Kate's emotional transitions are far too fast to be plausible. She's a wild animal one moment and a lovesick noodle the next, and I can't find the dramatic sense.

Suddenly, there's a breakthrough: I realize that *Shrew* is a farce, not a tragedy like *Onegin* or *Romeo and Juliet*. In farce, characters needn't have much depth, and the challenge is to sketch them as quickly as possible, whether or not you can find dramatic motivation that works for you as an actor. So I go with the staging as dictated and trust that I'll find ways to make Kate more than a stereotype later. I'm not entirely happy with forging ahead regardless, but that decision unblocks the impasse and lets me continue, and as the rehearsal progresses, I start to identify ways to make Kate more than a stereotype.

Yes, she's aggressive, contentious, and wilfully obnoxious. But, as I come to discover in later rehearsals, and still more once we get into performances, Kate's rapid changes from confusion to attraction to anger reflect the tensions between her determination to remain a feisty, independent hellion and her growing interest in Petruchio. She'll find herself enormously drawn to him one moment and then revert to her old combativeness the next as a defence against this alarming new emotion. What she really wants is love, and somehow I have to play her to elicit sympathy, as well as laughter and dislike. One key is showing that her bad temper derives from her pain when everyone admires her beautiful sister Bianca but scorns her. Petruchio, Kate's only suitor, has to play Kate's game, blow by blow, to earn her respect on her own terms. And though finally he thinks he's

*A feisty Kate breaks Hortensio's (Jeremy Ransom) mandolin over his head.*

*Kate tries to resist the charms of Petruchio (Robert Conn).*

conquered her, she has also conquered him; she's learned to play *his* game with her apparent acquiescence. Their growing love makes them better, more sensitive people, and the ballet ends not with Kate's taming but with her victory over her former self, and something like an equal relationship. What I eventually come to love about performing this ballet is the tremendous opportunity it offers for dramatic spontaneity: the laughs come in different places every night.

The acting would be challenging enough on its own, but there's also tremendous physical difficulty; the piece is crammed with steps that ballet class just doesn't prepare you for, so many pratfalls and such risky lifts that you end up black and blue, even when you *do* know what you're doing. Here's one place it helps to be a little older and wiser. I've spent hours studying a videotape of Haydée and Cragun to learn as much as I can before I get out on the floor and actually risk my neck. In early rehearsals, the three other couples learning Kate and Petruchio have been throwing themselves into their roles, trying everything twenty-five different ways at top speed, as if to prove themselves. I calmly watch them, recalling artist Jack Shadbolt's words in a 1992 *Globe and Mail* interview, "I think I've grown more patient . . . knowing not to jump too fast." Over the years, I've learned both patience and the dangers of being swept up in the blind enthusiasm of nerves and adrenalin, so Serge and I observe quietly until we've profited from the others' mistakes; only then do we tackle a difficult lift – and we experiment cautiously until we've mastered it.

We're working on "the helicopter," a lift in which Petruchio raises Kate in arabesque, holds her above his head as he rotates her three hundred and sixty degrees, and drops her to within an inch of the floor, catching her in exactly the same position as he originally lifted her. *The Taming of the Shrew* requires more upper-body strength – for both men and women – than any ballet I've done, and while I have less-powerful arms than Marcia Haydée, at least I'm confident that Serge, one of the strongest dancers I know, would never drop me. We take the movement apart step by step as Reid sits by the wall-long mirror, occasionally adjusting a space-heater to make the room bearable.

"Start the partnered fouetté earlier," says Reid when I find myself wincing and faltering. He claps his hands for the pianist to stop. "Turn, then fouetté."

"I'm afraid of overturning," I tell him. "I wish there was more time in the music." We take it more slowly, and it works better, but when Serge turns me in arabesque, I'm a little off-balance.

"Am I tilting my head too much, or is Serge putting me off my leg?" I ask Reid. It's a bit of both, so we tinker away to get it right.

Movements that are second nature in a solo have to be modified when someone's partnering you. Reid notices that I'm getting into trouble when I change my pirouette to avoid kicking Serge: "You wobbled because you pulled your leg in too much."

"I was afraid I'd knock him over," I explain.

"It's okay. I stood back," Serge reassures me.

Sometimes the sheer effort of partnering me causes problems. "Try not to flap your hands," Reid shouts when I struggle for balance as Serge carries me across the room high above his head.

"I'll try to run more smoothly," says Serge.

"Or I can pretend I'm shaking with laughter," I suggest.

"You can pretend you're laughing because it's the second-to-last lift of the ballet," Reid comments wryly.

*Kate begins to melt, to the amazement of her father (Laszlo Surmeyan), her sister (Chan Hon Goh), and Lucencio (Raymond Smith).*

Not infrequently Serge and I are both so out of breath that we double over, hands on our knees. This is what the audience never sees: the absolute fatigue as you try to do the equivalent of one hundred-yard dash after another without showing the effort and exertion. Sore all over, I gingerly rub my ribs, bruised from a previous rehearsal. Full of falls and lifts and fights, *Shrew* demands that you portray intense physical discomfort, and that's the only easy part of the whole process: behind our smiles and beautiful poses, dancers are often in pain, and injuries are a professional hazard, if not an inevitability.

*ℱ℈*

The first and most basic requirement for every professional dancer is a strong, healthy body, but ironically that's one of the hardest things to achieve and maintain. A proper diet, well-planned supplementary exercises, the judicious care of massage therapists, physiotherapists, and podiatrists, and prompt medical attention when problems arise are absolute essentials if we're to dance at all, let alone dance well. You can't push your body to its limits day after day, in choreography that becomes more demanding, violent, and dangerous every year, without the occasional injury. In 1979, New York's Institute of Sports Medicine reported that professional ballet is second only to professional football in the severity of its physical demands, which means that dancing is harder than hockey, baseball, basketball, or tennis.

Dancing is almost always painful, but it gets worse over the years, as sprains, strains, bruises, stress fractures, and general wear and tear take their accumulated toll. When we turn out at the hips, point our feet for long periods of time, and dance on pointe on those tiny bones in our feet, we strengthen some muscles but weaken others. With the constant emotional and physical stress, it's no wonder that we have problems. We have to learn how to look after our instruments – our bodies – at the same time as we're learning our craft, our roles, and new dance styles. Many dancers past their mid-twenties take anti-inflammatories routinely (under careful medical supervision) and deal with the unpleasant side-effects as best they can; the only alternative is to stop dancing. Fortunately, the older we get, the more tricks of the trade we acquire to cope with the daily battering we give our bodies.

I've been luckier than most dancers in having relatively few injuries. When I was younger, I occasionally strained my neck, which is very long and therefore quite vulnerable to muscle spasms and inflammation. The only time Rudolf Nureyev ever snapped at me – he called me a traitor – was when I had to cancel a performance of *The Sleeping Beauty* in Australia because my neck was so severely injured that the muscle spasms made me look like Quasimodo. Over time, I learned how to strengthen and protect my neck with exercises, a special pillow, the proper placement of neck rolls during long plane trips, and massage. A torn hamstring, due to dancing some tough roles too soon after a three-week holiday in 1983, was probably my worst injury, requiring intensive physiotherapy for five months before I could dance again. More recently, in 1989,

I injured my foot so badly by enthusiastic jumping on some of the hardest stages in the country that I considered retiring. The initial pain, which felt like hot knives being plunged into my foot, was agonizing, and I was able to finish a performance of *Giselle* only by having my foot frozen. But the worst was yet to come: despite months of physiotherapy, I was in pain for two years, and the injury is still aggravated by jumping. I now wear specially made orthotics in street shoes and I even have fashioned flexible arch supports for my pointe shoes. The only good thing about injuries is that you learn about your body and its weak points in the process. It's taken me years of experience to develop an understanding of what my body needs and deserves to function at its best.

For years we had to find appropriate doctors and physiotherapists outside the company, but eventually, insisting that we deserved the best possible care, we negotiated a part-time physiotherapist and massage therapist in our union contract. We found a sympathetic ear in associate director Valerie Wilder, who had discovered for herself the benefits of such therapy as a marathon runner training to be a triathlete.

Among the women in the company, even those rare dancers who manage to avoid serious injury suffer from the pain of dancing on pointe, so for more than twenty-five years we've had a resident podiatrist, Dr. Peter Walpole, who arrives every week with new inventions and aids for our sore feet with their bruises, blisters, and corns. Sometimes he sets up a little table, puts on a hat with a light like a miner's cap, and examines our troubled feet under a magnifying glass. When I started at the National, all we had to soften the impact of dancing on pointe was lamb's wool or Kleenex; now there are so many aids – from special foam-rubber pads to a marvellous invention called Second Skin, a jelly that cushions the toes from repeated impact – that I order my shoes a full size larger to accommodate them.

In recent years, there's been an explosion of knowledge in sports medicine and kinesiology; it's a little surprising that, with all that we now know about the body, there hasn't been a more dramatic decrease in pain, injury, and exhaustion. Part of the problem is that we still have to dance on hard floors when we're on tour. But even if all floors were "sprung," the demands made on us as dancers – in the studio, the theatre, and society at large – have grown far greater. Thirty or forty years ago, most dancers danced only one way, in one style, but now we're increasingly expected to be able to do any kind of dancing, in pointe shoes or in running shoes (much more comfortable), and to learn an entirely new physical vocabulary with every new work. The ballets of John Alleyne, William Forsythe, and Jirí Kylián, to name just three choreographers, are tremendously exciting for both dancers and audiences, but the innovative challenges in movement that they pose add considerably to our physical stress. Regular extracurricular strengthening, tailored to the individual physique, is essential; daily ballet class doesn't begin to be enough any more.

Ever since I fell off those pipes in our basement when I was six, I've known that my own greatest problem was upper-body strength. When I first danced Aurora, I had trouble in the infamous Rose Adagio because my arms weren't powerful enough, so I promptly started to work on the problem. When I came to learn the intricate lifts in ballets like *Onegin* and *Shrew* that had been choreographed for Marcia Haydée, who was renowned for her upper-body strength, I realized how much I'd improved over the years.

The technique that has helped me most, both in building strength and recovering from injuries, is the Pilates method, invented by Joseph Pilates, a German-born American who died in 1967. Focusing on the creation of a strong, flexible centre, involving both mind and body, he developed a combination of exercise and physiotherapy, adaptable to any physique, that yields better posture, greater strength, and a reduction in back injury. Unlike regular weightlifting, which many dancers have now taken up, in Pilates you work against resistance in a full range of motion while lying on the Universal Reformer, a wooden frame with a gliding platform that looks like a cross between a torture rack and a mousetrap. Pilates requires intense coordination – it's almost like dancing – but it doesn't stress the joints, and I've found it so beneficial that I'll continue even after I've stopped dancing.

One problem that remains unsolved is the discrepancy between what we now know about the most effective methods of physical training and the requirements of daily rehearsals and performances. There's evidence that working at peak intensity every day, as professional dancers are obliged to do, actually damages the muscles, which don't have time to recover, so that eventually they become weaker, not stronger. Even though our contract now requires the company to give us an hour's rest after every three hours of rehearsal and short breaks within each three-hour span, we can't afford the luxury of cross-training or a physiologically rational workload pattern. It's not surprising that overuse injuries are so common in dancers; there's never enough time for recuperation. A marathoner might begin with a twenty-five-mile week, running long and short runs on alternate days and building up gradually to a forty- or fifty-mile week, slowing down the schedule as the race approaches to ensure optimal muscle recovery. But a dancer typically learns a strenuous full-length role like Giselle over a period of four or five weeks, with the workload and pressure increasing in intensity towards the end. The physical consequences are exhaustion and injury because of the lack of adequate recovery time, and the emotional consequences – as I found – can be burn-out and depression. If there's a positive side to this pressure, it's that sometimes it teaches you more about your instrument, so that you can learn to strengthen your innate weaknesses and compensate for any deficiencies in your training.

Enlightened artistic directors like Reid Anderson are genuinely concerned with our welfare and allow principal dancers to opt out of rehearsals if they feel close to injury, but even so, taking proper care of ourselves isn't always possible. For instance, company finances allow only one full dress rehearsal on-stage, with all the dancers, technicians, and orchestra together. The opening-night cast typically takes this rehearsal, and, because it's our only chance to practise in full-performance conditions with lights, costumes, and music, we feel obliged to dance full out instead of "marking," or running through the steps primarily for tempi and spacing without doing the more strenuous movements. This means that just when we should be resting our muscles and minds, we exhaust ourselves physically and emotionally, becoming more prone to injury – or at least to a less-impressive performance – on the opening night.

❧

In a December 21, 1992, article in *People*, choreographer Mark Morris dismissed classical ballerinas as "dead virgins . . . encouraged to be stupid, pale, underweight, irresponsible children. They're raised like veal in those little sheds. They're unhappy, illiterate, inartistic, manic-depressives with eating disorders and no menstruation." Of course, he's exaggerating wildly, but he's close to the truth in one particular – and controversial – area.

One of the most difficult things about being a dancer is adapting to the profession's unnatural weight demands. I've felt the strain myself ever since the days when, year after year, Betty Oliphant would repeat the dreaded litany to my parents, "She's talented, but she's too fat. She has to lose weight." Early in my career, before I knew the dangers, I sometimes responded unwisely to the relentless pressure by living on lettuce and tomatoes, or even fasting for several days, despite the fact that I was quite slim by reasonable standards (at five feet seven, I normally weigh between 115 and 120 pounds).

Unfortunately, the glorification of excessive thinness is part of the ideal of female beauty throughout western society. You see it in magazines, television shows, movies: thin is beautiful, and very thin is even better. A study by American University researchers in 1991 found that the body weight of Miss America and of *Playboy* centrefold women between 1979 and 1988 was 13 to 19 per cent below the healthy weight range for women of a similar age – and weighing 15 per cent less than normal is one criterion of anorexia nervosa. According to Naomi Wolf in *The Beauty Myth*, women's anxiety about their weight supports a $33-billion-a-year diet industry.

But if many perfectly healthy North American women consider themselves fat, the problem is magnified many times over in ballet, where the rewards – the best roles, promotions, popular adulation – go to the unnaturally thin. This wasn't always the case, and many great ballerinas of the past look positively pudgy by current standards, but classical dancers now must look as fragile, sylphlike, and delicate as possible, even though we must also be physically stronger than ever. The exceptions who've managed to triumph despite a "weight problem," including Lynn Seymour and me, have faced constant criticism from colleagues and the press, even though we're at the low end of the normal weight range. The ballet public has embraced the anorexic image, expecting and applauding it regardless of the cost in malnutrition and injury.

Sometimes when I come back from vacation, I'm shocked to see how scrawny and unhealthy some dancers look. But the shock fades quickly because we see our bodies differently when we're honing them for the stage; unfortunately it *is* true that most choreography looks more elegant on attenuated bodies. But there must be a happy medium between aesthetics and health. Our distorted view of what constitutes an appropriately lean physique makes it dangerously easy for some dancers to slip from being lean to being painfully thin, while still believing that they're too heavy. Some of the greatest dancers – Natalia Makarova, Gelsey Kirkland, Evelyn Hart – appear anorexic; once Evelyn, who's as tiny as a newborn fawn, actually complained to me that her hips were too large. Many of these artists paid an enormous price for the way they look. Gelsey Kirkland's career was cut short by her self-destructive lifestyle, including obsessive dieting. Evelyn survived her anorexia, but it left her susceptible to frequent stress fractures. Countless young women over the years have damaged their health permanently by trying to look like Gelsey and Evelyn, deceiving themselves with the belief that, if they're as thin as their idols, they'll be able to dance as well.

Part of the secret to keeping the right weight is a careful diet. Rudolf Nureyev ate a rare steak almost every day, because he thought it gave him the energy for eight shows a week. Recently we've learned that complex carbohydrates – pasta, vegetables, and grains – are the mainstay of a healthy diet, and that's how I enjoy eating now.

Perhaps because dancers need to curb their appetites and reduce the stress of rehearsals and performances, smoking remains surprisingly prevalent, even though dancers know it will affect their stamina and health in the long run.

Occasionally, there are even more serious addictions like alcoholism or the sad descent into drugs that I witnessed with Patrick Bissell. But the drug use described by Gelsey Kirkland in *Dancing on My Grave* is very much the exception: few dancers could afford cocaine and other illegal drugs even if they wanted them, and those who indulged would quickly discover that you can't survive professionally if you don't stay healthy. Most dancers have only to behave irresponsibly or miss class for about a week and they're out of a job.

The sharp contrast between the realities of the dancer's life and the visions we create on-stage often comes as a shock to people who visit us backstage. They may have just seen me in *The Merry Widow* as the glamorous Hanna Glawari, tossing back champagne in Maxim's in a glittering gown, but they discover me peeling off my false eyelashes in my dressing room with my swollen feet in a bucket of ice water. The fantasy we concoct on-stage is made possible only by the disciplined ability to rise above the trials and tribulations involved in getting there.

❧

A dancer's life may be hard, but I wouldn't have chosen any other. All the pain, the exhaustion, the injuries, the depression, the dieting, and the hardships of touring have been negligible compared to the joys of creating a new role or learning an established classic and then getting out on the stage and performing, and the older I get, the more I relish it all.

One of the greatest pleasures for me has always been the music, from Bach (Balanchine's *Concerto Barocco*), Gluck (Neumeier's *Don Juan*), Mozart (Kudelka's *Musings*), Beethoven (Kudelka's *Pastorale*), Adam (*Giselle*), Bizet (Balanchine's *Symphony in C*), and Brahms (*Intermezzo*) to the great twentieth-century composers such as Mahler (*Song of the Earth*), Stravinsky (*The Rite of Spring*), Prokofiev (*Romeo and Juliet*), Bartok (*The Miraculous Mandarin*), Britten (Kylián's *Forgotten Land*), Martinú (Tetley's *Sphinx*), and Hindemith (Balanchine's *The Four Temperaments*). And then, in a class by himself, there's the greatest of all ballet composers, Tchaikovsky, whether the score was specifically written for the extraordinary Petipa–Ivanov ballets (*Swan Lake, The Sleeping Beauty, The Nutcracker*) or adapted (Balanchine's *Serenade*, one of the loveliest of all the ballets, or the score for *Onegin*).

*With Serge Lavoie in Jirí Kylián's Forgotten Land.*

Many dancers live and breathe the music when they're learning a role, partly so that they'll learn it perfectly; it's a good thing that I learn the music quickly, because it affects me so strongly that I can't bear to listen to it unless I'm actually rehearsing or on-stage. The problem is that, like Pavlov's dog, I'm

programmed so that my nerves and muscles automatically respond: if I hear the *Sleeping Beauty* waltz, I get as tense as I do before my first entrance as Aurora, and the music from *Romeo and Juliet* makes me cry, even if I'm in public. I've often had to ask restaurants to change the tape if they're playing something from the ballet, because I find myself so drawn into the music that I can't take part in conversation. Over the years, I've come to realize that what makes daily ballet class stimulating or dreary for me is more the pianist's selection of music than who is teaching or how intriguing the exercises are.

Certainly one of the reasons I never tire of so many of the great roles is the possibilities that they offer of changing the tempi and dynamics of my response to a great score as I continually explore the fresh interpretive possibilities in some of my favourite works. It still amazes me that Tchaikovsky wrote such brilliant scores in response to the demanding shopping lists given him by Marius Petipa for the St. Petersburg Ballet. For example, Petipa prescribed a section that would be "abruptly coquettish, 3/4. Thirty two bars. Finish with 16 bars. 6/8 forte. *Pas d'action, Grand adagio,* very animated." And from those specifications Tchaikovsky created the astonishingly beautiful music for the entrance of Aurora and the Rose Adagio in *The Sleeping Beauty.*

One of the difficulties of dancing to nineteenth-century ballet music is that most of the musical and choreographic phrases are repeated four times almost identically. This convention allows even an unknowledgeable audience to detect any deviation from perfect technique, which is one of the reasons the Tchaikovsky ballets, with their intricate steps, are technically so demanding; there's no room for error or for glossing over a mistake, and when you know that the audience can spot every minor flaw, it can unnerve you for a whole scene if you have one slightly imperfect pirouette. Contemporary choreography tends to be more forgiving.

In *The Sleeping Beauty* and *The Nutcracker*, movement doesn't express emotion and character as it does in romantic ballets like *Giselle*; you can't hide any technical inadequacies behind a dramatic performance. Since I've never thought of myself as technically proficient, I've always been amazed at my success as Aurora, which some people consider my most memorable classical role. Probably it helped that there are many more jumps – my strong point – than in most classical ballets, and that I had the benefit of Nureyev's coaching.

*The Sleeping Beauty*, especially in Rudolf's version, is very taxing in both technique and stamina. Aurora's sixteenth birthday is the culmination of her years of training to be a princess; she must sparkle like champagne but also possess a regal bearing, and there should be a hint of the nervousness of youth. That last quality isn't hard to achieve, because the most famous part of the first

*Wonderful romance in* The Merry Widow *with* John Meehan.

act, the Rose Adagio, is extremely difficult; it's only the sweet grandeur of the music that carries me through. At the climax of this adagio, one by one Aurora's four suitors take her hand and turn her slowly as she balances on pointe; as each suitor is replaced by the next, she raises her hand and then lowers it graciously to take the next prince's hand. This sequence is a real test of the ballerina's balance, control, and stamina, and can easily become either a showy circus act or a disaster if Aurora wobbles desperately, trying to stay on pointe. Knowing what is coming, the audience gets as anxious as Aurora, and when the dancer makes it to the end without falling over, she's given a huge round of sympathetic applause. Fonteyn, the most honoured Aurora of our time, was by no means a brilliant technician, but her charm overshadowed the difficulties of this passage; somehow she conveyed the impression of an enchanting young girl having a wonderful time as she proffered her hand to each suitor. I try to emulate that effortlessness, that easy graciousness, and I no longer frustrate myself by trying to hold long balances with the assurance of Veronica Tennant; instead, I focus on the musical accents to guide me through.

For me, the highlight of *The Sleeping Beauty* is the last act pas de deux, which must reflect maturity, radiance, strength, and confidence – and if you've made it through Acts I and II without catastrophe, you've earned the right to those qualities. Aurora is now an adult, warm, regal, outgoing; her personal happiness bestows a blessing on her whole court. This pas de deux is the ultimate in classical grandeur, and the opulence of the Georgiadis sets and costumes in our production do it full justice; there's incredible richness in both the choreography and the look of it all. For me, this sequence is the epitome of what it feels like when everything in life is going perfectly.

A good partner can transform this difficult ballet from a trial to a joy in both the rehearsal process and the performance itself. In recent years, it's been my good fortune to have Laurent Hilaire of the Paris Opéra Ballet as my partner in several performances of *The Sleeping Beauty*, including one that opened the National's spring season in April 1994. Each time, I have been tremendously inspired by his warmth, his musicality, his exceptional dancing, his brilliant partnering, and his nobility of bearing and character – and these last qualities must be innate, for I've never seen anyone succeed in teaching them. I've had many partners throughout my career, and Laurent ranks with the greatest. I've decided that I will not dance Aurora again (or at least not the full ballet), and it delights me to have been able to dance it with Laurent in one of my final performances.

৪৯

*The Sleeping Beauty* is the unquestioned masterpiece of
the grand Russian imperial style, spectacular, lavish, and
reliant on pure technique. It's the work Sir Frederick
Ashton used to watch when he wanted "a private lesson"
from the master choreographer. In *Swan Lake*, Petipa's
French brilliance is complemented by the profound origi-
nality and Russian spirituality of his assistant, Lev Ivanov,
who choreographed the White Acts; this ballet has a Tchaikovsky score as great as *Beauty's*, but with far more emotional intensity. The characterization of the ballerina is
more complex. Instead of a story-book princess, the heroine
is a dark, enchanted creature, half-woman and half-swan,
who, in Erik Bruhn's version, knows that her terrible fate
is to be forever alone, the unwilling cause of destruction
for any man who loves her.

Bruhn found traditional interpretations far too sim-
plistic dramatically, so he added great psychological depth
to the Prince, a troubled young man who is dominated by
his widowed mother. It is his yearning for something more meaningful than
the shallow pleasures of court that leads him to seek the darkness of the forest,
where he is startled and enthralled by the mythical White Swan. Dancing
either the White Swan (traditionally named Odette) or her evil double, the
Black Swan (Odile), would be sufficient challenge for any ballerina. But in
most modern productions, the challenge is compounded by having the same
dancer take both roles, and inevitably a young dancer finds that one comes
much more naturally than the other. For me, it was the White Swan, whose
sorrowful movements are like one long sigh of resignation; the music itself
tells you almost everything you need to know about her.

*The White Swan
pas de deux with
Frank Augustyn.*

The famous violin and cello adagio, in which the White Swan reveals herself and falls in love, has three distinct musical sections. In the first, she is
drawn to the Prince but, knowing his inevitable fate if he loves her, she tries to
warn him of his danger. In the second, she tries to flee in an attempt to dissuade
him, but he continually pulls her back from her flight, symbolized by beautiful,
floating lifts. And then, in the most haunting section of the music, she experiences a transcendent moment of hope and succumbs to her yearning for human
love. The steps here are as intimate as lovemaking; she nestles her head against
his shoulder and they sway to and fro as he folds her wings in front of her. Erik
ended this adagio not with the languorous notes and slow pirouettes of most
versions, but with a more excitable passage from the original Moscow score;

The White Swan pas de deux with Serge Lavoie.

while this choice is certainly different, and I've gotten used to it over the years, it may be one of the few places where our production would be more moving if it were more traditional.

In the next act, the dazzling Black Swan, the deceitful antithesis of her white counterpart, so captivates the Prince that he forgets his promise of eternal love to the White Swan, and for years I couldn't get the emotional feel of the character. As ballet master David Scott used to say, I always looked as if I couldn't tell a lie, so my characterization consisted of a brittle, smiling, unconvincing mask. Like most dancers, I probably tried to be too evil, and no young man in his right mind would have been attracted by such malice. It took me the experience that comes only with age to realize that the Black Swan has to be genuinely inviting if the Prince is to fall in love and to understand the devious, heartless attitude she displays in her seduction, the completely immoral delight she takes in playing him like a fish, in exercising her power for the sheer fun of it.

*Pleading with the Black Queen (Victoria Bertram).*

In most versions, Odette is an enchanted princess and Odile is the daughter of the magician, Von Rothbart, but Erik saw the White Swan and Black Swan as two opposites within one body, one representing spiritual love, the other representing carnal love. This is why the Prince is so easily deceived; in the Black Act, he really is seeing the same woman, but here her blatantly sexual aspect is brought out by the Black Queen, another evil female figure with whom Erik replaced the traditional male villain. This is an interpretation of the ballet in which domineering women pull all the strings, and I've found it fascinating in recent years to work with Vicki Bertram as the Black Queen; I'm constantly aware of where she is on the stage, for she controls me completely, as both the Black and the White Swan, and we've worked out places where she gives me my freedom and others where she pulls me back sharply in a struggle as dynamic as any interaction between either of the swans and the Prince. The ballet reveals a contest between two views of woman: as a manipulator of men and as a genuinely loving partner.

Time and training have dramatically changed my interpretation in other ways as well. The last time we performed the ballet in Toronto, Magdalena Popa and I worked on the moment when the White Swan first sets eyes on the Prince. I used to become excessively agitated at this point, flapping around like a mad thing – in part because I couldn't control the adrenalin rush at my first entrance. Now, having studied these large birds, I realize that they never move so frantically. Instead, they freeze when they're startled, and then they decide whether to attack or flee. Now, for me, the challenge in that first scene is to convey fear with less movement rather than more.

Similarly, when I was young I exhausted myself with the technical difficulties of the Black Swan pas de deux, for Erik's version is much harder than the traditional choreography. Now that I understand that the Prince would never have been seduced by a creature so totally, salaciously evil, I've found technical as well as dramatic ways to solve the problem; for example, I contrast the sharp attack of the legwork with a more sensuous, alluring carriage, combining aspects of the White and Black Swans to make the Black Swan more genuinely appealing as she simmers with the promise of unrestrained sexual pleasure.

Erik's version is much darker but more realistic than the traditional version, where the lovers drift off into eternal happiness, usually in a silly little boat, as if love really did conquer all. Instead, the Prince is driven to his death by the enchanted swans, and Odette is forced to rise from her misery, spread her wings, and face her solitude – and an unending cycle of tragic betrayals – once again. This may be why grown men and women sometimes cry at the end of Erik's version. On paper, it may seem a ridiculous story of an oversized bird and a prince who is unduly excited by receiving a crossbow for his birthday, but it contains far deeper symbolism and beauty; Erik's *Swan Lake* is about the desires of the flesh and the torments of the soul, the struggle between instinct and idealism, power and submission, carnal and spiritual love.

The plot and motivation of Erik's version may not be entirely consistent and convincing; in some ways this *Swan Lake* might have been more coherent if it had been a little more daring in stating its implicit premise that, while the Prince may safely accept and admire female beauty, he is destroyed when he yields to his attraction to the darker side of female sexuality. However, the ambiguities in the production can stimulate uniquely imaginative interpretations by the principal dancers, and the resulting performance is often undeniably moving for dancers and audience alike. The inconsistencies and uncertainties contribute to the mystery at the ballet's core.

ℱᶺ

*Giselle* also deals with the grand themes of innocence betrayed, the loss of love, and the conflict between vengeance and forgiveness, but in quite a different style. After all, the heroine is a peasant girl, and her noble lover is disguised

*The Mad Scene from* Giselle, *with Victoria Bertram as my mother.*

as a humble villager. Many of the steps in the first act are quite realistic. For example, when Giselle meets Albrecht, she stands normally, both feet facing forward; Aurora and the Swan Queen would never be seen in such a casual pose. Similarly, Giselle's Mad Scene – a commonplace in nineteenth-century opera but rare in ballet – is often most effective when it's done as realistically as possible. The real test in *Giselle* is not so much the dancing as the emotional involvement, which saps your strength as thoroughly as the toughest variation.

Ever since I saw Lynn Seymour and Peter Martins do *Giselle* with the company in my first season, I've known how heartbreaking the Mad Scene can be. Unlike the stiff, stylized acting of several Soviet dancers I'd seen, so remote that you couldn't relate what you saw to any recognizable human emotion, Seymour's unaffected acting was so believable that I couldn't stop sobbing on-stage. She relived the memories of past happiness, reproduced in the music, by dancing the old steps disjointedly, like a broken doll. Unable to recognize her friends and family, she grew increasingly distracted by memories of old tales of the dreaded Wilis, the vengeful ghosts of betrayed women, and, as her mind became ever more unhinged, she suddenly began to see them beckoning to her. She had already left this earth in her mind and was halfway into the world of the dead.

There's long been a controversy over whether Giselle dies of a weak heart or kills herself with Albrecht's sword, though her burial in the unconsecrated ground of the forest indicates that she must have committed suicide. But for years I experimented with what has become the more popular interpretation, namely, that she dies of a broken heart and the shock of betrayal. I saw her madness as a consequence of the physical process of death, with loss of oxygen making her dazed, cold, and weak, adding panic and terror to the misery of Albrecht's desertion. Perhaps the strangest thing about dancing the Mad Scene – and it's different every time – is that I can never tell if I've done it well. I only know whether I've convinced myself.

I've never seen myself as an ideal Giselle, since I consider myself too tall and far too healthy-looking, so I try to make her death touching, because she is so innocent and trusting. The second act comes more naturally, perhaps because Act I is so physically and emotionally draining that the fatigue helps create the trance-like calm that characterizes Giselle at this stage. She is truly a spirit now, floating and illusory, so she must be quite different from the living peasant girl, and her emotions must be intelligible but otherworldly, distant. I particularly love the moments when Albrecht senses Giselle behind him – Does he hear something? Feel a sudden chill? – and then, when he looks, she has gone.

It took me a long time to master Giselle's run, which must be smooth, silent, and weightless; you can't bob up and down, and absorbing the impact as you traverse the stage takes a great deal of control in the legs and feet. I learned a lot from watching Veronica, and I studied the old lithographs of Carlotta Grisi, the original Giselle, to find the right angle of the body and the elongation of the neck that suggests that you're being invisibly controlled by the Queen of the Wilis.

The very end of the ballet is still magical for me after all these years. By then I'm so exhausted that I feel almost like a spirit, and it's easy to imagine myself becoming ever more fragile, more transparent, as the sun rises. I feel love, regret, and the peace that comes from forgiving and having that forgiveness accepted, but most of all I sense the finality of that moment: when Giselle fades into thin air, there can be no return. She is a suicide, and she and Albrecht will never be reunited before or after his death. There can be no future beyond this last, generous, loving act; Giselle will be no more.

ያ∂

Contemporary works can be just as challenging and demanding as the classics, and one of my favourites in this category is Cranko's *Romeo and Juliet*. In fact, ask any woman in the corps de ballet what role she craves most and the answer is likely to be Juliet, not least because it would be a rare young woman who can't identify with a girl who is totally captivated by a mysterious stranger of whom her parents disapprove. That the story is set to Serge Prokofiev's hypnotic, passionate score makes it all the more moving. I had loved the ballet from the first moment I saw it, and, when I joined the company and was merely a "citizen on the bridge," as one group of extras is called, I'd linger in the wings to watch Karen Bowes or Veronica as Juliet.

Cranko's version isn't too difficult technically – there's actually very little dancing for Juliet – but, like *Giselle*, it's exhausting emotionally. When I first learned the ballet, I was taught only the steps, which was fine for the first act, when the steps can carry the story and Juliet's emotions are those that every young girl has shared. But the third act is virtually all acting, with no steps to speak of once the farewell pas de deux is over. You have to find a meaning for each beat, each pulse of the music, and then project your thoughts to the audience that is watching you on the half-lit stage. For inspiration I turned to

Shakespeare. For example, when Juliet's parents try to force her agreement to a marriage with Paris and she responds with a frenzied tantrum, they leave her angrily. Desperate, exhausted with grief, and at the lowest point of her young life, she sits on the bed "past hope, past care, past help." I find these words and this moment so powerful that every time I perform it, I have to fight back my own tears.

Perhaps the hardest part of this act is the Potion Scene, in which Juliet tries to summon the courage to take the potion that will make her appear to be dead until Romeo can return to spirit her away from Verona. I'd been given a road-map of instructions: "Drink the bottle for so many bars, then drop the bottle on this note of the music, feel dizzy here, retch and stagger there, then collapse just here so you can crawl onto the bed." The music seems to go on for hours, and it's abrupt and dramatic, but you have to find ways to fill it, both for yourself and for the audience. Here, developing your own script helps a great deal, even if that script, and your performance, varies from night to night. Juliet thinks about calling her nurse back – surely she will have some sympathy? – but then she remembers her nurse's betrayal in recommending that Juliet wed Paris ("I think you are happy in this second match / For it excels your first") and realizes, "My dismal scene I needs must act alone."

The choreography tells Juliet simply to stand up, sit down on the bed, dart away, and then rush back to sit again. These actions depict her feverish state, her fears about what could go wrong if she takes the potion, and while a dancer may not be able to communicate all the details to the audience, it gives her movements point and force if she thinks through the words of Shakespeare's Juliet. She worries that the potion won't work, and she'll have to marry Paris after all; even worse, she fears that the potion will wear off too soon: "How if, when I am laid into the tomb, I wake before the time that Romeo come to redeem me? There's a fearful point. Shall I not then be stifled in the vault . . . and there die strangled ere my Romeo comes?" Most terrible of all, she imagines waking up to see her murdered cousin Tybalt "festering in his shroud," which may drive her mad. But finally her terrors resolve: "Romeo, I come. This do I drink to thee!"

Once Juliet has swallowed the potion, she traces its course through her body with trembling hands, and I recall the lines, "I have a faint cold fear thrills through my veins, that almost freezes up the heat of life." I have to conjure up these images every time I dance the role, or my acting becomes stale. The spontaneity of this scene must be measured by the demands of the music, but you can never be contrived or the audience will sense it immediately. It's a delicate balancing act.

✧

Another Cranko ballet that gives me a great deal of pleasure is *Onegin*. Like Juliet, Tatiana is initially an easy role to relate to, and the famous Letter Scene, with its fantasy of romance with a brooding stranger, reflects a favourite fantasy of every teenaged girl – at least, it was a favourite fantasy of mine. It strikes me as quite realistic that a dream of passionate love could give such a girl the courage to write a love letter to the object of her affections, only to be devastated when he rejects her. I love dancing the young Tatiana, but even more fascinating is her development from lovelorn child to mature, responsible wife. The adult Tatiana feels the compelling power of her old love when, years later, Onegin rediscovers her and declares his adoration, but by then she has developed the moral fortitude to reject him, asserting the strength of reason over passion. Emotionally, this is a very painful ballet: as a girl, Tatiana is so vulnerable and impetuous and so humiliated by Onegin's dismissal of her; then, as a grown woman, she's so tempted by the intensity of his love when it erupts to disturb the calm order of her marriage. Making Tatiana credible both as a girl and as a woman is a dramatic challenge, and it's particularly satisfying to be able to dance a full-length role in which the ballerina is allowed to become a mature adult faced with realistic moral decisions.

✧

Sir Frederick Ashton's *La Fille Mal Gardée* has the basic story-line of every ballet from *Giselle* to *Romeo and Juliet* to *Don Quixote*: the heroine loves a young man of whom her parents disapprove. This jewel of a comic ballet is both old and new. It was originally staged in 1789, and many versions are still danced, but the best of all – and one of the greatest of all ballets, in my view – is Ashton's 1960 production, full of mischief, fun, and some of the most brilliant choreography ever invented. Learning *Fille* was also one of the few times in my life (*The Merry Widow*, by Ronald Hynd, was another) when I've been able to learn a full-length role from the choreographer and see what a difference that can make.

Before Ashton arrived from England to work with us, we had learned the steps through Benesh notation (a method of recording choreography on a musical stave, which allows a trained choreologist to reconstruct both the steps and their relationship to the music). But while Benesh is a wonderful tool and a useful supplement to videotapes, as I discovered, it can be a very mechanical way of learning, far removed from the original inspiration of the choreographer.

We'd been taught, for example, that at her entry "Lise opens the door – four counts – she closes it – four counts – she yawns – 1, 2, 3, 4 – she lowers her arms – 5, 6, 7, 8 – she runs down the stairs – 1, 2, 3, 4 – she runs toward the hayloft – 5, 6, 7, 8" and so on and on, through the whole ballet.

When Sir Fred took his first rehearsal, after about thirty seconds he stopped me in dismay to ask, "What on earth are you doing?" I dutifully explained the counts that had been drilled into me, and he said, "Forget all that nonsense. Just come out on your music and close the door, and then when you feel like it, go down the stairs. All you have to do is make sure you are at the edge of the stage when you hear this piece of music, because then something else happens." What a relief! From then on, the steps felt spontaneous and real instead of the actions of a wind-up toy.

I was even more delighted when, for the first time in my career, Ashton gave me an option in the steps. In the second act, Lise's mother, the Widow Simone, locks her in the house to keep her away from her sweetheart while Simone goes to town. Left to her own devices, Lise behaves like many young adolescents, a child one moment, a young woman the next. Sulking, she bumps her way down the stairs on her behind – very painful, until you find the right angle – and winds up in a disgruntled heap on the floor. That's where I was given my option.

"Some dancers have a tantrum here," said Ashton, "and some sit on the couch and pout. Which would you prefer?"

I chose the tantrum, flying across the room to beat my hands and feet on the sofa; this seemed right because I felt Lise was spunky – or rather, I would have been spunky in her shoes, and, since I identified with this role so easily, I followed my instinct.

*Fille* is technically challenging, full of twists and reversals of position at full speed, yet the virtuosity is overshadowed by a wonderful comic tone straight out of British pantomime. The Widow Simone is the "Dame," a man dressed as a woman, with bold and bright costumes and a wonderful clog-dance routine, and the spirit of the music hall is so much present that at various points in the ballet, I half expect the characters to break into a "Oh no, I'm not! Oh yes you are!" routine.

*Fille* is as great a masterpiece as anything in the ballet repertoire, and it is only because it is a comedy – and a very English one at that – that it's not universally recognized as such. Perhaps also its great appeal for children, with its chickens, its obstreperous rooster, its live pony and cart, blinds some adults to both its beauties and its deep wisdom. Like the best, most-enduring fairy tales, it can too readily be dismissed by those who value only what is serious and ponderous. It's one of my greatest sorrows that I'm unlikely to dance *Fille* again.

ൠ

*The Nutcracker* also has a great deal of comedy and spontaneity, but the funniest parts may not always be apparent to the audience. This ballet, a Christmas institution and a great moneymaker for the company, comes round relentlessly like a yearly tune-up, and what really makes it amusing for the dancers year after year is its controlled unpredictability, which results from several elements.

First, there's the audience, as much as 75 per cent of it children. Their applause is very warm and immediate, but usually doesn't last very long, and their reactions are wonderful. Every time there's a lift or a big crescendo in the music, the kids laugh and shriek and carry on, and at any hint of romance on the stage, there's such a loud collective "Ugh!" from a large segment of the audience that even the dancers find it hard to stifle their laughter.

Then there are the young dancers from the Ballet School who participate in most scenes. Whenever I descend in the balloon as the Sugar Plum Fairy, I look down to see some faces gazing in delight while others are absolutely rigid with fright – and I'm sure some of the latter realize then and there that being on the stage isn't the life for them.

But who needs real children when the company members take this opportunity to let loose? Every year, the battle between the Mice, Gingerbread Cookies, and Soldiers grows more chaotic. At one point the Mouse King is supposed to improvise, and the rest of the dancers often do the same, performing little send-ups of other ballets – a mini-*Giselle*, a fragmentary *Swan Lake* – or playing tricks on each other. The rumours fly backstage, "Watch out for so-and-so! The Mice are going to gang up on him." And so the wings are crowded with Snowflakes getting ready for the next scene but eager to see what will happen to the poor victim this time, or, until she retired several years ago, having hysterics at Linda Maybarduk's antics as Ms. Mouse. There's so much noise from the laughing and pranks that the dancers often get disciplined, but the spirit of Christmas misrule prevails, and after a few performances, it's back to chaos. It's a terrific way to relieve the boredom of annual *Nutcrackers*.

ൠ

While most audiences still prefer the full-length ballets, one-act ballets can be just as exciting, and sometimes even more intense. The Balanchine repertoire is very dear to me: *Serenade*, *Concerto Barocco*, and *The Four Temperaments* are all masterpieces, with their glorious scores and their demands that you devour space with power, speed, and freedom. These ballets are intensely musical – I've seldom danced anything in which the steps reflect the music so perfectly – and they're so exquisitely conceived that the brilliant choreography shines through even a mediocre performance. Balanchine's work incarnates the joy of sheer dancing, and the jumps, the subtle and unusual changes of direction, and the pure inventiveness are perpetually delightful.

The works of Sir Kenneth MacMillan have also been a great joy to dance: *Solitaire*, *Concerto*, and one of the greatest of all ballets, *The Song of the Earth*, with its poignant Mahler score. I don't think the company has ever danced *Concerto* or *Song* as well as we might have done, chiefly because they were recreated from Benesh notation, and we didn't have the sustained and inspirational coaching that their great interpreters – Lynn Seymour, Marcia Haydée, Monica Mason, and Donald MacLeary – could have provided. Many of MacMillan's works, and especially *Song*, have such profundity that, without such coaching, it's difficult for younger dancers to discover and communicate their real and moving spirituality, and while the choreography in itself is beautiful, it becomes truly convincing only when its psychological motivation is understood. Older, more experienced dancers can find some of that motivation for themselves, but younger dancers typically need help to go beyond the steps. Knowing the counts and the positions isn't nearly enough. I've danced only a few performances of *The Song of the Earth* – I missed our first season because I was pregnant – but it remains one of the works I most look forward to dancing in the coming years, for it provides me with a great role in which I feel I can continue to grow as time goes on.

There are several one-act ballets, now out of the repertoire, that I'd love to see return. One of these is Hans van Manen's *Four Schumann Pieces*, which we have danced with Anthony Dowell (for whom it was made) and Rudolf Nureyev, and in which Frank Augustyn found one of his greatest roles. The elegant clarity of its choreography and score, the freshness of its style, and the sensitive story lying just beneath the surface, to be interpreted anew by each performer and the audience alike, make it a very fine work.

*The Seven Daggers*, an interpretation of Garcia Lorca's *Blood Wedding* by the great flamenco dancer Susana with a fine original score by her husband, Antonio Robledo, is a powerful ballet, with the added benefit of having been created especially for our company at Alexander Grant's request. For many years, Susana and Antonio taught Spanish dance at the National Ballet School, and each of them satisfies my definition of a brilliant and inspiring

*The Bride in* The Seven Daggers.

teacher – Susana with her earthy metaphors, perceptive warmth, and passionate wisdom, and Antonio with his gentle perfectionism, serenity, and musical intelligence. I wasn't fortunate enough to study with them at the school, since their guest-teaching engagements started after my time, but they trained a generation of National Ballet dancers (Peter Ottmann, Gizella Witkowsky, Sabina Allemann, David Nixon, Amalia Schelhorn, and many others) whose classical dancing seems to have derived an extra edge and flair from their experience with flamenco. The weeks I spent in Spain with Susana and Antonio learning the basics of Spanish dance in preparation for *The Seven Daggers* are one of my most treasured memories. Susana taught me the paradoxical importance of relaxation in achieving the staccato footwork of Spanish dance and sharpened my ability to isolate movements in one part of the body. I adored my experience with Spanish technique and found the role of the Bride dramatically

fascinating, a kind of opposite to Tatiana in *Onegin* in that the Bride, impris-
oned in a loveless marriage by the highly repressed village morality, abandons
everything for love and reaps disaster.

Ann Ditchburn's ballets will always be very dear to me. I've known Annie
since Grade 6, when we both commuted to the National Ballet Summer School
on the GO train. We didn't become friends immediately (I've found that my
closest friendships develop very gradually over the years), but when, through
my involvement with Tim Spain, I became part of that talented, rebellious
group of choreographers at the ballet school, Annie and I grew – and still remain – as close as sisters, with the same kind of unconditional love. She's always
there for me, even when we don't get to see much of each other, and I admire
her enormously as a choreographer-writer-filmmaker and, even more, as a strong,
gifted, intensely caring human being.

I remember vividly the joy of working with her on a three-minute pas de
deux, *Emily*, during my first year in the company, on *Mad Shadows*, and on her
beautiful pas de deux *Nelligan*, inspired by the life of the Quebec poet and created for Claudia Moore and Robert Desrosiers in 1976.

The ballets of James Kudelka, who is now, once again, our resident choreographer, are very precious to me; he's one of the most musical choreographers I
know, and, as the years pass, his mastery of both classical and more contemporary dance idioms continues to grow. I first worked with James in 1980 in a
workshop production, *The Rape of Lucrece*, which in my view was one of the
first ballets of his full choreographic maturity, but, unlike Veronica Tennant
and Cynthia Lucas, I hadn't been one of his favourite dancers in his earlier
years. In fact, when Reid Anderson told me a few years ago that James was coming back to the National to create something for the Mozart Festival, I told him
that, while I was delighted for the company and thought James was probably the
greatest living Canadian choreographer, I didn't think he'd use me. I felt quite
sure he didn't much like my dancing, or at least that I didn't inspire him. No
dancer can inspire every choreographer, and I'd learned not to take that personally as a reflection on my own abilities. Oddly enough, when Reid called James
to invite him, James said that he didn't think I'd want to work with *him*. We
never talked about it at the time, but recently, when I was learning *Pastorale*,
James said, "Isn't it nice that we've found each other before it was too late?"

I've found some of my greatest satisfaction as a dancer recently in James's
work. When he created *Pastorale* (to Beethoven's *Pastoral Symphony*) for the

*James Kudelka's* Musings.

company in 1990, I loved the ballet so much that I was a little hurt not to be dancing in it. After he'd created *Musings* for me, he asked somewhat hesitantly if I'd be willing to dance in the revival of *Pastorale* as second cast, and I accepted with enthusiasm. Unlike many choreographers, James often doesn't tell his dancers a great deal about motivation or story; instead, he may give you books to read or slight verbal hints. He told me that, while *Pastorale* was an abstract ballet, my role had been inspired by an historical character, the Empress Elisabeth of Austria (mother of Prince Rudolf of Mayerling fame), and suggested some books about her. Reading them, I grew fascinated by her anorexia, her obsession with exercise and riding, her loneliness and isolation, and the madness that ran in her family; although none of these things appears literally in the ballet, they gave me a great deal of inspiration.

*Musings* is also a ballet I find profoundly moving to dance. The lovely Mozart score is complemented beautifully by the choreography, and once again I'm able to be a complex and mature woman on-stage, not a perpetual teenager. I've always thought that the most severe test of a powerful stage presence is the ability to hold an audience while you stand still or walk slowly across the stage, and, quite apart from its glorious dancing, *Musings* gives me the challenge of instilling such simple moments with significance.

The Miraculous Mandarin *with Reid Anderson.*

*The Miraculous Mandarin*, which premièred in the spring of 1993, is one of the most extraordinary ballets I know. Many choreographers have tackled the Bartok score and its grim story of prostitution and murder, and most have failed; in my view, James has succeeded brilliantly. His transformation of the traditional story into an examination of child abuse and repressed sexuality offers me one of the most demanding roles of my career: a woman in a brutally destructive marriage who takes out her own frustrations in some rather perverse sexual exploitation of her youngest son. This highly disturbing subject matter has led many viewers to dislike the ballet itself, but I have always believed that ballet should be free to deal with any topic, any aspect of human life, and I welcome James's courage in confronting the ugly underside of the human soul.

Too often it seems that North American ballet audiences want productions to be all sweetness and light or, if there's tragedy, then it should be tragedy in the grand manner: *Romeo and Juliet* or *Giselle*. Modern dance has historically been far more receptive to drawing subject matter from all of life, and while I, too, appreciate the beauties of the Balanchine ballets or James's own *Pastorale*, I hope that, as time goes by, our ballet audiences will come to value the truth and intelligence of a work like *The Miraculous Mandarin*. I hope we have the opportunity to show the ballet in Europe, where I think it would be far better received. Above all, I look forward to working with James on other new ballets; although he's still a young man, the scope, inventiveness, and depth of his work continue to astonish me.

❧

When I think back on the thousands of performances I've given in nearly a quarter of a century of dance, I'm amazed to realize that only a small fraction – perhaps a dozen – completely satisfied my own standards. Such is the perfectionist nature of this art, and of my own psychological make-up, that I've hardly ever been able to say to myself, "There. That's what I wanted to do. I knew I was capable of it, so why can't I do it all the time?"

For years, like most dancers, and indeed most professional athletes, I deluded myself by thinking that there was a formula for giving a good performance. Whenever I felt I'd done well, I'd search my memory carefully for any identifiable tidbit that I could cling to as a talisman or make into a superstition. If I had taken class from a certain teacher before a good performance of *The Sleeping Beauty* or had started my preparations at precisely six thirty-five that evening, I would repeat the procedure before every *Sleeping Beauty*. And, of course, none of the rituals I put myself through worked.

In fact, one of the strangest and most frustrating things about my dancing is that the quality of my performance doesn't necessarily have any relation even to my physical state. I can prepare for days, be flawless in rehearsal, get a good night's sleep – and then go out on stage and do hardly anything right. Or I can be so exhausted that I honestly don't know where the strength for the next step will come from – and give one of those few performances that satisfies my every desire. I remember one *Giselle* in particular: with Frank, in Fredericton, New Brunswick, in the late seventies, during the period of my depression. On this occasion, I felt overworked and tense, and the physical conditions were far from ideal. The stage was small and the orchestra was in the basement, so that all we could see of them was conductor George Crum's eyebrows through a hole in the floor. But everything went right. Frank and I felt the spirit of the dancing surging through us, and we simply had to ride the wave. Every arabesque was so easy and natural it was almost as though an invisible partner was holding me there. Technically, I had a sensation of perfect balance and poise; emotionally, I felt I *was* Giselle. Perfect physical command, perfect conviction, perfect concentration; what more could anyone ask?

That's really why we dance. It's not for the applause, the good reviews, or the bouquets of flowers, and certainly not for the money, but for the anticipation of a perfect performance. What makes the waiting even more exciting and suspenseful is that you can never predict when it will happen. I've learned that I can't force a good performance; all I can do is prepare for one physically and emotionally. Finally, every performance is unique, and I can't hang on to the memory of past failures or successes or partners for support. In this most ephemeral of arts, I have only *this* performance, the one I'm dancing or about to dance. How oddly liberating this knowledge is – and how I wish I'd understood it sooner!

What is most important is taking pleasure in the process of preparation: the process of class, of rehearsing, of warming up for what you hope will be the performance of your dreams. Nobody has ever found the magic formula for a great performance, and nobody ever will. There is no formula. That's why, when it happens, it's magic.

Now and Then

*"If fate throws a knife at you, there are two ways of catching it: by the blade or by the handle."*
– Oriental proverb

*"All stages are slippery one way or another."*
– Karen Kain

February 1, 1994, began for me like any other day for the past twenty-five years: with class at the St. Lawrence Hall. But this particular morning, I quickly changed into street clothes and ran downstairs to the press conference, at which plans for the coming season were to be announced. Two parts of the announcement concerned me, and Reid wanted me there to answer questions. The bittersweet news was that on November 25, 1994, I would dance my last *Swan Lake* in a gala performance to commemorate my twenty-five years with the National Ballet. The joyful announcement, far more important in my view, was that next year's repertoire would include two ballets very dear to my heart: *Now and Then*, which John Neumeier had made for me in 1993, and Sir Frederick Ashton's *A Month in the Country*, originally created in 1976 for Lynn Seymour. (Lynn was the Royal Ballet's noted Canadian ballerina whose dramatic intensity I had so admired ever since my school days.)

One of the first questions the press asked was whether I was relinquishing the Swan Queen, my very first principal role in the company, voluntarily. After all, they seemed to think, I was on the brink of forty-three, and many an artistic director over the years has had to take the painful decision to remove his senior principals from roles they could no longer perform well. In this case, however, the decision was entirely my own, and Reid had tried hard to persuade me to change it.

In my own mind I had already given my last performance of *Swan Lake* on our Asian tour in 1992. I had told only a few close friends in the company that I intended this to be my goodbye to the ballet, but somehow many company members seemed to sense my decision, and a number of dancers who weren't performing that night came back to the theatre to watch. I danced my heart out to a small house of about two hundred people, few of whom seemed very knowledgeable about ballet, but that didn't matter – I was dancing for myself, and I gave it everything I had. After the final curtain call, the company lingered on the stage, and I noticed tears in the eyes of some of the younger dancers. These signs of affection and respect from my colleagues touched me deeply, and when I left the theatre that night, I was content.

Of course, my feelings about giving up *Swan Lake* for the second and last time are mixed. The Swan Queen was not only my first leading role in 1971; it was also the first role I danced with Rudolf Nureyev in 1972. I've always considered *Swan Lake* the most passionate, musical, and spiritual of all of the Russian ballets, and the role I treasure most from that repertoire. But while Fonteyn and Kolpakova, who were physically right for the classics, were able to go on dancing them past the age of fifty, it's been clear to me from the start that, because my body wasn't ideally suited to these roles, I would have to leave the Petipa ballets behind at a somewhat earlier age. In fact, I suspect I've already danced my last Aurora and *Nutcracker*.

I've chosen to relinquish *Swan Lake* now for several reasons. The Petipa repertoire requires very pure and very specific shapes, which depend on very correct placement. I've never really had that placement, so the classics have always been a struggle for me. Now, increasingly, I find it difficult to achieve the purity of shape and line that *Swan Lake* requires without so much effort that I've begun to wonder when that effort will start to show; a visible struggle to attain the impossible would be fatal in so pristine and passionate a role, whose choreography relies so heavily on the arabesque, the position that's given me trouble throughout my career.

I've reformed a little, but I'm still a perfectionist; simply maintaining a standard isn't good enough, and I won't go on dancing any role unless I'm reasonably confident that each time I have a good chance of improving on my previous performances. I can't accept the frustration of feeling unable to take the role even farther physically than I have before – to jump higher, spin faster, attain an even purer line. Rudolf taught me to bring that commitment to the classics, so, like an athlete, I'm trying to pace myself to peak at the right time. I'll dance *Swan Lake* in November and then let it go after what I hope will be the best performance I'm capable of giving, even if my eyes will probably be unusually bright with tears. It's time to let a few more of the very talented younger women have their chance at the Swan Queen.

Oddly, I won't feel deprived the morning after my last *Swan Lake* because there are so many other roles to anticipate, equally challenging and probably better suited to the dancer I'm still striving to become, roles in which I can continue to find and to give more each time. The really important news for me at that press conference wasn't my final *Swan Lake*; it was that, after years of seemingly futile phone calls and letters to Anthony Dowell, artistic director of the Royal Ballet, Reid had managed to wangle for me the twenty-fifth-anniversary present of my dreams, *A Month in the Country*.

Lynn Seymour's dancing has always dazzled me; I agree with Dame Ninette de Valois, founder of the Royal Ballet, who wrote, "Lynn Seymour will go down in the history of the first fifty years of the Royal Ballet as the greatest dramatic dancer of that era" (in her foreword to Richard Austin's *Lynn Seymour*. Ashton had always adored Lynn, and it was for her that he created some of his last works, most notably *A Month in the Country*, a retelling of Turgenev's poignant and subtly ironic play. With its lush sets and costumes by Julia Trevelyan Oman and its romantic Chopin score, *Month* has exquisite choreography, a strong dramatic structure, and an atmosphere that evokes both Mozartian opera and Chekhov. The leading roles – the slightly neurotic, slightly pretentious Natalia Petrovna and the young tutor Beliaev, with whom everyone falls in love (created by Anthony Dowell) – have both delicacy and passion, and the supporting roles, including Natalia's husband (created by Alexander Grant), are each as meticulously crafted in their own way. One of the work's many strengths comes from Ashton's decision to work with an ensemble, including mature character dancers like Grant, principals in their prime, such as Seymour and Dowell, and even a young corps de ballet dancer, to whom he gave her first big opportunity. Ashton knew all about the rich dramatic textures that are made possible in a narrative ballet only by taking the talents of mature artists as seriously as the virtuoso technique of the youngest, most beautiful dancers.

From the first time I saw *A Month in the Country*, I've coveted Lynn's role. Back in 1976, when Sir Fred came to set *La Fille Mal Gardée* on the company, an odd thing happened. We were at a party at Tomas Schramek's house, in the wee hours of the morning, a time when Sir Fred always blossomed as the rest of us started to sag with physical exhaustion. Suddenly, he turned to me and said, "In ten years' time, you'll be ready to dance Natalia Petrovna." I was exhilarated that Sir Fred thought I might eventually grow into the role, and from that moment on, dancing Natalia Petrovna was a constant dream.

When Sir Fred died in 1986, I thought my chance was gone forever. I would never have dared to raise the subject with him again, and it seemed unlikely that the National Ballet might acquire the ballet, for over the years the Royal has jealously (and rightly) guarded Ashton's last masterpiece. Every company needs some works that no one else performs, and I couldn't imagine that a treasure like *A Month in the Country* would be shared with anyone else.

Nevertheless, several years ago, when Reid asked me what I would most like for a twenty-fifth-anniversary ballet, *Month* was what came to mind. Reid began a succession of calls to Anthony Dowell, but, each time, Anthony was reluctant to let the ballet go. I almost considered writing Anthony a letter explaining how much the role would mean to me, but I held back. No matter how much I wanted it, I wouldn't put Anthony in the position of having to say no to me, and I was a little afraid that he might think I wasn't good enough. I had almost given up hope, but fortunately Reid had not. He decided to make one last call in December 1993, and this time Anthony agreed. Giving up *Swan Lake* hurts a little less when you can look forward to *A Month in the Country*.

Actually, Anthony's long hesitation wound up serving me well. Instead of getting one item from the top of my wish-list, I'll have two: not only *A Month in the Country*, but also James Kudelka's *The Actress*, which premièred February 16, 1994. Knowing that at this stage of my career new roles are what inspire me to keep dancing, Reid had responded to Anthony's early refusals by commissioning James to create a new work for me. That ballet – which uses a Chopin score, like *Month*, and challenges my dramatic capabilities as greatly as *Month* will do, though in a very different way – turned out to be *The Actress*, a series of vignettes and memories from a day in the life of a famous ballerina.

Every young classical dancer longs for her first *Sleeping Beauty*, her first *Giselle*, her first *Swan Lake*; in works like these a ballerina tests herself against the long history of great interpretations and establishes her own credentials as a principal dancer. Here, too, she responds to a challenge even more difficult than the choreography: Can she make the role her own, bringing some beauty so unique that, years later, people will still remember her as they remember Fonteyn's Aurora, Makarova's Odette/Odile in *Swan Lake*, and Seymour's Giselle?

But for the experienced artist, there's something better still: creating a role made for and with you by a great choreographer. The roles that Ashton created for Fonteyn, that MacMillan created for Seymour, that Cranko created for Haydée, carry the stamp of those ballerinas even more indelibly than our memories of their great interpretations of the classics. It was the desire to create new roles that took me to France to work with Roland Petit early in my career, and lately I've had this supreme pleasure at home: Alice Hargreaves in Tetley's

*With Graeme Mears in* Now and Then.

*Alice* in 1986, Kudelka's *Musings* in 1991, and, in the past year or so, three more extraordinary roles – the lead in Neumeier's *Now and Then* (February 24, 1993), the Mother in Kudelka's *The Miraculous Mandarin*, and the title role in *The Actress*. Each of these works has drawn on not only my physical and musical abilities but also, and even more importantly, on whatever wisdom I have acquired over the years. Other dancers can and will perform these roles, but I'll always be proud of having been the first, of having offered everything I'd learned as a gift to the choreographer, who could then choose and shape and refine whatever he found to inspire him. Because both John Neumeier and James Kudelka are generous and highly creative men, my roles in these ballets are children of my artistic maturity, created during long, sometimes intense, sometimes humorous hours in the studio, the product of the intimate interplay between the choreographer's genius and my own talents and experience. These created roles fit me as no pointe shoes and no classical roles ever could.

Working with John and James, I came to realize that what I value most in the dancer's life has changed almost imperceptibly through the years. Early in my career, performance was everything. I'd slave to approach perfection in rehearsal, lie awake at night agonizing over my shortcomings, and live for the moments on-stage, only to have nightmares in which everything that had gone wrong assumed monstrous proportions, while everything that had gone well became skewed and distorted. Of course, performances still matter enormously – there's nothing like feeling you've just given one of the best of your life – but these days I take equal or even greater pleasure in the creative process, especially with choreographers like Glen Tetley, James Kudelka, John Neumeier, and Christopher House.

Christopher, one of Canada's greatest modern dance choreographers, created *Café Dances* for the company's Concert Group in 1991. He showed me more clearly than anyone else ever has done how exciting and liberating a spontaneity can arise when blocks of choreography are fitted loosely to blocks of music, so that steps and music are sometimes independent and sometimes joined together. That very contemporary attitude to the marriage of music and movement initially violated all my instincts, but, as Peter Ottmann and I worked with Christopher on our pas de deux, I came to delight in the wit and freedom that that choreographic approach permits.

I loved every moment of working with John Neumeier, because of the man he is and the way he works with his dancers. He has incredible intellectual and emotional depth that I could tap into. Even though *Now and Then* is an abstract ballet, it has strong emotional overtones, and on one level it describes the difference between a ballerina "now," in full maturity, and "then," as an aspiring artist. Dancing it, I find myself reflecting on my own past and contemplating the differences between youth and maturity in us all. In the studio, John worked from an emotional point deep within himself, which he was articulate enough to be able to pass on to us; he let us enter his imagination and ideas, his thoughts, emotions, and dreams, and then try to translate them into movement. I've never enjoyed the purely technical side of dancing. To me, technique is merely the tool that allows you to express what you want in a role, and sometimes working on technique feels rather like swallowing some nasty medicine that you know will do you good. So when I find someone who motivates me from some deep emotional core, I respond with joy. I haven't often worked with people who can

*With Nils-Bertil Wallin.*

Now and Then.
*My partner is Graeme Mears.*

do that to me. Working with John, I discovered that it didn't really matter to me whether the ballet was a popular or critical success, because the creative process itself was so enlightening and enriching.

*Rehearsing with John Neumeier (in dark clothing).*

Working with James Kudelka brings very similar rewards, even though he's far more enigmatic in rehearsal. He has his own agenda, which he doesn't necessarily share with you, but I'm so conscious of his enormous intelligence and talent that I turn myself over to him completely – and there aren't many people I trust that much. Often he doesn't tell you what you're doing or why, so you start off with a sense of mystery; probably he's so close-mouthed because he wants us to use our own intelligence and instincts to the fullest. He knows what he's doing, but he wants you to bring something of your own to the piece. He'll show you what he wants, he may dole out a hint or two, he'll delight you with his dark sense of humour, but then he'll watch to see how the movement sits on your body, how you fit it to the music. He lets you share in the creative process, and then suddenly there will be a moment of discovery far more intense and satisfying than what you might experience at the denouement of a mystery story.

James's work is a special challenge because he likes to see a struggle – not necessarily on-stage, but in the process of creation. If something is pat and pre-dictable, it's boring. Anything worth doing doesn't come easily, so whether or not it's visible on-stage, the tension of the struggle to accomplish a movement is what makes it interesting. His choreography has turned out to be more diffi-cult than anything I've ever done, and a ballet like *The Actress*, where I'm on stage for almost forty-five minutes, demands emotional and physical stam-ina unlike anything I've ever experienced. In all his works, the most difficult parts come when you're past the point of fatigue, wondering how you can man-age to take another step. You have to draw on every inner resource, every bit of determination.

It's in moments of near collapse in ballets like *The Actress* or James's *Pastorale* that I particularly appreciate Rex Harrington's gifts as a partner. I can throw myself into abandoned pirouettes or terrifying lifts with complete confi-dence that, if something goes wrong, I can rely on Rex not only to save my life and solve the problem but also to make the solution as beautiful as the choreog-raphy. Even when Rex is standing to one side, I feel that he's dancing with me; he reads my moods, movement, and momentum almost instinctively. The more often I dance a role with him, the farther I can go with it.

In James's ballets, I'm on call as a full human being. He's not just interested in whether I can do an arabesque or a pirouette; he wants all my musicality, my

*A pas de deux from* The Actress *with Rex Harrington.*

physicality, my emotions, intelligence, instinct – everything I can give. He'll take what he wants, edit judiciously, and guide me without my even knowing I'm being guided. Nothing is wasted – no time, no effort; I'm completely involved every instant. That involvement, that experience of working beyond my limits, is the only reason I'm still dancing.

It's probably no coincidence that many roles created for me in recent years – Alice Hargreaves, the leads in *Musings* and *Now and Then*, The Actress – are not only as difficult technically as the classics, though in a different way, but also deal more or less explicitly with the situation of a mature woman surrounded by youth. In a sense, all these works are sensitive case studies of what is lost and what is gained as we grow older, of the beauties and knowledge and richness of character that is possible at each stage of life.

It's not so long ago that the mention of a woman's age, let alone a ballerina's, was taboo. That is changing, however, thanks to factors such as the influence of the women's movement, the emergence of vibrant, intelligent, attractive female role models who are proudly over the age of fifty, and, of course, the aging of the baby boomers, so that "they" have become "we," the forty-something generation. Books like Betty Friedan's *The Fountain of Age* reflect and encourage our growing awareness that aging brings strengths as well as losses, and that the former may far outweigh the latter. Women of my age in other professions are seen as just entering their prime.

But despite the advances outside the ballet world, despite the wonderful performing longevity of dancers like Fonteyn, Kolpakova, Ulanova, and Haydée, or of Bruhn and Nureyev on the masculine side, the world of ballet and ballet audiences can sometimes be a little backward. The classical ballets have young girls and boys, often little more than children, as leading characters: Aurora, a perpetual sixteen; Prince Siegfried, just twenty-one; Giselle, almost certainly under twenty; Franz and Swanilda, teenaged village brats. Even modern classics like *Romeo and Juliet* and *La Fille Mal Gardée* tell the story of children, and works for adults, like Ashton's *A Month in the Country* and *Enigma Variations* or Kudelka's *The Actress*, are conspicuous by their rarity. The historical practice of addressing professional artists as the "boys" and "girls" of the ballet no doubt reflects ballet's marked preference for youth, though I must admit that youthful bodies are frequently considered more conventionally beautiful than middle-aged ones, and too often ballet has been dedicated to the pursuit of beauty above all else.

I don't mean that older dancers can't do younger roles. At fifty, Fonteyn and Kolpakova danced some of their best, most-credible Auroras, and Carla Fracci, Marcia Haydée, and Ekaterina Maximova are among the large group of

*The final moments of* The Actress.

ballerinas who have danced convincing teenagers in their forties. I'm told that I've danced roles like Giselle, Juliet, and Tatiana at least as well after turning forty as I did before, and – so long as it isn't a steady diet – I enjoy the challenge of finding the right simplicity for youthful roles. But there's a special joy in being able to dance a mature woman, or to show a young girl who grows up during the ballet, as Tatiana does in *Onegin*. It's wonderful to feel that you can use on-stage everything you've learned in life.

Like most women of my generation, I've always been completely honest about my age; I'm proud of every year that has brought me new knowledge, and I wouldn't trade that for any magic potion from the Fountain of Youth. Perhaps that's one reason choreographers with real emotional and spiritual depth haven't hesitated to reveal me on-stage as the adult I'm proud to be in real life. We've been part of a real pioneering movement in ballet that recognizes that adults are much more interesting than teenagers. While some friends don't like me to appear in roles that acknowledge my age and experience, or to talk about my age with interviewers, I'm happy to reveal the woman and the dancer I have become over the years; I have no interest whatsoever in attempting to be a perpetual sixteen-year-old, on or off the stage. If the classical repertoire gives pride of place to youth, it's the narrower because of it. I'm thankful to be a dancer at a time when there are choreographers who want to explore all of life, not just to exploit the physical beauty and energy of youth.

Of course, aging in the ballet world has liabilities I very much appreciate as I watch one friend after another move into character roles, like Tomas Schramek, or into the studio, like Cynthia Lucas, or into another career altogether, like Veronica Tennant. Every day when I have to drag myself out of bed and into the studio, it's a little harder, and I feel the aches and pains more acutely. Keeping my muscles warm enough to dance is more and more difficult. I remember Rudolf's constant massages and complaints about how cold the studios and theatres were, and I laugh to myself as I book another urgent massage appointment and wrap myself in layer upon layer of warm clothing.

Oddly enough, I have as much stamina as I've ever had, which is a very good thing, because I never have and never will pace myself on-stage or withhold my energy and full commitment even in rehearsal, and the day I have to start holding back is probably the day I'll decide to retire. As Valerie Wilder joked recently, "After twenty-five years you still haven't learned to mark!" I don't believe in "saving myself"; nothing less than 100 per cent will do. So it doesn't bother me to dance full out in rehearsals day after day, and I have no problems with ballets that keep me dancing for an hour, though I prefer not to dance every evening if I can avoid it. What's hard is those full-length ballets

The Miraculous Mandarin *with Martine Lamy and Jeremy Ransom.*

with long stretches when I'm not dancing, like *Romeo and Juliet*, where I barely appear in the second act and have a terrible time keeping warm while I'm waiting. During intermissions, swaddled in almost every item of apparel I can find, I sometimes find myself thinking, "If they stretch the interval out any longer, I'm going to be in rigor mortis by the third act!" I can't deny it; my muscles just don't stay supple as long as they used to, and it takes longer now for my body to recover from exhausting performances.

Occasionally, I wake up and wonder why I'm putting my body through the stress and pain of class, rehearsal, and performance. But every day that I wake up and find that I can still move, that nothing's broken, and know that I'm about to go into the studio to work with people like James on roles like The Actress, I thank my lucky stars.

In *Alice*, my younger counterpart was the story-book Alice danced by Kimberly Glasco; in *Now and Then*, Margaret Illmann is my youthful shadow-self; and, in *The Actress*, just before the end, Chan Hon Goh dances a very classical variation as the Young Ballerina, while I dash off-stage for a quick change into evening clothes and high-heeled red shoes. If real life imitated ballet novels and movies, I'd be intimidated or threatened by these young and very talented dancers, and I'd think that the choreographers had it in for me to play me against them like this.

Fortunately, the truth couldn't be farther from the stereotype. The wonderful thing about my life now is that I feel absolutely no competitiveness with

anyone else, because we're at such different stages as dancers. For many years I felt insecure; I was never really competitive, but I always felt extreme pressure to prove that I deserved the roles I was dancing. That was part of the price of early stardom. Now, I don't need to prove anything. I just have to dance as well as I possibly can for myself and for the choreographer who has entrusted me with a role. I know who I am as a woman and what I can and cannot do as an artist; on-stage there's a sense of calm and a savouring of the moment that I could never achieve when I was young. Maturity confers the ability to stand centre stage, totally still, and fill the theatre with the power of your memories and emotions in moments that are far more compelling than multiple pirouettes.

Because I rejoice that there are certain things I can explore only as a mature dancer, it's easy to delight in the special gifts of dancers like Kim and Margaret, with whom I share a dressing room, or Chan, Martine Lamy, Jennifer Fournier, and so many others with whom I share the stage or a role. Contrary to popular opinion, many older dancers encourage and help younger ones whom they admire. Margot Fonteyn was very generous with me, and I know that, if we'd danced in the same company, she would have given me the same artistic and moral support she gave many young women in the Royal Ballet. At the National, Veronica Tennant was the dancer who might have felt most threatened by my quick rise in the company, yet she was the person who most actively encouraged me. She had enough self-confidence to realize that my own particular abilities took nothing away from her own exceptional talent. Her steady focus and constant determination in combatting a series of injuries that would have felled many other performers were an inspiration, and when she retired in 1989, there were many tears at her final performance, including my own. At the party that followed, I remarked that she set standards for every dancer who came after her – and I was referring to much more than the unique expressiveness of her dancing.

Margot and Veronica set an example that now gives me the greatest pleasure to follow. Recently, I've had the privilege of working with some of the younger dancers – Chan in *La Fille Mal Gardée* and *The Sleeping Beauty*, and Sarah Green, Jenny Fournier, and Robert Conn in *Coppélia*, for instance – as they prepared for their debuts. I don't concentrate so much on steps and technique as on trying to help them find the essence of a sequence, an incident, or a character – the meaning behind the steps, the artistry beyond technique. I haven't tried to persuade them to do a role the way I did; I firmly believe there are as many right ways to do a role as there are performers, perhaps even as many as there are good performances by one performer. Rather, I want to help them find their own way and encourage them to have confidence once they've

*With my partners from* The Actress.

found that way. Watching them later, feeling more nervous for them than I do now for myself, and hoping that I might have contributed something to the beautiful performances I was witnessing, gives me a new and very special kind of joy and satisfaction. The art of dance passes down through the generations by a sort of oral transmission, and I begin to feel that I may have some talent for passing the torch in this way even when my dancing career is over.

But I hope that won't be for some time. In addition to the wonderful roles that are still coming my way, there's another source of inspiration that helps give me the emotional energy to push on, and that's the opportunity to work with partners who bring out new qualities in my own dancing. I've been singularly blessed in my partners: Nureyev, Frank Augustyn, Denys Ganio, Rex Harrington, Peter Ottmann, Laurent Hilaire, and many others, not least Graeme Mears, my partner in *Now and Then*, whose sensitivity is combined with a strong, serene stage presence. In the past year, quite unexpectedly, I've acquired two more.

I had danced *Onegin* with Reid Anderson some years ago, but he had long since retired from the stage when James Kudelka asked him to appear in *The Miraculous Mandarin* as the Father, my husband. That worked so well that James once again asked Reid to appear in *The Actress* as A Former Acquaintance. This pas de deux was one of the first things James created in the new ballet, and what happened took us all by surprise. James had conceived Reid's character as someone from the Actress's past, perhaps a former partner or choreographer, possibly a lover from very long ago. But the darkness that had possessed us in *Mandarin* somehow took over as we worked – James said he has no idea where that particular pas de deux came from – and once again we found ourselves creating a highly charged duet, filled with the tensions and resentments of long-unfinished business. It was as if the ghost of Antony Tudor had walked into the room and seized control. Reid is a very generous, concerned, and innovative artistic director, but when he gets on-stage with me these days, there's a sinister quality that I find quite unparalleled. I love dancing against type, and dancing with Reid brings out the wintry depths of our souls. Anyone who has seen us in those ballets knows exactly what I mean by roles that only mature artists can possibly perform.

At the other end of the spectrum is Robert Conn, a young soloist whom Reid had originally invited to dance with us for a season as part of an artist exchange with American Ballet Theatre, where he was a member of the corps de ballet. When Serge Lavoie was injured in September 1993, Reid asked whether I'd consider dancing with Robert in *The Taming of the Shrew* in November. Normally I'm an agreeable sort, so I said I'd give it a try – but I also

*With Robert Conn in* The Actress.

warned Reid that I couldn't imagine there'd be enough time to rehearse the difficult partnering (the company was on tour and Robert was in Toronto). I'd heard that this Conn person was very strong and very talented, but privately I was concerned that we couldn't develop a real partnership so quickly, if only because Robert was twenty-four and, in my mind, unlikely to be able to give me the dramatic and comic flair I wanted in my Petruchio. At this stage in my career, I simply won't dance if I don't think I can give a full-out performance both technically and dramatically, and I was prepared to cancel at the last minute if the artistic level we'd managed to reach in so short a time wasn't up to the standard everyone expects for the opening night of a season.

When we finally rehearsed, Robert delighted me with his great talent (which I'd expected), his ease in lifting me in Cranko's intricate choreography (which I'd also expected), and, even more, with his quick intelligence and his attitude (which I *hadn't* expected). I could see that he shared my belief that a dancer's highest goal is to do justice to the work he or she is dancing, so that the integrity of the ballet takes precedence over the advancement of one's own career (that's one reason I've always been happy to take small or even "cameo" roles in ballets I admire). Giving ourselves over to the choreography and the music, we worked very hard but very easily. Robert was extremely open; he would try anything, and he would both offer and accept suggestions with the good-humoured equanimity of an artist who can transcend ego. This meant that I, too, could suggest and adjust without worrying that I'd intimidate Robert or hurt his feelings. So far, so good – but as late as the Sunday before our Wednesday performance, I quietly told a friend that I wasn't sure the show would go on with this particular cast.

The dress rehearsal conquered my doubts, and we went on to give two performances that I felt were as good as any I'd ever done as Kate and, quite possibly, better.

ℰ𝔞

I get very tired of being asked when I'm going to retire; the question is as impossible to answer as "When are you going to get pregnant?" or "When are you going to die?" or "When will you have the flu this year?" And, frankly, it's boring. People have been asking me about retirement since I was twenty-nine, as if I were already over the hill and nastily preventing bright young dancers from getting the leading roles they want. Dame Margot Fonteyn had to put up with queries about retirement for decades. I'm not quite sure why retirement is such a preoccupation with interviewers or casual acquaintances, and I often have to remind myself that people usually don't mean to be offensive when they ask, that the question itself doesn't necessarily reflect a desire for the old girl to get off the stage. Sometimes I wish I were a writer or physician or actor so the question wouldn't arise.

On the other hand, I can understand why people who enjoy my dancing are upset at the thought that someday, inevitably, I'll stop, so I'll take this opportunity to answer a more sensible question: how long do I hope to go on dancing? I want to dance as long as I'm able to expand my artistic horizons; as long as there are challenging new roles and exciting partners and brilliant choreographers who want to work with me; as long as I can happily hurl myself about the rehearsal studio and stage; as long as I feel I can improve artistically in the roles I choose to do; as long as the joy of performances that meet or surpass my expectations outweighs the occasional aches and pains and longings to stay in bed instead of getting up for class; as long as I'm sure the applause at the end of a ballet is for what I've just done, not for what I've been in the past; and as long as my dancing satisfies my own standards. In the meantime, like every other dancer, I'll take it one day at a time, knowing that injury is the unpredictable factor that could curtail the career of a twenty-year-old as quickly as it could my own.

In dance, as in life itself, it's important to appreciate what you have while you still have it, for who knows what tomorrow may bring. That awareness supports my determination to make every single performance as good as it can possibly be. I remember wondering how Rudolf Nureyev could dance every night of those long, exhausting tours in the seventies. When I finally got the nerve to ask him, he replied, "If I didn't get on-stage this often, I'd be too frightened to do it at all." I understand that perfectly now.

✍

Meanwhile, my personal horizons have expanded considerably over the years, so I now have a much richer, happier, and better-balanced life than I did as a young corps member, or even as a precocious principal dancer. I haven't talked much about my family, but my mother, father, sisters, brother, and nephews have helped me keep my feet on the ground, although my adorable nephews have proven to be even more adept at running me off my feet when I've done any extensive babysitting. The love of my family sustains me and grows more precious every year, and I find myself on the phone with one or another of them as often as I can when it's impossible to get together in person. Close friends offer a safe haven where I know I'm loved, and can offer love in return, no matter what, whether we see each other every day or not for months. The Kain–Petty cats, Billy and Betty, arouse outrage, delight, worry, and laughter. And Ross – Ross brings me so much joy, understanding, stimulation, and support on every level that I wonder almost daily how I can possibly have had the good luck to meet and marry a man who would make our garden grow so beautifully, both literally and metaphorically.

I'm well aware that the hardest thing for any performing artist is to find such contentment in private life, and although I paid my dues in my early years with the company and continually work hard at my personal relationships, I feel blessed far beyond my deserts. It should be quite clear from what I've said that the long string of limited and generally unsatisfactory relationships that afflict my character in Kudelka's *The Actress* don't reflect the realities of my own life, however fascinated audiences may be with trying to translate what happens on-stage to characters and events in my own biography. As James and I joked after creating yet another pas de deux in which The Actress is left vaguely unsatisfied, I've had much better luck myself.

*(Left to right) With Mom and Dad; my nephews, Dylan and Taylor; a night out with Ross.*

My life has been greatly influenced – usually for the better – by three strong women: Betty Oliphant, Celia Franca, and (in a separate and quite special category) my mother. I love and admire all of them, and in most respects I strive to achieve the same strength of character they exemplify. But there's one way in which I try to follow a different course. Betty, Celia, and my mother, at least in their younger days, shared a kind of rigidity in their principles, a conviction that they're right and everyone else must be wrong. That quality may well have been what gave them strength in an era when women were often undervalued by society in general, but I've also come to see how determined self-confidence, whether real or assumed, can sometimes be counter-productive. In contrast, I have always tried very hard to keep an open mind. I've come to realize that what I also learned from these women, and what attracts me most in my close women friends, is a certain depth of soul, a profound ability to care about other people, and a willingness to show that caring, even if it means risking being hurt by others. When I was very young, I wanted to be a nice person. That ambition has changed, in subtle but very crucial ways: now I try to find the right mix of hard-won strength and the ability to care, the willingness to remain vulnerable and open to those I love.

In the past few years, there have been a few external signs of my new inner strength and independence of spirit. First, several years ago, I cut my hair. This may not seem like much of an achievement, but to someone like me, whose first accomplishment at ballet school was perfecting the flattening of the bun and who continues to work in a world of "bunheads," it's almost a revolutionary act. Shortly after I took the bold step, someone pointed out to me that in most ballet companies the women with short hair tend to be senior ballerinas who have gained a certain self-confidence; if that's true, then I gladly show my solidarity.

My second declaration of independence was learning how to drive. It's amazing how many dancers – especially women dancers – don't drive, possibly because when we're young we'd much rather spend the time in the studio than in driver-education courses. Like most dancers, I always lived very close to work, so there seemed to be no reason to incur the expenses of buying, insuring, maintaining, and parking a car. But after I'd lived almost twenty years in Cabbagetown, Ross and I fell in love with a beautiful old restored farmhouse in North York, and a major consequence of the move was that I had to learn to drive. I enrolled in the Young Drivers of Canada course, where I sat in a classroom hour after hour with a group of sixteen-year-old boys listening to exhortations on the dangers of speed on the highway. I had to laugh at this; as Ross says, I may take risks on the stage, but I'm far likelier to dawdle on the road. Circumstances may have forced me into getting my driver's licence, but now I relish my new freedom and wonder why it took me so long to find it.

*My new look.*

That having short hair and driving a car would be remarkable rites of passage for me tells you something about the sheltered nature of the ballet world in which I grew up and the sacrifices many dancers, especially those of my generation, make completely unawares. Recently, a radio interviewer in Toronto asked me, "So what are you going to be when you grow up?" I knew she was just being flippant, but I was furious at the implication that what we do is childish, a kind of leisure activity through which we postpone our entry into real life. All our lives, we dancers have had to deal with the attitude that we're well-meaning and talented children, ill-equipped to do anything but dance. Our fight to be treated as adults with real jobs worthy of respect is just beginning, and the older I get, the more determined I am to make this fight a personal campaign.

Dancers spend as much time training and learning as any other professionals, and we do it so intensively, and from such a young age, that we often sacrifice our childhoods to be able to arrive at professional status by the age of nineteen or twenty. With other artists, we contribute – socially, economically, and culturally – to the enrichment of society in ways that are often discounted or overlooked. For example, a 1992 report on Canadian culture found that the federal government's investment of three billion dollars in culture generated a direct economic impact of over eleven billion dollars and supported almost half a million jobs. These figures are impressive, but many people still see the arts as a frill to be trimmed when times are bad. I know that not everyone would agree that the arts are essential to any and every civilization, part of what makes life worth living, in a very real sense. But surely the economic value of the arts ought to convince even the Philistines of our dollars-and-cents importance to society in general.

However, dancers and other artists see very little of the money our activities generate. We remain, after old-age pensioners, the lowest-paid and least-protected sector of Canadian society, and many of us have little or no access to social services and benefits enjoyed by other Canadian workers, such as collective bargaining, unemployment insurance, and company pensions. Things are getting better – for instance, in 1992, Bill C-7 recognized the status of the artist as an independent, self-employed member of society – but all dancers continue to be underpaid, overworked, and constantly in the position of having to justify their existence. Unionization has helped National Ballet dancers in many ways in recent years, but most of us still make very little money during our careers and find ourselves having to start again from scratch in a new career when we retire. The average Canadian professional dancer makes about $13,500 a year, and when you consider how hard dancers work and how uncertain our future is, it's not surprising that many people in other professions think dancers must be single-minded to the point of simple-mindedness to enter a profession that pays so poorly.

Comparatively speaking, dancers at the National are a privileged lot; starting pay is about $23,000, so we don't have to wait tables or do telemarketing to be able to continue dancing, as many modern dancers must. But even at the National, and even after concerted efforts by Erik Bruhn and Reid Anderson to improve the situation, we work in terrible conditions. After twenty-five years, I currently share a ten-by-twelve-foot locker room with eight or nine other dancers and at least twice as many cockroaches. Lockers are piled high with tutus, practice skirts, and travelling boxes that are used to store make-up and props. Our rehearsal studios have low ceilings (through which we crash every now and then) or supporting pillars (around which we veer at perilous speeds). We can afford only one dress rehearsal with costumes, lights, and orchestra, so only one cast can experience what a work will be like on-stage before a run in which often three or four casts perform. We arrive on-stage under-rehearsed and frustrated. Ultimately, it's the audience who is short-changed. That is why we all remain angry and somewhat embittered several years after our hopes for a new Ballet-Opera House were dashed, apparently once and for all, by politicians who simply don't consider cultural spending a priority. I don't regret having chosen to follow my career in Canada, but I can't help thinking longingly of what life might have been like had I been willing to join a highly subsidized European company.

Some politicians have been sympathetic to the arts and artists. In the eighties, then-Communications Minister Flora MacDonald and Employment and Immigration Minister Barbara McDougall – is it coincidence that both are women? – lent moral and financial support to an organization in which dancers learn how to help themselves.

Joysanne Sidimus, one of my close friends, danced with George Balanchine's New York City Ballet before becoming a principal dancer with the National Ballet of Canada. Although she became one of the few people authorized to teach the Balanchine ballets to other companies, she found retirement from the stage such a traumatic experience that she decided to do extensive research on how other dancers were coping. The result was her book *Exchanges: Life After Dance* (1986). One of her conclusions was that dancers in North America faced severe poverty upon retirement, unlike European dancers, for whom respectable pensions are often provided after a working life of twenty or so years. As two Canada Council reports had also confirmed, there was an urgent need for post-career support for dancers, and Joysanne, one of the most determined, well-organized, energetic, and compassionate of human beings, decided to accept the challenge. After nine months' research and a systematic survey into dancers' most-pressing needs, Joysanne opened the Dancer Transition Centre's main office in Toronto on September 1, 1985, with a mandate to provide dancers who have become members during their careers with the financial, legal, personal, and career-counselling assistance they need when the moment comes to withdraw from the stage.

Sharing Joysanne's concerns – I had seen many former colleagues devastated when injury or age forced them off the stage – I offered my assistance as soon as I read the survey we all received, and at the first meeting of the founding board of directors, I was elected president. Despite my initial discomfort with having to chair meetings, I recently accepted the title of "president for life," and I consider my commitment to the centre permanent.

I'm extremely proud to be part of what Joysanne has accomplished; since 1985, we have helped more than two thousand dancers with advice, counselling, and our resource library, and we have provided grants to more than eighty dancers in training for new professions, from gourmet chef to physician to computer programmer. The skills that dancers acquire during their years in the profession – discipline, focus, determination, complete commitment to hard work – tend to make them particularly fine students and practitioners in their new fields. In the days of *The Red Shoes* and even later, dance was almost a form of religion: you took the veil and put every part of your life but dance on hold. The centre has reminded dancers of the need to be prepared for life outside and beyond dance, and, perhaps for the first time in Canada, there are new generations of dancers coming along who have learned to find a better balance in their lives while they're still dancing and the hope of a satisfying future when they decide to stop.

ॐ

Having reached that balance in my own life later, perhaps, than many of the younger dancers I see around me, I have finally arrived at the point where I can value my own talent and abilities. For years, I never displayed any awards or photographs of memorable performances on my walls; instead, with some embarrassment, I relegated them to the basement. But now I treasure them, and whenever I look at them I realize the richness of my career.

In the traditional *Sleeping Beauty*, the Fairies bring gifts to the baby Aurora, and although Rudolf's production suppresses that spiritual message, the story is a good parable for the creation of a ballerina. To have a career like mine, you need many gifts, many generous fairy godmothers. To start with, you need some innate special talent, some ability to communicate with and please an audience. From your parents' genes, you need the gift of a body more or less suitable for dancing. Then you need the gifts of discipline, determination, training, and encouragement supplied by teachers like Betty Oliphant and Daniel Seillier. You need careful coaches and well-matched partners like Frank, Rex, and Robert; you need demanding-but-sensitive ballet masters and mistresses like David Scott, Joanne Nisbet, and Magdalena Popa. You need mentors such as Rudolf Nureyev, comforters like Mary McDonald, examples of generosity like Veronica Tennant. You need visionary artistic directors like Celia Franca, Erik Bruhn, and Reid Anderson – and you need the luck to have the right artistic director at the right time, as I have had. You need choreographers like Ann Ditchburn, Constantin Patsalas, Roland Petit, Eliot Feld, Glen Tetley, John Neumeier, and James Kudelka. You need a repertoire of established works that allow your talent to flower, as the Ashton, Cranko, and Petipa works have done for me, and then, when you start to become a little pot-bound and require judicious transplanting, you need the right new roles. There must be a precious core of friends and family to sense your sorrows and uncertainties and hold your hand when you're down. And let's not forget the wardrobe people, the music directors and conductors and rehearsal pianists, the publicity directors, the designers and stagehands and set-builders and electricians. If *The Sleeping Beauty* Prologue really represented the bestowal of all the gifts you need for a successful career, the ballet wouldn't finish till dawn, and it still wouldn't show the special ingredient

The Sleeping Beauty *with Laurent Hilaire.*

*More* Sleeping Beauty *with Laurent.*

that pulls everything together: the spirit of cooperation and teamwork that takes all the gifts and doles them out at the right time and in the right proportions to everyone involved in the production. I've become the dancer I am because all of these gifts have been there when and as I needed them.

I'm a lucky, hard-working dancer who has had a long time in the spotlight, and I'm grateful for every moment, even if I don't always enjoy all the personal attention. I know that a large factor in my success was being in the right place at the right time, just coming to prominence during the dance boom of the seventies, when, thanks to Nureyev and Sol Hurok, the company and I gained experience and exposure that would simply be impossible in today's economic climate.

When I look back, I have only one regret: that I enjoyed so little of my career for the first decade or so. There was a time when I was a real sensation in New York, and everyone was clamouring to see me in *The Sleeping Beauty*. I'd make that terrifying entrance down the huge flight of stairs and leap right into my first solo with full energy, and the audience would explode. As Marcia B. Siegel wrote in the *Boston Globe* (May 4, 1973), I was "a tall, strong girl who hurls herself into space with reckless courage. When she comes galloping on for her first scene, the famous Rose Adagio, you admire her great vitality and spirit – she's the kind of beauty who's impressive when she's awake, not asleep." But that was Siegel's view, not mine; I always had trouble believing that all that commotion was for me, because I didn't actually like my own performances very much, and all I really cared about was preparing for the next show, hoping I'd do somewhat better. Tension and insecurity completely overshadowed any pleasure I might have taken from my successes.

Now I'm able to savour each performance and accept the joy that comes from pleasing both yourself and your audience. I can let myself go and disarm the old censorious critic crouching invisibly on my shoulder, as each performance becomes an opportunity to draw upon everything I've learned over the years: technique, musicality, emotion, artistry, love of risk. Instead of the blind, forgetful panic of my youth, I find myself plunging into the moment and into a deeper part of myself where words rarely enter. Later, I often recall Isadora Duncan's comment, "My dance is not a dance of the body, but of the spirit. My body moves because my spirit moves it."

How can I describe the power of some moments of performance? Sometimes through dancing you experience the deep pleasure of simply being alive, of moving, of breathing. Dancing is so intensely physical, so ecstatic, so personal. When I dance in MacMillan's *The Song of the Earth*, I'm in touch with universal truths that I would never have the courage to put into words; to the very core of my being I feel the joy of life, the sorrow of death, the desperate rage of struggling against the laws of nature, and the peace that finally comes from accepting those laws. At moments like these, dancing remains what it was in prehistory: a religious experience in the most profound sense. Superficially, *Swan Lake* is about a confused young man who is deceived into committing a terrible betrayal of love, but it is really about far more: the hidden desires of the flesh and the torments of the mind, the battle between the body's instincts and the soul's aspirations.

For Michelangelo, the human body was an instrument of the soul, the noble means by which we reach towards God, and in rare performances I have felt something similar. I hesitate to speak of such things – to speak of them is almost to profane them, or to risk the chance that they will never happen again – but every now and then, in a ballet like *The Song of the Earth* or *Swan Lake*, I begin to understand the ancient belief that the true artist is possessed by some power, some spirit. I feel touched and elevated by something that far transcends the merely human; I sense that for a few moments I am the privileged instrument for higher truths, in reality the "chosen maiden" of *The Rite of Spring*; and I feel deeply blessed to be part of an art form that somehow allows the wordless communication of matters so deep, so important. Make no mistake about it – at its highest, dance involves both body and soul. If it didn't, I wouldn't still be dancing.

# Acknowledgements

As in any project of this sort, there have been many whose help and encouragement have been essential, and it is with gratitude and affection that I acknowledge their contributions.

I would like to thank:

The National Ballet of Canada, especially the Publicity Department and its director, Julia Drake, and her assistants, Terri MacFarlane and Allan Brown, and the Archives, formerly under Assis Carreiro and now under Sharon Vanderlinde, for their support and tireless efforts on my behalf;

Avie and Beverly Bennett, nurturing patrons of the arts, for their constant support, encouragement, and wisdom;

My dear friend the late Stephen Godfrey, for undertaking this project with his usual unbridled passion for the arts;

Penelope Reed Doob, for assuming the project after Stephen's untimely death and for expanding the manuscript in light of new developments and further conversations (one of the most rewarding aspects of our collaboration has been the discovery of a warm and generous new friend in a long-time acquaintance);

Pat Kennedy, my editor, for her patience and expertise, and Trish Lyon and Kong Njo, photo researcher and designer, for their help in adding another dimension to my words;

My sisters, Sandra and Susan, my brother, Kevin, and my friends, Gary, Ann, Joysanne, and especially Marley, for their wise and loving counsel throughout the project;

My parents, Wynne and Charlie, for their painstaking labours in sorting and cataloguing my photos and clippings – and, of course, for their love and support for so many years;

And, above all, Ross, for his constant love and understanding during the course of what turned out to be a much longer and more difficult process than either of us had envisioned.

# Photo Credits

A & A Studios, 15

Jim Allen, 176

Heidi Bassett, 266 (middle)

BIPNA (London), 159

Judy Cameron, 101 (small photo)

Canadian Broadcasting Corporation, from Norman Campbell's CBC Television productions of "Karen Kain: The Pleasure of Your Company," 37, and "La Fille Mal Gardée," 87

Canada Wide, 19 (*Toronto Telegram*)

Canapress, 45, 160, 213 (Bill Becker)

Joseph Ciancio, title page, vi, 211, 214, 215, 245, 267

Anthony Crickmay (courtesy The Theatre Museum, London, England), 25, 52, 57, 60, 63, 64, 71, 72, 110, 111, 155

Marina Donatti, 123

R. Faligant, 132

Beverly Gallegos, 116

*Globe & Mail*, 9 (Eric Christensen), 35 (Dennis Robinson)

Barry Gray, 38-39 (all photos), 68, 74, 75, 77, 79 (far left, near left, far right), 80, 81, 85 (both), 138 (background), 145 (both), 166, 195, 227, 230

Hurok Productions, 102, 115

Karen Kain and the Kain family, 1, 3, 4, 5, 6, 23, 169, 178, 266 (right)

Winnie Klotz, 100-101 (large photo)

Francette Levieux, 130 (background and left inset), 131

Arnaud Maggs, 32

Colette Masson, 133

MIRA (Myra Armstrong), 96, 97, 108

*Mississauga News*, 17

Desmond O'Neill, 118

Andrew Oxenham, 29, 40, 62, 79 (second from right), 84, 103, 142-43, 200-201, 208, 239

Lydia Pawelak, 251, 255, 263

Louis Peres, 98 (background)

Peter of Holland, 12

Photo Lavolé, 130 (right inset)

Reilly, 98 (right inset)

Tom Sandler, 209, 266 (left)

Garth Scheuer, 172, 173

David Street, 47, 120, 148, 171, 175, 190, 204, 217 (all photos), 222, 228-29, 252-53 (all photos), 256

Martha Swope, 181, 186-87

Michel Szabo, 125, 134, 135

*Toronto Star*, 82, 138 (inset), 141 (Doug Griffin)

Jack Vartoogian, 86, 89, 202

Linda Vartoogian, 30, 51, 91, 98 (left inset), 106, 109

Cylla von Tiedemann, 198, 199, 232, 241, 242, 250, 254, 259, 260, 271, 272

Unidentified, 33, 94, 113, 127, 161 (both), 196, 224

Max Waldman (courtesy of the Max Waldman Archives, Westport, Ct.), 65, 66-67

# Index

Page numbers in italics refer
to photographs.


*Actress, The,* 249, 250, 254, *255, 256,* 257,
    259, *260,* 262, *263, 265*
Adams, John, 196
Adams, Lawrence, 13
*Adieu,* 195
*Afternoon of a Faun, 74, 75,* 112
AIDS, effect on dance world, 121-22
*Aladdin,* 175, *175, 176*
*Alice,* 14, 120, 139, 197, *197-205, 202,*
    *204, 206,* 250, 257, 259
Allan, David, 196
Allemann, Sabina, 239
Alleyne, John, 19, 42, 210, 218
Alonso, Alicia, 75
American Ballet Theatre, 114, 121, 165,
    167, 183, 184, 190, 197, 262
Amyot, Luc, *142-43*
Anderson, Reid
    as dancer, *242,* 262
    as National's director, 37, 149, 208, 209,
    *209*-10, 212-15, 220, 240, 246, 248,
    249, 262-63, 268, 270
Arias, Roberto "Tito," 114
Ashton, Frederick, 31, 104, 120, 124, 184,
    185, 227, 246, 257, 270
    curtain calls, 53
    work with National Ballet, 86, 144-46,
    235-36, 248
Astaire, Fred, 19, 121
*At Midnight, 181,* 195
Atanassoff, Cyril, *125*
Aubrey, John, 121
Augustyn, Frank, 68, *75, 79,* 80, *82,* 119,
    124, 125, 139, *159,* 165-66, 167, 172,
    177, 238, 262, 270
    in *Afternoon of a Faun, 74, 75*
    in *Ballet Revue, 146, 148*
    in *Bayadère, La,* 40
    character, 80-83
    in *Coppélia, 187*
    early life, 61
    in *Fille Mal Gardée, La,* 85-88, *86,*
    *87, 89*
    in *Giselle, 77, 85, 85, 86,* 243-44
    in *Intermezzo,* 59-61, *60*
    in *Loup, Le,* 64, 73
    at Moscow International Ballet
    Competition, 64-75, *68, 77*
    Nureyev's influence on, 93, 108-11
    partnership with Kain, 78-90; *see also*
    individual ballets
    in *Romeo and Juliet,* 61-63, *62,* 85-86
    in *Sleeping Beauty, The,* 63-64, *64, 65,*
    *66-67,* 70-73, *72, 75,* 80-82, *81*

    in *Swan Lake,* 64, 73-74, 79, *227*
Austin, Richard, 248


Baignères, Claude, 131, 132
Baker, Peggy, 21
Balanchine, George, 20, 23, 34, 43, 112,
    185, 188, 197, 237-38, 243, 269
Ballet of the 20th Century, 113-14
Ballet British Columbia, 19
Ballet National de Marseille, Le, 125-26,
    137, 151-53
Ballet Rambert, 32
Ballet Revue, 146-47, *148*
Ballets de Paris, 15, 125
Ballets des Champs-Elysées, 125
Bardot, Brigitte, 137
Barnes, Clive, 107, 159, 204
Baryshnikov, Mikhail, 64, 69, 76, 94,
    112-13, 183-84, 205
*Bayadère, La,* 31, 38-40, *41*
Béjart, Maurice, 108, 113-14, 136
Belle, Anne, 26
Benesh notation, 235
Berlin, Christina, 183
Berlin Opera Ballet, 88
Berlioz, Hector, 196
Berman, Janice, 204
Bernheimer, Martin, 56
Bertram, Victoria, 9, 230, *230,* 232
Bissell, Patrick, 165-67, *166,* 223
Blanton, Jeremy, 53, 83
*Blood Wedding,* 238
*Blue Snake,* 197
Bolshoi Ballet, 69-71, 77
Bornhausen, Angelica, 54
Bortoluzzi, Paolo, 113, 117
Bournonville, August, 34, 111
Bowes, Karen, 27, 44, 46, 233
Bruhn, Erik, 92, *118,* 120, 156
    character, 191-92, 205-7
    as choreographer
    of *Coppélia,* 129
    of *Swan Lake,* 31, 54, 74, 79, 99-103,
    227, 230-31
    as dancer, 19, 34, 58, 93-94, 125, 140,
    189-90, 191, 257
    death, 206
    as National's director, 88, 149-50, 174,
    189, *190,* 191-92, 193-95, 196-97,
    204-5, 209, 210, 268, 270
    choice of successors, 207-9
Bryans, Rudy, *123*
Bucharest State Opera Ballet, 192-93
Bujones, Fernando, 188


*Café Dances,* 251
Campbell, Douglas, 139
Campbell, Norman, 139
Canada Council, 269

Canadian Dance Teachers' Association, 8
Carey, Betty, 7-9
*Carmen,* 125, 131-32, *132, 133,* 137,
    152-53
Caron, Leslie, 131
Charles, Prince of Wales, 139, *160*
Chase, Lucia, 183
Chopin, Frédéric, 248, 249
*Cinderella,* 175
Coe, Kelvin, 75, 121
Cohen, Judy, 209
Cohen, Nathan, 18
*Components,* 196
*Concerto,* 238
*Concerto Barocco,* 238
*Concerto for the Elements: Piano Concerto,*
    197
Conn, Robert, *214,* 261, 262-64, *263,* 270
Constant, Marius, 134-36
Cooper, Elizabeth ("Babette"), 128-29
*Coppélia,* 13, 107, *123,* 129-31, *130, 131,*
    139, 152, 184-85, *186-87,* 188, 190,
    261
corps de ballet
    of National Ballet of Canada, 31, 37-43,
    *38-39*
    of Royal Ballet, 41
*Corsaire, Le,* 114, *116,* 117, 121
Cousineau, Yves, 13
Cragun, Richard, 212, 214
Cranko, John, 43, 183, 197, 209, 212, 233,
    235, 249, 263, 270
Crum, George, 49, 193, 243-44
Cumberland, Christy, 12
Cunningham, Merce, 29


Dancer Transition Centre, 269
*Dancing for Mr. B.,* 26
*Daphnis and Chloë,* 114
Darcus, Jack, 139
Davies, Robertson, 3
de Valois, Ninette, 32, 248
Del Tredici, David, 197
Desrosiers, Robert, 19, 196, 197, 240
Diaghilev, Serge, 92, 188
*Diary,* 167
Ditchburn, Ann, 16, 18, 124, 134, 137,
    146, 147, 148, *148,* 168, 240, 270
Domingo, Placido, 120
*Don Juan,* 107-8
*Don Quixote,* 76, 183, 194, *195*
Doob, Penelope, 179
Dowd, Irene, 22
Dowell, Anthony, 188, 189, 238, 248
*Dream, The, 142-43,* 145, *145*
*Dresser, The,* 53
Dudinskaya, Natalia, 75, 96
Duncan, Isadora, 273
Dutilleux, Henri, 73

Earle, David, 196, 197
*Echo*, 195
*Eh!*, 58-59
Elisabeth, Empress of Austria, 241
*Elite Syncopations*, 13
*Emily*, 240
Empry, Gino, 153, 169
*Endangered Species*, 196
*Enigma Variations*, 257
Erik Bruhn Dance Competition, 179

*Falcon and the Ballerina, The*, 139
Farrell, Suzanne, 27, 49
Feld, Eliot, 58, 59, 124, 195-96, 209, 270
Ferns, Pat, 139
Festival of Two Worlds (Spoleto), 168, 183
*Fille Mal Gardée, La*, 42, 53, 69, 85, 86-88, 86, 87, 89, 91, 139, 140, 144-45, 235-37, 248, 257, 261
Finlay, Terence, Jr., 171
Finney, Albert, 53
Fisher, Juliet, 49
floors for dancing, 37, 139-40
Fonteyn, Margot, 20, 27, 104, 113, 140, 144, 145, 157, 184, 226, 247, 249, 257, 264
   character, 50, 114-17, 174, 261
   partnership with Nureyev, 92, 95-96, 105, 107, 113-17, 120, 121, 131
Ford, Robert, 68
*Forgotten Land*, 222
Forrester, Maureen, 139
Forsythe, William, 42, 210, 218
Fotheringham, Alan, 81
*Four Schumann Pieces*, 43, 108, 238
*Four Temperaments, The*, 43, 238
Fournier, Jennifer, 261
Fracci, Carla, 27, 190, 257
Franca, Celia, 159, 189, 266
   character and background, 31-33, 45-46, 51, 59, 69
   as choreographer, 58
   in *Giselle*, 2-3, 8, 13
   as National's director, 9, 22-23, 31-33, 32, 41, 43, 51-55, 59, 61, 63-64, 69, 73, 75, 78, 83, 86, 95, 96-99, 104, 107, 124, 125, 126, 191, 209, 270
   retirement, 141-44
   in *Romeo and Juliet*, 45
   in *Swan Lake*, 49
Fraser, John, 77, 108-11, 112, 161, 170, 177, 183
Freedman, Harry, 196
Friedan, Betty, 257
Frigerio, Ezio, 136

Gagnon, André, 137, 139
Ganio, Denys, 126, 128, 132, 133, 188-89, 262
Geddes, Lorna, 9, 42
Georgiadis, Nicholas, 70, 96, 99, 226
Gerussi, Bruno, 175
Giggs, Iris, 10
*Giselle*, 8, 13, 28, 36, 41, 53, 77, 84, 85, 85,

86, 107, 108, 108, 109, 118, 139, 144, 160, 218, 225, 231-33, 232, 243-44, 249, 258
Glasco, Kimberley, 202, 202, 259, 261
Godfrey, Stephen, 149-50
Godunov, Alexander, 76
Goh, Chan Hon, 215, 259, 261
Gorlinsky, S. A., 113
Gorrissen, Jacques, 59, 142-43, 145, 186-87
Goss, John, 172
Goss, Pat, 61
Gould, Glenn, 94, 121
Grace, Princess of Monaco, 129
Graham, Martha, 104, 157, 197
Grand Ballet du Marquis de Cuevas, 15
Grant, Alexander
   as dancer, 248
   as National's director, 77, 77, 81, 124, 144-45, 147-51, 159-60, 183, 184, 191, 197, 208, 238
Great Artists Management Inc., 146
Green, Sarah, 261
Gregory, Cynthia, 188
Grigorovich, Yuri, 69, 75
Grisi, Carlotta, 233
Grossman, Danny, 196, 197

Haber, David, 124, 144
Harrington, Rex, 86, 89, 120, 196, 196, 198-99, 201, 254, 255, 262, 270
Harris, Susan, 12, 13
Harwood, Vanessa, 9, 59, 97, 104-5, 108, 154, 165, 193
Haydée, Marcia, 27, 48, 212, 214, 219, 238, 249, 257
Hecht, Paul, 172, 174
Hechter, William, 140
Helpmann, Robert, 145
Hicklin, Ralph, 18
Hilaire, Laurent, 90, 226, 262, 271, 272
Holm, Hanya, 197
*Hot House: Thriving on a Riff*, 197
House, Christopher, 251
Hurok, Sol, 99, 124, 273
Hynd, Ronald, 139, 235
Hyslop, Jeff, 139, 175

*Île Inconnue, L'*, 196
Illmann, Margaret, 259, 261
*Impromptu*, 195
*Intermezzo*, 59-61, 60, 195
*Intermittences du Coeur, Les*, 126-28, 127
Ivanov, Lev, 34, 223, 227

Jago, Mary, 36, 59, 108, 154, 193
Jarvis, Lillian, 13
Jeanmaire, Zizi, 125, 126, 131-32, 152

Kain, Charles, 3-8, 4, 10, 13, 17, 172, 174, 266
Kain, Dylan, 180, 266
Kain, Karen
   as actor, 48, 137, 212-14

on age, 257-62
and animals, 5-6, 15-16, 140-41, 178, 265
backstage, 35, 47, 82, 119, 120, 135, 159, 160, 196, 208, 267
in Ballet Revue, 146-47, 148
childhood, 1, 2-3, 4, 5-8, 5, 6
daily class, 28-29, 30
on dance for TV, 139-40
on dancing as spiritual experience, 270-74
early ballet lessons, 7-8
on economic position of dancers, 267-70
emotional life, 15-17, 151-54, 156-65, 167, 264-67
and family, 2-7, 161, 172, 265, 266; see also individual family members
guest appearances, 77, 124-37, 151-53, 156, 184-89, 195-96
hair and make-up for stage, 12, 50, 105, 266
injuries, 216-20
interviews, 149-50, 151
marriage, 170-80; see also Petty, Ross
   wedding, 170-74, 172, 173
at Moscow International Ballet Competition, 64-75, 68, 192
on music for ballet, 223-25, 227
National Ballet of Canada audition, 22-24
in National Ballet of Canada corps, 26-54, 144
National Ballet of Canada debut, 30-31
at National Ballet School, 10-24, 12, 17, 19, 23, 161-62
National Ballet School audition, 8-10
partners: see individual dancers
performance rituals, 47-56, 243-44
physique, 10, 13-14, 20, 27-28, 247
in rehearsal, 32, 79, 80, 85, 94, 125, 217
on retirement, 264-65
reviews, 18, 28, 56, 63, 75, 81, 107, 136, 152, 159, 184, 204-5, 273
solo debut, 54-56
teaching in China, 161
on television, 37, 139-40
weight, 15, 21, 22-24, 220-22 see also individual ballets; National Ballet of Canada
Kain, Kevin, 4, 5, 6, 172, 172, 180
Kain, Sandra, 4, 5, 6, 172, 172
Kain, Susan, 4, 5, 6, 172, 172
Kain, Taylor, 180, 266
Kain, Winifred, 3-8, 3, 4, 6, 10, 11-12, 13, 17, 172, 205, 266, 266
Karsavina, Tamara, 8
Keil, Birgit, 195
*Khachaturian Pas de Deux*, 196
Kirkland, Gelsey, 112-13, 167, 221, 223
Kirov Ballet, 192
Kisselgoff, Anna, 107, 159, 184, 204-5
Kolpakova, Irina, 75, 247, 257
*Kraanerg*, 30-31, 43, 125

Kraul, Earl, 13, 53
Kudelka, James, 16, 19, 42, 148, 210, 240,
    242, 249, 250, 251, 254-57, 257, 259,
    262, 265, 270
Kylián, Jirí, 197, 210, 218, *222*

Laidlaw, Robert A., *23*
Lamberts, Heath, 179
Lamy, Martine, *259, 261*
Lander, Judith, 167
Lavoie, Serge, 89, 213, 214-16, *222*,
    *228-29*, 262
*Legend of Joseph, The*, 183
Leigh, Angela, 13
Liepa, Maris, 69
Limón, José, 114, 196
Linehan, Brian, 177
Littler, William, 152
London Festival Ballet, 193
Lorca, Garcia, 238
*Loup, Le*, 73, 125, 126
Love, Betty Carey, 7-9
Lucas, Cynthia, 146, *148*, 240, 258

Macdonald, Brian, 139, 177
MacDonald, Flora, 269
McDonald, Mary, 33, 64, 68-69, 80,
    144, 270
McDougall, Barbara, 269
McFall, John, 196
MacLeary, Donald, 238
MacLeod, I. H., 111
MacMillan, Kenneth, 13, *31, 33*, 144,
    238, 249, 273
*Mad Shadows*, 16, 134, 137, *138*, 240
Mahler, Gustav, 238
Majors, Lee, 165, 167
Makarova and Company, 188
Makarova, Dina, 183
Makarova, Natalia, 49-50, 76, 112, 128,
    188-89, 190, 205, 221, 249
Malinowski, Barbara, 22
Mallet, Gina, 185
Marceau, Marcel, 129
Marcus, Howard, 46
Margaret, Princess (Countess of
    Snowdon), *159*
*Marguerite and Armand*, 114
Markova, Alicia, 190
Martha Graham Company, 197
Martins, Peter, 41, 112, 232
Mason, Monica, 96, 238
Massine, Léonide, 188
Massine, Lorca, 188
Maximova, Ekaterina, 257
Maybarduk, Linda, 22, 26-27, 64, 96,
    191, 237
Maynard, Olga, 56
Meadows, Howard, 121, 168
Mears, Graeme, *250, 252-53*, 262
Meehan, John, *224*
Meredith, Burgess, 165
*Merry Widow, The*, 139, 223, *224*, 235
Metropolitan Ballet, 189
Michelangelo, 274
Michener, Roland, 99

Michener, Wendy, 18
Millay, Edna St. Vincent, 124
*Miraculous Mandarin, The*, 16, 242-43,
    *242*, 250, 259, 262
*Mirror Walkers, The*, *52*, 53, 83
Molloy, Molly, 160
Montague, Owen, *202*
*Month in the Country, A*, 246, 248, 257
*Monument for a Dead Boy*, 108
Moodie, Susanna, 3
Moore, Claudia, 19, 240
*Moor's Pavane, The*, *113*, 114, 117, 190,
    196
Morris, Mark, 220
Moscow International Ballet
    Competition, 64, 192
Munroe, Alistair, 121
music for ballet, 223-25; *see also* com-
    posers by name
*Musings*, 241, *241*, 250, 257

Nagy, Ivan, 167
*Nana*, 125, 132-36, *134, 135*, 137
*Napoli*, 34
Narrizano, Silvio, 139
National Ballet of Canada, 13, 26-27, 32,
    119, 124, 137, 151, 153, 165, 167,
    174, 175, 190, 249, 269, 273
  artistic directors: *see* Anderson, Reid;
    Bruhn, Erik; Franca, Celia; Grant,
    Alexander; Haber, David
  casting policy, 78, 95, 148-49, 182
  corps de ballet, 31, 37-43, *38-39*
  criticism of, 108-11
  formation of, 9
  guest artist policy, 125, 149-50,
    183, 195
  style, 34, 46-47
  tours, 43-45, 54-56
  working conditions for dancers, 268-70
  *see also* ballets by name; Kain, Karen
National Ballet School, 9-22, 150, 190
  dedication of students, 17
  matrons, 11-12, 16
  in *Nutcracker*, 237
  Oliphant's training style, 18-21
  Staines's training style, 21-22
*Nelligan*, 240
Neumeier, John, 108, 203, 210, 246, 250,
    251, 254, *254*, 270
New York City Ballet, 269
Nijinska, Kyra, 112
Nijinsky, Vaslav, 69, 112
Nisbet, Joanne, 27, 33, 144, 270
Nixon, David, 239
*Notre Dame de Paris*, 152
*Now and Then*, 203, 246, 250, *250*, 251,
    *252-53*, 257, 259, 262
Nureyev, Rudolf, *51, 74, 75, 76, 83, 91*,
    *104, 111, 118, 120*, 221, 270
  character, 102-11, 117-20, 122, 129,
    136, 156-57, 159, 179, 216
  as choreographer
    of *Don Quixote*, 183
    of *Sleeping Beauty, The*, 63, 93, 94-96,
    99, 225-26

of *Swan Lake*, 111
  curtain calls, 5
  as dancer, 19, 58, 64, 69, 90, 94, 94, 111-
    12, 140, 191, 238, 247, 257,
    258, 262
  in *Corsaire, Le*, *116*, 117
  in *Giselle*, *108, 109*, 118
  in *Moor's Pavane, The*, 117
  in *Sleeping Beauty, The*, 98, *100-101*,
    106-7, 118-19, 120
  in *Swan Lake*, 99-103, *102*, 104-5,
    106, 115
  in *Sylphides, Les*, *110*
  death, 121-22
  influence in west, 92-94
  Kain's guest engagements with, 111-20,
    141, 149, 153, 184
  and National Ballet of Canada, 93-113,
    119, 209, 273
  partnership with Fonteyn, 92, 95-96,
    105, 107, 113-17, 120, 121, 131
  Rosa (Nureyev's sister), 76
*Nutcracker, The*, 12, 59, 93, 157, 208, 225,
    237, 247

Ohno, Kazuo, 212
*Oiseaux Exotiques*, 196, *200-201*
Oliphant, Betty, 8-13, *9, 13*, 15, 17, 18-21,
    23, 49, 58, 150, 160-61, 190, 193,
    220, 266, 270
Oman, Julia Trevelyan, 248
*Ondine*, 114, 116
*Onegin*, 183, 197, 209-10, *210*, 219, 235,
    258, 262
Osborne, Gregory, 121
Ottawa Ballet, 90
Ottmann, Peter, 168, 239, 251, 262
Oxenham, Andrew, 50

*Paquita*, 188, 189
Paris Opéra Ballet, 15, 121, 125, 132,
    134, 136
*Pas de Chance*, 13
*Pastorale*, 240, *241*, 243, 254
*Patineurs, Les*, 148
Patsalas, Constantin, 121, 124, 134, 148,
    190, 196, 197, 205, 207-8, 270
Peckinpah, Sam, 12
Penderecki, Krzysztof, 196
Pérusse, Sonia, 97
Peterson, Jim, 112
Petipa, Marius, 31, 34, 63, 73-74, 93, 96,
    188, 197, 223, 225, 247, 270
Petit, Roland, 15, 30-31, 73, 124, 125-37,
    *125, 130*, 139, 141, 149, 151, 156,
    167, 170, 183, 184, 185-88, 196,
    249, 270
  character, 126, 153, 157, 179
*Petrushka*, 190
Petty, Ross, 141, *169, 171, 172, 173*,
    *175, 176, 178*, 185, 266, 267
  career, 168-70, 174-75
  meets Kain, 167-68
  "roast" speech, 175-78, 179
Petty, Victor, 169
Petty, Violet, 169, *172*

Pickford, Mary, 156
Pilates, Joseph, 219
Plisetskaya, Maya, 73, 75
pointe shoes, 35-37, *35*
Popa, Magdalena, 75, 192-93, 230, 270
Porter, McKenzie, 6, 152
Potts, Lucy, 11, 24
Potts, Nadia, 9, 11, *47*, 49, 53, 64, 108, 154, 193
Poulenc, Francis, 58
Prokofiev, Serge, 233

Rainier, Prince of Monaco, 129
Rambert, Marie, 32
Ransom, Jeremy, *213, 259*
*Rape of Lucrece, The,* 240
*Rashomon,* 190
*Raymonda,* 188, 197
Read, Alexander "Ragtime," 12-13
*Realm,* 197
*Red Shoes, The,* 140, 188, 269
Reeves, Maggie, 172
Reich, Steve, 195
Reiser, Wendy, 64, 96
*Rendezvous, Les,* 31
*Rite of Spring, The,* 112, 274
Robbins, Jerome, 60, 75
Robledo, Antonio, 238, 239
*Romeo and Juliet,* 13, 14, 17, 43, 45, 48, 61-63, *62,* 85-86, 137, 165-66, 198-99, 225, 233-34, 243, 257, 258, 259
*Ronde, La,* 139
Rowe, Marilyn, 75
Rowes, Barbara Gail, 56, 63, 156
Roxander, David, 146-47, *148*
Royal Academy of Dancing, 32
Royal Ballet, 41, 92-93, 95-96, *96,* 114, 159, 183, 208, 248, 249, 261
Royal Danish Ballet, 189, 190
Ruther, Doris, 12

Sadler's Wells Royal Ballet, 32
St. Laurent, Yves, 129
St. Petersburg Ballet, 225
Samsova, Galina, 107
Schaufuss, Peter, 75, 188
Schelhorn, Amalia, 207, 239
Schönberg, Arnold, 197
Schramek, Julia, 180
Schramek, Milan, 180
Schramek, Tomas, 27, 61, 108-11, 119, 146, 147, *148,* 180, 248, 258
Scott, David, 27, 33, 75, 83, 86, 144, 193, 230, 270
*second detail, the,* 42
Seillier, Daniel, 15, *15,* 21, 162, 270
*Serenade,* 43, 238
Sergeyev, Konstantin, 96
*Seven Daggers, The,* 238-40, *239*
Sever, Peter, 146
Seymour, Lynn, 36, 41, 92-93, 96, 157, 221, 232, 238, 246, 248, 249
Shadbolt, Jack, 214
Shaughnessy, Kate, 12
Shearer, Moira, 140

shoes: *see* pointe shoes
Sibley, Antoinette, 50
Sidimus, Joysanne, 269
Siegel, Marcia B., 273
*Sinfonia,* 197
*Sleeping Beauty, The,* 28, 36, 50, *51,* 80-81, *81,* 118-19, 120, 121, 146, 159, 165, 247, 249, 261, *271, 272,* 273
   Bluebird pas de deux, 64, 70-73, *71, 72,* 75
   Fonteyn in, 114, 116
   Nureyev's, 63-64, *64-67,* 93, 94-96, *96, 97,* 98, 99, *100, 101, 102,* 105-8, 225-26
   Petipa's, 34, 93, 96, 226-27
   spiritual message of, 154, 270-72
Smith, Lois, 13
Smith, Raymond, *215*
Sniderman, Marlaina (Marley), 164, 172, 174, 180
Sniderman, Robert, 164, 180
Sniderman, Zachary, 180
*Snow White,* 175
*Solitaire,* 31, *33,* 144, 238
*Song of the Earth, The,* 238, 273-74
*Songs of a Wayfarer,* 108, 114
Spain, Tim, 18, 240
*Spartacus,* 69
*Sphinx,* 197
Staines, Mavis, 21-22
Stefanschi, Sergiu, *52,* 59, 108-11, 183
Stewart, Frances, 3
Stewart, Henry Louis, 3
Stewart, Thomas Alexander, 3
Strate, Grant, 13
*Straw Hearts,* 195
Stuttgart Ballet, 209
styles and traditions of ballet: *see* Training and technique
Surmeyan, Hazaros "Laszlo," 23, 49, 54, 55, 61, *138, 215*
Susana, 238, 239
Swados, Elizabeth, 146
*Swan Lake,* 12, 22, 24, *25,* 49, 53, 54-56, 59, 64, 95, 107, 111, 114, 116, 152, 154, 156, 246-48, 249, 273-74
   Black Swan pas de deux, 64, 73-74, 79-80, *166*
   Bruhn's, 31, 79-80, 93, 99-105, *102, 103, 106, 115,* 190, 227-31, *227-30*
   corps de ballet in, 41, 42
   Petipa's, 34, 73-74, 227
*Sweeney Todd,* 168-69
*Sylphide, La,* 34, 107, 190, 191
*Sylphides, Les, 110,* 159
*Symphonic Variations,* 114
*Symphony in C,* 197

*Tales of Hoffmann, The,* 149, 185
Tallchief, Maria, 26, 190
*Taming of the Shrew, The,* 212-16, *213, 214, 215,* 219, 262-64
Taylor-Corbett, Lynne, 167
Tchaikovsky, Peter Ilyich, 53, 224, 225, 227
technique: *see* training and technique

television, dance on, 139-40
Tennant, Veronica, 9, 13, 27, 54, 59, 96-99, 193, 208, 209, 226, 233, 240, 258
   character, 43, 55, 206, 261, 270
Terabust, Elisabetta, 152, 188
Tessmer, Karyn, 146
Tetley, Glen, 14, 139, 179-80, 197, 197-205, 249, 250, 270
Tharp, Twyla, 184
Till, Eric, 139
Tippett, Clark, 121
Tobias, Tobi, 28
Todd, Deborah, 180
Traill, Catharine Parr, 3
training and technique, 20, 35, 219
   Balanchine, 34
   Bournonville, 34, 111
   British, 19-20, 95-96, 114
   dancing on, before, or after the music, 15
   National Ballet of Canada, 34, 46-47
   National Ballet School, 18-22
   Nureyev's, 111-12
   Russian, 19, 34, 94, 95-96, 107, 111
   Vaganova method, 21
*Transfigured Night,* 197
Trudeau, Pierre Elliott, 99, 139
*Truth and Variations,* 146
Tudor, Antony, 32, 60, 157, 197
*Two Pigeons,* 148

Ulanova, Galina, 192, 257

Valukin, Eugen, 70
van Dantzig, Rudi, 108
Van Hamel, Martine, 23, 27, 64, 197
van Manen, Hans, 43, 108, 238
Vasarely, Victor, 30
Vasiliev, Vladimir, 69
Vivaldi, Antonio, 197
Volkoff, Boris, 9

Wallin, Nils-Bertil, *251*
Wallis, Lynn, 206, 207, 208, 209
Walpole, Peter, 218
Warhol, Andy, 140-41
   portrait of Kain, *141*
Wilder, Valerie, 206, 207, 208, 209, 218, 258
Witkowsky, Gizella, 239
Wolf, Naomi, 221
Wright, Peter, 53
*Wuthering Heights,* 185

Xenakis, Iannis, 30

Yvaral, Victor, 30

Zakariasen, Bill, 204